Fortran 90
A Reference Guide

Luc Chamberland
With contributions by John Russell

For book and bookstore information

http://www.prenhall.com

Prentice Hall PTR
Upper Saddle River, NJ 07458

Library of Congress Cataloging-in-Publication Data

Chamberland, Luc.
  Fortran 90 : a reference guide / Luc Chamberland.
    p. cm.
  Includes index.
  ISBN 0-13-397332-8 (paper)
  1. FORTRAN 90 (Computer program language)   I. Title.
QA76.73.F28C47   1995
005.13'3--dc20   95-32303
                                                            CIP

Editorial/production supervision: *Patti Guerrieri*
Cover design direction: *Jerry Votta*
Cover designer: *IBM (Julie Santilli) and Design Source*
Manufacturing buyer: *Alexis R. Heydt*
Acquisitions editor: *Mike Meehan*
Editorial assistant: *Dori Steinhauff*

Published by Prentice Hall PTR
Prentice-Hall, Inc.
A Simon & Schuster Company
Upper Saddle River, NJ 07458

The publisher offers discounts on this book when ordered in bulk quantities. For more information, contact: Corporate Sales Department, Prentice Hall PTR, One Lake Street, Upper Saddle River, NJ 07458, Phone: 800-382-3419, Fax: 201-236-7141, e-mail: corpsales@prenhall.com

Portions of the Fortran 90 Standard are reprinted with permission of the American National Standards Institute (ANSI) under an exclusive licensing agreement with the International Organization for Standardization (ISO). No part of ISO/IEC 1539-1:1991 (E) may be reproduced in any form, electronic retrieval system or otherwise without the prior written consent of the American National Standards Institute, 11 West 42nd Street, New York, New York 10036.

IBM, AIX, and RISC System/6000 are registered trademarks of International Business Machines Corporation. UNIX is a registered trademark in the United States and other countries licensed exclusively through X/Open Company Limited.

Printed in the United States of America
10 9 8 7 6 5 4 3 2 1

ISBN   0-13-397332-8

Prentice-Hall International (UK) Limited, *London*
Prentice-Hall of Australia Pty. Limited, *Sydney*
Prentice-Hall Canada Inc., *Toronto*
Prentice-Hall Hispanoamericana, S.A., *Mexico*
Prentice-Hall of India Private Limited, *New Delhi*
Prentice-Hall of Japan, Inc., *Tokyo*
Simon & Schuster Asia Pte. Ltd., *Singapore*
Editora Prentice-Hall do Brasil, Ltda., *Rio de Janeiro*

Contents

Part 2. Statements

Acknowledgments

This book would not have been possible were it not for the help I received from my numerous reviewers.

John Russell helped out immensely with the writing on intrinsic procedures and arrays. He also brought a large dose of common sense to the book's organization.

Special thanks go to Henry Zongaro, who reviewed this manuscript in its entirety and provided innumerable suggestions on how the text could be improved. His comprehensive knowledge of Fortran 90 was available to me at all stages of writing.

The entire IBM XL Fortran team provided many helpful comments and suggestions on the AIX version of this work. Some members' tireless commitment to technical accuracy must be acknowledged: Janice Shepherd, Lisa Martin, Melanie Ullmer, Jim Clark, Graham Warren, Gordon Slishman, Lee Johnson and Dick Weaver each made hundreds of valuable suggestions.

Thanks also to Mike Meehan and the staff at PTR Prentice Hall for their support and encouragement.

Preface

A Brief History of Fortran

The first generation of computing focused on the needs of the machine s, not the programmers. Programming was incredibly tedious. Programmers had to contend with coding in machine or assembly language, facilities for I/O were often very restrictive, machine memories were very small and program portability was unknown. As much as 50% of computer resources was spent debugging programs, rather than solving the problems for which they had been intended.

The First FORTRAN Compiler

In 1954, a group at IBM, led by John Backus, proposed a system for programming computers in a high-level language, in a paper entitled, "PRELIMINARY REPORT, Specifications for the IBM Mathematical FORmula TRANslating System, FORTRAN". Among the features proposed were assignment statements, DO-loops and I/O statements. In addition, some very ambitious facilities for performing matrix arithmetic, solving simultaneous systems of equations and solving differential equations were proposed as features that might be added in the future.

The IBM effort was not unique; over the preceding five years, many proposals and prototypes for interpreters and compilers of high-level programming languages were put forward. Some of these had such prosaic names as "A-2". However, none of these systems was so ambitious as FORTRAN, which offered a clearer syntax and made promises of excellent run-time performance.

From the very start, the main objective of the FORTRAN project was to automate the effort of producing very efficient machine code. It was felt that if some FORTRAN programs suffered a significant performance degradation (where significant meant more than 50%) over functionally equivalent hand-coded machine language versions, FORTRAN would not be accepted. So, the implementers spent considerable effort designing algorithms to generate very efficient code, pioneering optimization techniques. Their success was often so remarkable, it surprised the implementers themselves.

The first FORTRAN compiler, FORTRAN I, was finally made available in the spring of 1957. By late 1958, it is estimated that more than half of the customer installation base used FORTRAN for the majority of their problems.

FORTRAN 66

Within a few years, FORTRAN compilers began to appear on computers produced by other manufacturers. Each of these provided different extensions or implemented existing features in slightly different ways. Indeed, IBM itself supported different machine-dependent language constructs in FORTRAN compilers for different IBM machines!

Eventually, the need to write portable programs was so great, that the Business Equipment Manufacturers Association (BEMA) began to work to produce a standard FORTRAN. This effort culminated in what is now known as FORTRAN 66. The FORTRAN 66 standard consisted of a common subset of features available in all existing FORTRAN compilers. By using only those features specified in the standard, the programmer was guaranteed program portability (ignoring, of course, implementation-specific features, such as the precision and range of numeric data).

However, by the time FORTRAN 66 arrived, FORTRAN was already showing signs of age. Newer programming languages had facilities for handling character data, structured data types, structured constructs and recursion. In addition, FORTRAN had well-known problems with features that tended to be error-prone, such as nonsignificant blanks and implicit data typing.

FORTRAN 77

Eventually, the need for new features was so great, that the standard was revised by the American National Standards Institute (ANSI) X3J3 committee. The result was FORTRAN 77, which added much needed features like the character data type and the IF construct. In addition, the standard restricted the definition of features that had been left unspecified by FORTRAN 66, or whose use in FORTRAN programs tended to be error-prone. For example, FORTRAN 66 specified that, in certain circumstances, the target of a branch from outside a DO-loop could be inside the DO-loop; FORTRAN 77 prohibited this.

The changes made by FORTRAN 77 were necessary, but did not address all of the needs of the science and engineering community, so work began almost immediately on a new revision of FORTRAN. This eventually appeared in the form of the Fortran 90 standard.

Fortran 90

Fortran 90 was a significant and extensive revision of the Fortran language. A number of commonly used extensions were added, improving the portability of programs that use such extensions. Some of these included the DO WHILE, END DO and IMPLICIT NONE statements, bit manipulation procedures, the INCLUDE line and namelist I/O.

The most important features of Fortran 90, however, are those that make Fortran programs easier to write and maintain. Use of the new array facilities, new intrinsic procedures and elemental invocation of intrinsic procedures help to make code more readable than it would be if it were written using multiply-nested DO-loops. Derived types and pointers permit the creation of complex, abstract data structures, such as linked lists and trees. Dynamic storage allocation facilities are provided through allocatable arrays, pointers and automatic objects. Data hiding and data abstraction can be achieved through the use of modules, generic procedures and derived types. In the past, programs that required these facilities had to use vendor-specific extensions; otherwise, the only choice was to use a different programming language.

The features of Fortran 90 also provide alternatives to the FORTRAN 77 language constructs that were most prone to error, such as implicit type declaration and nonsignificant blanks, which can be avoided through the use of IMPLICIT NONE and free source form, respectively.

All of Fortran 90's features, coupled with the continuing focus on efficiency of execution, serve to make Fortran a fully modern programming language, and an excellent language for solving the problems encountered in scientific, numerical and engineering applications.

The Future of Fortran

Since the appearance of the new Fortran standard, there have been a number of developments in the world of Fortran. A new dialect of Fortran, known as High Performance Fortran (HPF), was defined by the High Performance Fortran Forum (HPFF). HPF grew out of ideas implemented in earlier data-parallel Fortran compilers, such as Fortran D (Rice University) and CM Fortran (Thinking Machines).

HPF consists of a set of machine-independent compiler directives for data distribution and language constructs (extensions to Fortran 90), such as PURE procedures and FORALL statements and constructs. These features are designed to facilitate the efficient execution of Fortran programs on massively parallel computers. In addition, HPFF added features to HPF that it felt were badly needed in Fortran 90. Thus, outstanding performance remains a key concern in the definition of Fortran dialects.

Meanwhile, the X3J3 committee has been busily preparing the next Fortran standard (tentatively known as Fortran 95), which is expected to include some of the language constructs specified by HPF, thereby enhancing the portability of most HPF programs. In addition, it is expected to include some new features, such as default initialization of structure components, pointer initialization and the ability to invoke user-defined procedures on an element-by-element basis.

The current plan for the Fortran language is that there should be a major revision of the standard produced in 2000. Some of the proposed additions for this revision include object-oriented features, exception handling and improved interoperability with procedures written in languages other than Fortran. As always, the emphasis will be on code maintainability, programming ease and efficient program execution.

Ease of programming is the central idea behind this book. While the list of Fortran 90 tutorial books grows, there are no books that provide quick access to information for Fortran 90 programmers who already understand the basics of the language — until now. *Fortran 90: A Reference Guide* is organized to help you find the syntax details, languages rules and examples you need without having to wade through chapters of instructional material. This is a book that Fortran programmers will actually use.

Henry Zongaro
An IBM representative to the X3J3 and HPFF committees
Toronto

Chapter 1. Introduction

How to Use This Book

This book is intended as a reference tool, organized to help you find information as quickly as possible. The use of color, alphabetized sections, and extensive cross-referencing ensure that you will not need to sift through whole sections to find the facts you need.

This book is not intended as a Fortran tutorial. Some knowledge of Fortran concepts, particularly FORTRAN 77, is assumed.

Color Highlighting

All Fortran 90 material that has been added to FORTRAN 77 is highlighted in blue. At a glance, you can see the dozens of new features added by Fortran 90, and how far-reaching and comprehensive the efforts of the Fortran standards committees have been in upgrading the language. A light skim will show you how every area of the Fortran language has been revisited and enhanced for today's programming needs.

Note that although the primary description of a given feature is highlighted, not all other material that may mention the feature is highlighted. For example, the description of the **ALLOCATABLE** statement (see "ALLOCATABLE" on page 184) is highlighted, but not all lists, tables, or secondary references that may refer to the **ALLOCATABLE** statement are highlighted.

Organization

The book is divided into three main parts:

- *Concepts and Elements* provides some general background on the items and multi-statement constructs you can use to write Fortran programs. When specific syntax information on a particular statement or intrinsic procedure is required, references to the alphabetized sections are provided.

- *Statements* provides an alphabetical reference of all Fortran statements. Each statement description includes a brief explanation of purpose, a syntax diagram, a detailed discussion of rules concerning the statement, examples, and references to any related information. This section is particularly useful to programmers who know which statement is needed and simply require details on syntax or rules.

- *Intrinsic Procedures* provides an alphabetical reference of all Fortran intrinsic procedures.

Also, *Appendix A* discusses FORTRAN 77 compatibility, and the Glossary provides an alphabetical reference to terms commonly used in this book.

To illustrate how the *Concepts and Elements* section and the *Statements* section complement each other, the following table provides references to thematic groups of statements. The first two columns refer to *Concepts*, while the last two columns refer to the corresponding *Statements*.

Group/Concept	Page	Statements	Page

IF Construct	88	IF (block)
		ELSE IF
		ELSE
		END IF
			265
			233
			232
			237

CASE Construct	90	SELECT CASE CASE END SELECT	330 196 237
DO / DO WHILE Construct	93, 97	DO DO WHILE END DO EXIT CYCLE	225 227 237 248 214
WHERE Construct	81	WHERE ELSEWHERE END WHERE	351 234 237
Module	122	MODULE CONTAINS PRIVATE PUBLIC END MODULE USE	288 212 310 313 235 348
Interface Block	112	INTERFACE MODULE PROCEDURE END INTERFACE	281 290 239
Derived-type Definition	28	Derived Type PRIVATE SEQUENCE END TYPE	223 310 332 240
Subprogram	127	FUNCTION SUBROUTINE ENTRY CONTAINS RETURN	257 336 243 212 324

Group/Concept	Page	Statements	Page
Input/Output	141, 149	BACKSPACE	191
		CLOSE	203
		ENDFILE	241
		FORMAT	252
		INQUIRE	270
		OPEN	295
		PRINT	307
		READ	315
		REWIND	326
		WRITE	353

How to Read Syntax Diagrams

Throughout this book, the syntax of Fortran statements and elements is illustrated by diagrams, using notation often referred to as "railroad tracks".

Fortran keywords are shown in uppercase bold; for example, **OPEN**, **COMMON**, and **END**. You must spell them exactly as shown, although a processor may support lowercase characters.

Variable names and user-specified names appear in lowercase italics; for example, *array_element_name*.

If a variable or user-specified name ends in *_list*, it means that you can provide a list of these terms separated by commas.

Punctuation marks, parentheses, arithmetic operators, and other special characters must be entered as part of the syntax.

Syntax Diagrams

- Syntax diagrams are read from left to right and from top to bottom, following the path of the line:

  The ►►── symbol indicates the beginning of a statement.

  The ──► symbol indicates that the statement syntax is continued on the next line.

  The ►── symbol indicates that a statement is continued from the previous line.

  The ──►◄ symbol indicates the end of a statement.

  Program units, subprograms, constructs, interface blocks and derived-type definitions consist of several individual statements. For such items, a box encloses the syntax representation, and individual syntax diagrams show the required order for the statements.

- Required items appear on the horizontal line (the main path):

►►—*keyword*—*required_argument*——————————————————►◄

- Optional items appear below the main path:

►►—*keyword*——————————————————————————►◄
        └─*optional_argument*─┘

Note: Optional items (not in syntax diagrams) are enclosed by square brackets ([and]). For example, [UNIT=]u

- If you can choose from two or more items, they appear vertically, in a stack.

If you *must* choose one of the items, one item of the stack appears on the main path:

►►—*keyword*——┬─*required_argument*─┬——————————————►◄
           └─*required_argument*─┘

If choosing one of the items is optional, the entire stack appears below the main path:

►►—*keyword*——————————————————————————►◄
          ├─*optional_argument*─┤
          └─*optional_argument*─┘

- An arrow returning to the left above the main line indicates an item that can be repeated, and the separator character if it is other than a blank:

             ┌─,←─────┐
►►—*keyword*—▼─*repeatable_argument*─┘——————————————►◄

A repeat arrow above a stack indicates that you can make more than one choice from the stacked items.

             ┌─,←─────┐
►►—*keyword*—▼─*required_argument*─┬─┘————————————————►◄
            └─*required_argument*─┘

Example of a Syntax Diagram

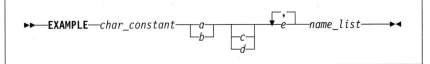

Interpret the diagram as follows:

- Enter the keyword **EXAMPLE**.

- Enter a value for *char_constant*.

- Enter a value for *a* or *b*, but not for both.

- Optionally, enter a value for *c* or *d*.

- Enter at least one value for *e*. If you enter more than one value, you must put a comma between each.

- Enter the value of at least one *name* for *name_list*. If you enter more than one value, you must put a comma between each. (The *_list* syntax is equivalent to the previous syntax for *e*.)

What's New to Fortran?

Fortran 90 adds a wealth of new features and functionality to FORTRAN 77, as defined by the ISO publication of the Fortran 90 standard: *International Standards Organization Programming Language Fortran*, ISO/IEC 1539-1:1991 (E).

Fortran 90 is an upward-compatible superset of FORTRAN 77. That is, any FORTRAN 77 program is a standard-conforming Fortran 90 program. Although a few FORTRAN 77 features have been reinterpreted, no FORTRAN 77 features have been deleted from Fortran 90. (See "FORTRAN 77 Compatibility" on page 415 for more details.)

The Fortran standard committees are responding to questions of interpretation about aspects of Fortran 90. This book attempts to reflect all approved modifications made to Fortran 90 up to the end of 1994.

You may have noticed the case distinction between "Fortran 90" and "FORTRAN 77". The name was modified to reflect the addition of Fortran 90 support for lower-case characters. The following outlines some of the key features that Fortran 90 brings to the Fortran language.

Free Form

In addition to the fixed form source format (defined in FORTRAN 77), Fortran 90 defines a free form source format. A statement can begin in any column, and blanks are significant.

See "Free Form" on page 16 for more information.

Parameterized Data Types

Although the length specification for a data type (e.g., INTEGER*4) is a common industry extension, Fortran 90 provides facilities for specifying the precision and range of noncharacter intrinsic data types and the character sets available for the character data type. When used with the **SELECTED_INT_KIND** and **SELECTED_REAL_KIND** intrinsic functions, parameterized data types become portable across platforms.

See "Type Parameters and Specifiers" on page 21 for more information.

Derived Types

A derived type is a user-defined type whose components are intrinsics and/or other derived types. Objects of derived type can be used in intrinsic assignment, in input/output, and as procedure arguments. When used with defined or extended intrinsic operations, derived types can be used to provide powerful data abstractions (e.g., linked lists).

See "Derived Types" on page 28 for more information.

Array Enhancements

With Fortran 90, you can specify array expressions and assignments. An array section, a portion of an array, can be used as an array. Array constructors offer a concise syntax for specifying the values of an array. Assumed-shape arrays, deferred-shape arrays, and automatic arrays provide more flexibility when using arrays. Use the **WHERE** construct to mask array expression evaluation and array assignment.

See "Array Concepts" on page 41 for more information.

Pointers

Pointers refer to memory addresses instead of values. Pointers provide the means for creating linked lists and dynamic arrays. Objects of intrinsic or derived-type can be declared to be pointers.

See "Pointer Association" on page 106 and "POINTER" on page 305 for more information.

Dynamic Behavior

Storage is not set aside for pointer targets and allocatable arrays at compile time. The **ALLOCATE** and **DEALLOCATE** statements let you control storage usage at run time. You can also use pointer assignment to alter the storage space associated with the pointer.

See "ALLOCATE" on page 186, "DEALLOCATE" on page 221, and "Pointer Assignment" on page 84 for more information.

Control Construct Enhancements

The **CASE** construct provides a concise syntax for selecting, at most, one of a number of statement blocks for execution. The case expression of each **CASE** block is evaluated against that of the construct.

The **DO** statement with no control clause and the **DO WHILE** construct offer increased versatility. In addition, the **CYCLE** and **EXIT** statements provide control over the execution of the construct from within the construct.

Control constructs can be given names, which is of particular use for nested constructs by enhancing readability and syntax checking.

See "Control" on page 87 for more information.

Procedure Enhancements

Fortran 90 introduces many new features that make the use of procedures easier. Functions can extend intrinsic operators and define new operators. With subroutines, you can extend intrinsic assignments. The actual arguments of a procedure can be specified with keywords, and you can explicitly indicate the intended use of dummy arguments and whether or not they are optional.

The interface or characteristics of a dummy or external procedure can be explicitly specified in an interface block. A generic interface block can specify a name that can be referenced to access any specific procedures defined within the block, depending on the nature of the actual arguments.

Internal procedures, contained within a main program or another subprogram, let you partition programs while allowing you to access entities defined in the host procedure.

Recursive procedures are allowed in Fortran 90; functions and subroutines can call themselves directly or indirectly.

See "Program Units and Procedures" on page 101 for more information.

Modules

Modules provide the means for data encapsulation and the operations that apply to the data. A module is a nonexecutable program unit that can contain data object declarations, derived-type definitions, procedures, and procedure interfaces. With modules, you can specify that some entities can be used only within the module, and other entities can be accessed from any program unit.

See "Modules" on page 122 for more information.

New Intrinsic Procedures

Fortran 90 brings dozens of new intrinsic procedures to Fortran. For example, a set of transformational intrinsics provides powerful array manipulation capabilities. Many new inquiry functions let you examine the properties of entities.

See "Intrinsic Procedures" on page 359 for details.

Part 1. Concepts and Elements

Chapter 2. The Language Elements

This chapter describes the elements of a Fortran program:

Characters

The character set is processor dependent. The following table represents the Fortran character set.

Letters		Digits	Special Characters	
A	N	0		Blank
B	O	1	=	Equal sign
C	P	2	+	Plus sign
D	Q	3	-	Minus sign
E	R	4	*	Asterisk
F	S	5	/	Slash
G	T	6	(	Left parenthesis
H	U	7	)	Right parenthesis
I	V	8	,	Comma
J	W	9	.	Decimal point / period
K	X		$	Currency symbol
L	Y		'	Apostrophe
M	Z		:	Colon
			!	Exclamation point
			"	Double quotation mark
			%	Percent sign
			&	Ampersand
			;	Semicolon
			?	Question mark
			<	Less than
			>	Greater than
			_	Underscore

A processor may also represent

- lowercase letters, which are equivalent to the corresponding uppercase letters except in a character context
- control characters (for example, "newline")
- other characters, which can appear only in character constants, character string edit descriptors, comments, and input/output records.

The default character type must support a character set that includes the Fortran character set. The processor can also support other character sets in terms of nondefault character types. Only the blank character (to be used for padding) is requisite for each nondefault character type.

The characters have an order known as a *collating sequence*, which is the arrangement of characters that determines their comparison status. A processor defines a collating sequence for each character type.

For the default character type, the following constraints apply to the collating sequence:

- `ICHAR('A') < ICHAR('B') < ... < ICHAR('Z')` for the letters
- `ICHAR('0') < ICHAR('1') < ... < ICHAR('9')` for the digits
- `ICHAR(' ') < ICHAR('0') < ICHAR('9') < ICHAR('A')` or `ICHAR(' ') < ICHAR('A') < ICHAR('Z') < ICHAR('0')`
- `ICHAR('a') < ICHAR('b') < ... < ICHAR('z')`, if the processor supports lowercase letters
- `ICHAR(' ') < ICHAR('0') < ICHAR('9') < ICHAR('a')` or `ICHAR(' ') < ICHAR('a') < ICHAR('z') < ICHAR('0')`, if the processor supports lowercase letters

A *lexical token* is a sequence of characters with an indivisible interpretation that forms a building block of a program. It can be a keyword, name, literal constant (not of type complex), operator, label, delimiter, comma, equal sign, colon, semicolon, percent sign, `::`, or `=>`.

Names

A *name* is a sequence of

- letters (A-Z, a-z)
- digits (0-9)
- underscores (_)

The first character of a name must be a letter.

The maximum length of a name is 31 characters.

The character contexts are: characters within character literal constants and character-string edit descriptors.

A name can identify entities such as:

- A variable
- A constant
- A procedure

- A derived type
- A construct
- A program unit
- A common block
- A namelist group

A subobject designator is a name followed by one or more selectors (array element selectors, array section selectors, component selectors, and substring selectors). It identifies the following items in a program unit:

- An array element (see "Array Elements" on page 51)
- An array section (see "Array Sections" on page 53)
- A structure component (see "Structure Components" on page 31)
- A character substring (see "Character Substrings" on page 27)

Statements

A Fortran statement is a sequence of lexical tokens. Statements are used to form program units.

See Part 2 of this book for details on all Fortran statements.

Statement Keywords

A statement keyword is part of the syntax of a statement, and appears in uppercase bold in the syntax diagrams in this book. For example, the term **DATA** in the **DATA** statement is a statement keyword.

No sequence of characters is reserved in all contexts. A statement keyword is interpreted as an entity name if the keyword is used in such a context.

Statement Labels

A statement label is a sequence of one to five digits, one of which must be nonzero, that you can use to identify statements in a Fortran scoping unit. In fixed-form, a statement label can appear anywhere in columns 1 through 5 of the initial line of the statement. In free form, such column restrictions do not apply.

You must not give the same label to more than one statement in a scoping unit. Blanks and leading zeros are not significant in distinguishing between statement labels. You can label any statement, but you can only refer to executable statements and **FORMAT** statements by using statement labels. You must place the statement making the reference and the statement you want to reference in the same scoping unit. (See "Scope" on page 101 for details).

Lines and Source Formats

A line is a horizontal arrangement of characters. By contrast, a column is a vertical arrangement of characters, where each character in a given column shares the same line position.

The kinds of lines are:

Initial Line Is the first line of a statement.

Continuation Line Continues a statement beyond its initial line.

Comment Line Does not affect the executable program and can be used for documentation. The comment text continues to the end of a line. Although comment lines can follow one another, a comment line cannot be continued. A line of all blanks or a zero-length line is a comment line without any text. Comment text can contain any characters allowed in a character context.

If an initial line or continuation line is not continued, or if it is continued but not in a character context, an inline comment can be placed on the same line, to the right of any statement label, statement text, and continuation character that may be present. An exclamation point (!) begins an inline comment.

INCLUDE line Indicates source text to be inserted during processing.

Source lines can be in fixed form or free form format. These source forms cannot be mixed within the same program unit. The means of specifying a program unit's source form is processor-dependent.

Fixed Form

If a fixed-form line contains only default kind characters, it must contain exactly 72 characters. Otherwise, the maximum number of characters is processor-dependent.

Columns beyond the right margin are not part of the line and can be used for identification, sequencing, or any other purpose.

Except within a character context, blanks are insignificant; that is, you can imbed blanks between and within lexical tokens.

Requirements for lines and for items on those lines are:

- A comment line begins with a C or an asterisk (*) in column 1, or is all blanks. Comments can also follow an exclamation point (!), except when the exclamation point is in column 6 or in a character context.

- For an initial line:

- Columns 1 through 5 contain either blanks or a statement label.
- Column 6 contains a blank or zero.
- Columns 7 through 72 contain statement text, possibly followed by other statements or by an inline comment.

- For a continuation line:

  - Columns 1 through 5 must be blank.
  - Column 6 must have a character that is not zero or blank. The character in column 6 is referred to as the continuation character. Exclamation points and semicolons are valid continuation characters.
  - Columns 7 through 72 contain continued statement text, possibly followed by other statements and an inline comment.
  - Neither the **END** statement nor a statement whose initial line appears to be a program unit **END** statement can be continued.
  - A statement can have up to 19 continuation lines.

A semicolon (;) separates statements on a single source line, except when it appears in a character context, in a comment, or in column 6. Two or more semicolon separators that are on the same line and are themselves separated by only blanks or other semicolons are considered to be a single separator. A separator that is the last character on a line or before an inline comment is ignored. Statements following a semicolon on the same line cannot be labeled. Additional statements cannot follow a program unit **END** statement on the same line.

Example of Fixed Form

```
C Column Numbers:
C       1         2         3         4         5         6         7
C23456789012345678901234567890123456789012345678901234567890123456789012

      CHARACTER ABC ; LOGICAL X           ! 2 statements on 1 line
      DO 10 I=1,10
        PRINT *,'this is the index',I  ! with an inline comment
10    CONTINUE
C
      CHARSTR="THIS IS A CONTINUED
    X CHARACTER STRING"
      ! There will be 38 blanks in the string between "CONTINUED"
      ! and "CHARACTER". You cannot have an inline comment on
      ! the initial line because it would be interpreted as part
      ! of CHARSTR (character context).
  100 PRINT *, IERROR
      END
```

Free Form

A free-form line can specify up to 132 characters on each line, with a maximum of 39 continuation lines for a statement.

Items can begin in any column of a line, subject to the following requirements for lines and items on those lines:

- A comment line is a line of blanks or begins with an exclamation point (!) that is not in a character context.
- An initial line can contain the following items in the following sequence:
  - A statement label
  - Statement text
  - Additional statements
  - The ampersand continuation character (&)
  - An inline comment
- A continuation line in a noncharacter context begins on the next noncomment line. If the first nonblank character is an ampersand, the statement continues at the next character position. Otherwise, it continues with the first position of the line.
- A character context can be continued if:
  - The last character of the continued line is an ampersand and is not followed by an inline comment. If the right-most character of the statement text to be continued is an ampersand, a second ampersand must be entered as a continuation character.
  - The first nonblank character of the next noncomment line is an ampersand.
- If a lexical token is continued, the ampersand must immediately follow the initial part of the token, and the remainder of the token must immediately start after the ampersand on the continuation line.

A semicolon separates statements on a single source line, except when it appears in a character context or in a comment. Two or more separators that are on the same line and are themselves separated by only blanks or other semicolons are considered to be a single separator. A separator that is the last character on a line or before an inline comment is ignored. Additional statements cannot follow a program unit **END** statement on the same line.

Blanks

Blanks must not appear within lexical tokens, except in a character context or in a format specification. Blanks can be inserted freely between tokens to improve readability, although they must separate names, constants, and labels from adjacent keywords, names, constants, and labels.

Certain adjacent keywords may require blanks:

Blanks Optional	Blanks Mandatory
BLOCK DATA	CASE DEFAULT
DOUBLE PRECISION	DO WHILE
ELSE IF	IMPLICIT *type_spec*
END BLOCK DATA	IMPLICIT NONE
END DO	INTERFACE ASSIGNMENT
END FILE	INTERFACE OPERATOR
END FUNCTION	MODULE PROCEDURE
END IF	RECURSIVE FUNCTION
END INTERFACE	RECURSIVE SUBROUTINE
END MODULE	RECURSIVE *type_spec*
END PROGRAM	*type_spec* FUNCTION
END SELECT	*type_spec* RECURSIVE
END SUBROUTINE	
END TYPE	
END WHERE	
GO TO	
IN OUT	
SELECT CASE	

See "Type Declaration" on page 343 for details about *type_spec*.

Example of Free Form

```
! Column Numbers:
!      1         2         3         4         5         6         7
!2345678901234567890123456789012345678901234567890123456789012345678901
 DO I=1,20
    PRINT *,'this statement&
    & is continued' ; IF (I.LT.5) PRINT *, I

 ENDDO
 EN&
         &D                   ! A lexical token can be continued
```

INCLUDE Line

The **INCLUDE** line inserts source text into a program unit. The **INCLUDE** line is not a Fortran statement.

```
►►──INCLUDE─char_literal_constant────────────────────►◄
```

char_literal_constant

specifies the name of source text (e.g., an include file). The optional kind type parameter cannot be a named constant. See "Character" on page 26 for details.

An **INCLUDE** line cannot be continued, nor can it contain a statement label. A Fortran statement cannot be added to the line, although you can add an inline comment.

An included file can contain any complete Fortran source statements, including other **INCLUDE** lines. Recursive **INCLUDE** lines are not allowed. An **END** statement can be part of the included group. The first included line must not be a continuation line, nor can the last included line be continued. The statements in the include file are processed with the source form of the including file.

Order of Statements and Execution Sequence

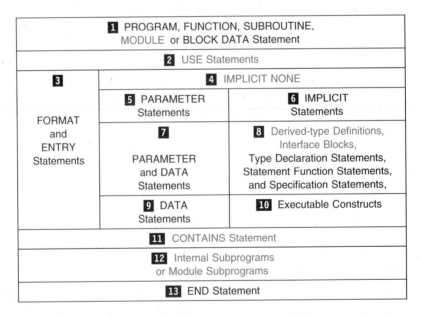

Figure 1. Statement Order. Vertical lines delineate varieties of statements that can be interspersed, while horizontal lines delineate varieties of statements that cannot be interspersed. The numbers in the diagram are used later in the book to identify groups of statements that are allowed in particular contexts.

Refer to "Program Units and Procedures" on page 101 or Part 2 for more details on rules and restrictions concerning statement order.

Normal execution sequence is the processing of executable statements in the order they appear in a scoping unit. It begins with the first executable statement in a main program. Nonexecutable statements and comment lines do not affect the normal execution sequence.

A transfer of control is an alteration of the normal execution sequence. Some statements that you can use to control the execution sequence are:

- Control statements
- Input/output statements that contain an **END=**, **ERR=**, or **EOR=** specifier

When you reference a procedure, the execution of the program continues with the first executable statement following the **FUNCTION**, **SUBROUTINE**, or **ENTRY** statement in the referenced procedure (or to a statement referenced by an alternate return specifier).

In this book, any description of the sequence of events in a specific transfer of control assumes that no event, such as the occurrence of an error or the execution of a **STOP** statement, changes that normal sequence.

Chapter 3. Data Types and Data Objects

This chapter describes:

The Data Types

A data type has a name, a set of valid values, a means to denote such values (constants), and a set of operations to manipulate the values. There are two categories of data types: *intrinsic types* and *derived types*.

The intrinsic types, including their operations, are predefined and are always accessible. There are two classes of intrinsic data types:

- **Numeric (also known as Arithmetic):** integer, real, and complex

- **Nonnumeric:** character and logical

Derived types are user-defined data types whose components are intrinsic and/or derived data types.

Type Parameters and Specifiers

A processor provides one or more representation methods for each of the intrinsic data types. Each method can be specified by a value called a *kind type parameter*, which is a scalar integer initialization expression that indicates the decimal exponent range for the integer type, the decimal precision and exponent range for the real and complex types, and the representation methods for the character and logical types. Each intrinsic type supports a processor-dependent set of kind type parameters.

The *length type parameter* specifies the number of characters for entities of type character.

A *type specifier* specifies the type of all entities declared in a type declaration statement. Some type specifiers (**INTEGER**, **REAL**, **COMPLEX**, **LOGICAL**, and **CHARACTER**) can include a *kind_selector*, which specifies the value range a type can represent. See *type_spec* on page 343 for details on using type specifiers.

The **KIND** intrinsic function returns the kind type parameter of its argument. See "KIND (X)" on page 384 for details.

Data Objects

A *data object* is a variable, constant, or subobject of a constant.

A *variable* can have a value and can be defined or redefined during execution of an executable program. A variable can be:

- A scalar variable name
- An array variable name
- A subobject

A *subobject* (of a variable) is a portion of a named object that can be referenced and defined. It can be:

- An array element
- An array section
- A character substring
- A structure component

A subobject of a constant is a portion of a constant. The referenced portion may depend on a variable value.

Constants

A *constant* has a value and cannot be defined or redefined during execution of an executable program. A constant with a name is a *named constant* (see "PARAMETER" on page 302). A constant without a name is a *literal constant*. A literal constant must be of intrinsic type. The optional kind type parameter of a literal constant can only be a digit string or a scalar integer named constant.

A signed literal constant can have a leading plus or minus sign. All other literal constants must be unsigned; they must have no leading sign. The value zero is considered neither positive nor negative. You can specify zero as signed or unsigned.

Automatic Objects

An *automatic object* is a data object that is dynamically allocated within a procedure. It is a local entity of a subprogram and has a nonconstant character length and/or a nonconstant array bound. It is not a dummy argument.

An automatic object cannot be specified in a **DATA**, **EQUIVALENCE**, **NAMELIST**, or **COMMON** statement, nor can the **PARAMETER**, or **SAVE** attributes be specified for it. An automatic object cannot be initialized or defined with an initialization expression in a type declaration statement. An automatic object cannot appear in the specification part of a main program or module.

Intrinsic Types

Integer

The integer type specifier must include the **INTEGER** keyword. See "INTEGER" on page 276 for details on declaring entities of type integer.

The form of a signed integer literal constant is:

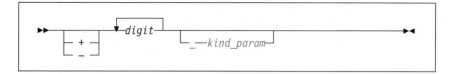

kind_param   is a kind type parameter

A signed integer literal constant has an optional sign, followed by a string of decimal digits containing no decimal point and expressing a whole number, optionally followed by a kind type parameter. A signed, integer literal constant can be positive, zero, or negative. If unsigned and nonzero, the constant is assumed to be positive.

If *kind_param* is specified, the magnitude of the literal constant must be representable within the value range permitted by that *kind_param*.

Examples of Integer Constants

```
0                       ! has default integer size
-173_2                  ! the value -173 with a kind type parameter of 2
9223372036854775807
```

Real

A real type specifier must include either the **REAL** keyword or the **DOUBLE PRECISION** keyword. The precision of double precision values is greater than that of default real values. See "REAL" on page 321 and "DOUBLE PRECISION" on page 229 for details on declaring entities of type real.

The forms of a real literal constant are:

- A basic real constant optionally followed by a kind type parameter
- A basic real constant followed by an exponent and an optional kind type parameter

- An integer constant (with no *kind_param*) followed by an exponent and an optional kind type parameter

A basic real constant has, in order, an optional sign, an integer part, a decimal point, and a fractional part. Both the integer part and fractional part are strings of digits; you can omit either of these parts, but not both. You can write a basic real constant with more digits than a processor will use to approximate the value of the constant. A processor interprets a basic real constant as a decimal number.

The form of a real constant is:

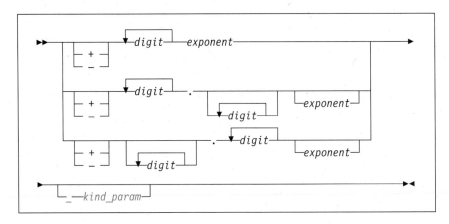

exponent

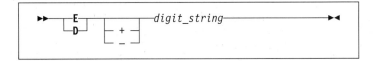

kind_param   is a kind type parameter

digit_string denotes a power of 10. **E** specifies a constant of type default real. **D** specifies a constant of type default double precision.

If both *exponent* and *kind_param* are specified, the exponent letter must be **E**. If **D** is specified, *kind_param* must not be specified.

A real literal constant that is specified without an exponent and a kind type parameter is of type default real.

Examples of Real Constants

```
+0.
+5.432E02_16
7.E3
```

Complex

A complex type specifier must include the **COMPLEX** keyword. The kind of a complex constant is determined by the kind of the constants in the real and imaginary parts.

See "COMPLEX" on page 209 for details on declaring entities of type complex.

Scalar values of type complex can be formed using signed literal constants of type real and/or integer:

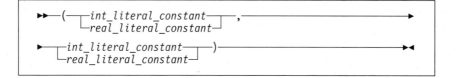

If both parts of the literal constant are of type real, the kind type parameter of the literal constant is the kind parameter of the part with the greater precision, and the kind type parameter of the part with lower precision is converted to that of the other part. If the precision of each part is the same, the processor determines that the kind type parameter is the same as one of the parts.

If both parts are of type integer, they are each converted to type default real. If one part is of type integer and the other is of type real, the integer is converted to a real with the precision of the real.

Examples of Complex Constants

```
(3_2,-1.86)        ! Integer constant 3 is converted to default real
                   ! for constant 3.0

(5.67D4,8.76543E-03)
```

Logical

The logical type specifier must include the **LOGICAL** keyword. See "LOGICAL" on page 285 for details on declaring entities of type logical.

The form of a logical literal constant is:

```
►►──┬──.TRUE.──┬──────────────────────────────────►◄
    └──.FALSE.─┘   └──_──kind_param──┘
```

kind_param   is a kind type parameter

A logical constant can have a logical value of either true or false.

Examples of Logical Constants

```
.FALSE._4
.TRUE.
```

Character

The character type specifier must include the **CHARACTER** keyword. See "CHARACTER" on page 199 for details on declaring entities of type character.

The form of a character literal constant is:

kind_param   is a kind type parameter

Character literal constants can be delimited by double quotation marks as well as apostrophes.

character_string consists of any characters capable of representation in the processor. The delimiting apostrophes (') or double quotation marks (") are not part of the data represented by the constant. Blanks embedded between these delimiters are significant.

If a string is delimited by apostrophes, you can represent an apostrophe within the string with two consecutive apostrophes (without intervening blanks). If a string is delimited by double quotation marks, you can represent a double quotation mark within the string with two consecutive double quotation marks (without intervening blanks). The two consecutive apostrophes or double quotation marks are treated as one character.

You can place a double quotation mark within a character literal constant delimited by apostrophes to represent a double quotation mark, and an apostrophe character within a character constant delimited by double quotation marks to represent a single apostrophe.

The length of a character literal constant is the number of characters between the delimiters, except that each pair of consecutive apostrophes or double quotation marks counts as one character.

A zero-length character object uses no storage.

Examples of Character Constants

```
''                      ! Zero-length character constant
1_"ABCDEFGHIJ"          ! Character constant of length 10, with kind 1
```

Character Substrings

A character substring is a contiguous portion of a character string (called a parent string), which is a scalar variable name, scalar constant, scalar structure component, or array element. A character substring is identified by a substring reference whose form is:

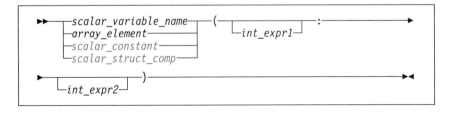

int_expr1 and int_expr2
specify the left-most character position and right-most character position, respectively, of the substring. Each is a scalar integer expression called a substring expression.

The length of a character substring is the result of the evaluation of MAX($int\_expr2 - int\_expr1 + 1, 0$).

If int_expr1 is less than or equal to int_expr2, their values must be such that:

$$1 \leq int\_expr1 \leq int\_expr2 \leq length$$

where length is the length of the parent string. If int_expr1 is omitted, its default value is 1. If int_expr2 is omitted, its default value is length.

A substring of an array section is treated differently. See "Array Sections and Substring Ranges" on page 57.

Examples of Character Substrings

```
CHARACTER(8) ABC, X, Y, Z
ABC = 'ABCDEFGHIJKL'(1:8)    ! Substring of a constant
X = ABC(3:5)                 ! X = 'CDE'
Y = ABC(-1:6)                ! Not allowed in either FORTRAN 77 or Fortran 90
Z = ABC(6:-1)                ! Z = '' valid only in Fortran 90
```

Derived Types

You can create additional data types, known as derived types, from intrinsic data types and other derived types. You require a type definition to define the name of the derived type (*type_name*), as well as the data types and names of the components of the derived type.

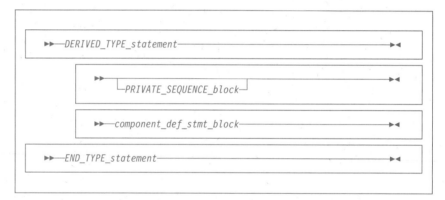

DERIVED_TYPE_statement

> See "Derived Type" on page 223 for syntax details

PRIVATE_SEQUENCE_block

> includes the **PRIVATE** statement (keyword only) and/or the **SEQUENCE** statement. Only one of each statement can be specified. See "PRIVATE" on page 310 and "SEQUENCE" on page 332 for details on syntax.

component_def_stmt_block

> consists of one or more type declaration statements to define the components of the derived type. The type declaration statements can specify only the **DIMENSION** and **POINTER** attributes and cannot contain initial values. See "Type Declaration" on page 343 for detailed syntax and information.

END_TYPE_statement

> See "END TYPE" on page 240

Each derived type is resolved into ultimate components of intrinsic data type.

The type name is a local entity. It cannot be the same name as any of the intrinsic data types.

The **END TYPE** statement can optionally contain the same *type_name* as specified on the **TYPE** statement.

The components of a derived type can specify any of the intrinsic data types. Components can also be of a previously defined derived type. A pointer component can be of the same derived type that it is a component of. Within a derived type, the names of components must be unique, although they can be different from names outside the scope of the derived-type definition. Components that are declared to be of type **CHARACTER** must have length specifications that are constant specification expressions; asterisks are not allowed as length specifiers. Nonpointer array components must be declared with constant dimension declarators. Pointer array components must be declared with a *deferred_shape_spec_list*.

By default, no storage sequence is implied by the order of the component definitions. However, if you specify the **SEQUENCE** statement, the derived type becomes a *sequence derived type*. For a sequence derived type, the order of the components specifies a storage sequence for objects declared with this derived type. If a component of a sequence derived type is of derived type, that derived type must also be a sequence derived type.

The size of a sequence derived type is equal to the amount of storage needed to hold all of the components of that derived type.

The **PRIVATE** statement can only be specified if the derived-type definition is within the specification part of a module. If a component of a derived type is of a type declared to be private, either the derived-type definition must contain the **PRIVATE** statement or the derived type itself must be private.

If a type definition is private, the following are accessible only within the defining module:

- the type name
- structure constructors for the type
- any entity of the type
- any procedure that has a dummy argument or function result of the type

If a derived-type definition contains a **PRIVATE** statement, its components are accessible only within the defining module, even if the derived type itself is public. Structure components can only be used in the defining module.

A component of a derived-type entity cannot appear as an input/output list item if any ultimate component of the object cannot be accessed by the scoping unit of the input/output statement. A derived-type object cannot appear in a data transfer statement if it has a component that is a pointer.

A scalar entity of derived type is called a *structure*. A scalar entity of sequence derived type is called a *sequence structure*. The type specifier of a structure must include the **TYPE** keyword, followed by the name of the derived type in parentheses. See the **TYPE** type declaration statement on page 339 for details on declaring entities of a specified derived type. The components of a structure are called *structure components*. A *structure component* is one of the components of a structure or is an array whose elements are components of the elements of an array of derived type.

An object of a private derived type cannot be used outside the defining module.

Determining Type for Derived Types

Two data objects have the same derived type if they are declared with reference to the same derived-type definition.

If the data objects are in different scoping units, they can still have the same derived type. Either the derived-type definition is accessible via host or use assocation, or the data objects reference their own derived-type definitions with the following conditions:

- The derived-type definitions have the same name. Renaming affects only the local name, not the original definition of the derived type.
- Each of the derived-type definitions contains the **SEQUENCE** statement.
- Each derived-type definition has components that do not specify private accessibility and that match the components of the other derived type in name, order, and attributes.

A derived-type definition that specifies **SEQUENCE** is not the same as a definition declared to be private or that has components that are private.

Example of Determining Type with Derived Types

```
PROGRAM MYPROG

TYPE NAME                          ! Sequence derived type
    SEQUENCE
    CHARACTER(20) LASTNAME
    CHARACTER(10) FIRSTNAME
    CHARACTER(1)  INITIAL
END TYPE NAME
TYPE (NAME) PER1
```

```
CALL MYSUB(PER1)
PER1 = NAME('Smith','John','K')    ! Structure constructor
CALL MYPRINT(PER1)

CONTAINS
  SUBROUTINE MYSUB(STUDENT)        ! Internal subroutine MYSUB
    TYPE (NAME) STUDENT            ! NAME is accessible via host association
       ⋮
  END SUBROUTINE MYSUB
END

SUBROUTINE MYPRINT(NAMES)          ! External subroutine MYPRINT
  TYPE NAME                        ! Same type as data type in MYPROG
    SEQUENCE
    CHARACTER(20) LASTNAME
    CHARACTER(10) FIRSTNAME
    CHARACTER(1)  INITIAL
  END TYPE NAME
  TYPE (NAME) NAMES                ! NAMES and PER1 from MYPROG
  PRINT *, NAMES                   ! have the same data type
END SUBROUTINE
```

Structure Components

Structure components can be of any explicit type, including derived type.

Note: The case in which a structure component has a subobject that is an array or array section requires some background information from "Array Sections" on page 53, and is explained in "Array Sections and Structure Components" on page 57. The following rules for scalar structure components apply also to structure components that have array subobjects.

You can refer to a specific structure component using a *component designator*. A scalar component designator has the following syntax:

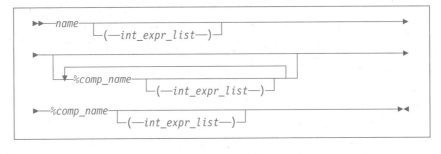

name is the name of an object of derived type

comp_name is the name of a derived-type component

int_expr　　　is a scalar integer expression called a subscript expression

The structure component has the same type, type parameters, and **POINTER**
attribute (if any) as the right-most *comp_name*. It inherits any **INTENT**,
TARGET, and **PARAMETER** attributes from the parent object.

Notes

- Each *comp_name* must be a component of the immediately preceding
  name or *comp_name*.
- The *name* and each *comp_name*, except the right-most, must be of derived
  type.
- The number of subscript expressions in any *int_expr_list* must equal the
  rank of the preceding *name* or *comp_name*.
- If *name* or any *comp_name* is the name of an array, it must have an
  int_expr_list.
- The right-most *comp_name* must be scalar.

Structure Constructor

```
►►—type_name—(—expr_list—)————————————————►◄
```

type_name　　is the name of the derived type

expr　　　　　is an expression. Expressions are defined under "Expressions
and Assignment", beginning on page 63.

A structure constructor allows a scalar value of derived type to be constructed
from an ordered list of values. A structure constructor must not appear before
the definition of the referenced derived type.

expr_list contains one value for each component of the derived type. The
sequence of expressions in the *expr_list* must agree in number and order with
the components of the derived type. The type and type parameters of each
expression must be assignment-compatible with the type and type parameters
of the corresponding component. Data type conversion is performed if
necessary.

A component that is a pointer can be declared with the same type that it is a
component of. If a structure constructor is created for a derived type containing
a pointer, the expression corresponding to the pointer component must evaluate
to an object that would be an allowable target for such a pointer in a pointer
assignment statement.

Examples of Derived Types

```
MODULE PEOPLE
  TYPE NAME
     SEQUENCE                         ! Sequence derived type
     CHARACTER(20) LASTNAME
     CHARACTER(10) FIRSTNAME
     CHARACTER(1)  INITIAL
  END TYPE NAME

  TYPE PERSON                         ! Components accessible via use
                                      ! association
     INTEGER AGE
     INTEGER BIRTHDATE(3)             ! Array component
     TYPE (NAME) FULLNAME             ! Component of derived type
  END TYPE PERSON
END MODULE PEOPLE

PROGRAM TEST1
  USE PEOPLE
  TYPE (PERSON) SMITH, JONES
  SMITH = PERSON(30, (/6,30,63/), NAME('Smith','John','K'))
                                      ! Nested structure constructors
  JONES%AGE = SMITH%AGE              ! Component designator
  CALL TEST2
  CONTAINS

  SUBROUTINE TEST2
    TYPE T
      INTEGER EMP_NO
      CHARACTER, POINTER :: EMP_NAME(:)  ! Pointer component
    END TYPE T
    TYPE (T) EMP_REC
    CHARACTER, TARGET :: NAME(10)
    EMP_REC = T(24744,NAME)                ! Pointer assignment occurs
  END SUBROUTINE                           ! for EMP_REC%EMP_NAME
END
```

How Type Is Determined

Each user-defined function or named entity has a data type. (The type of an entity accessed by host or use association is determined in the host scoping unit or accessed module, respectively.) The type of a name is determined, in the following sequence, in one of three ways:

1. Explicitly, in one of the following ways:

    • From a specified type declaration statement (see "Type Declaration" on page 343 for details).

- For function results, from a specified type statement or its **FUNCTION** statement.

2. Implicitly, from a specified **IMPLICIT** type statement (see "IMPLICIT" on page 268 for details).

3. Implicitly, by predefined convention. By default (that is, in the absence of an **IMPLICIT** type statement), if the first letter of the name is I, J, K, L, M, or N, the type is default integer. Otherwise, the type is default real.

In a given scoping unit, if a letter has not been specified in an **IMPLICIT** statement, the implicit type used is the same as the implicit type used by the host scoping unit. A program unit and interface body are treated as if they had a host with an **IMPLICIT** statement listing the predefined conventions.

The data type of a literal constant is determined by its form.

Definition Status of Variables

A variable is always defined or undefined, and its definition status can change during program execution. A named constant has a value and cannot be defined or redefined during program execution.

Arrays (including sections), structures, and variables of character or complex type are objects made up of zero or more subobjects. Associations can be established between variables and subobjects and between subobjects of different variables.

- An object is defined if all of its subobjects are defined. That is, each object or subobject has a value that does not change until it becomes undefined or until it is redefined with a different value.

- If an object is undefined, at least one of its subobjects is undefined. An undefined object or subobject cannot provide a predictable value.

Variables are initially defined if they are specified to have initial values by **DATA** statements or type declaration statements. Zero-sized arrays and zero-length character objects are always defined.

All other variables are initially undefined.

Events Causing Definition

Events that cause a variable to become defined are:

1. Execution of an intrinsic assignment statement other than a masked array assignment statement causes the variable that precedes the equal sign to become defined.

Execution of a defined assignment statement may cause all or part of the variable that precedes the equal sign to become defined.

2. Execution of a masked array assignment statement may cause some or all of the array elements in the assignment statement to become defined.

3. As execution of an input statement proceeds, each variable that is assigned a value from the input file becomes defined at the time that data are transferred to it. Execution of a **WRITE** statement whose unit specifier identifies an internal file causes each record that is written to become defined.

4. Execution of a **DO** statement causes the **DO** variable, if any, to become defined.

5. Beginning of execution of the action specified by an implied-**DO** list in an input/output statement causes the implied-**DO** variable to become defined.

6. Execution of an **ASSIGN** statement causes the variable in the statement to become defined with a statement label value.

7. A reference to a procedure causes the entire dummy argument data object to become defined if the entire corresponding actual argument is defined with a value that is not a statement label.

   A reference to a procedure causes a subobject of a dummy argument to become defined if the corresponding subobject of the corresponding actual argument is defined.

8. Execution of an input/output statement containing an **IOSTAT=** specifier causes the specified integer variable to become defined.

9. Execution of a **READ** statement containing a **SIZE=** specifier causes the specified integer variable to become defined.

10. Execution of an **INQUIRE** statement causes any variable that is assigned a value during the execution of the statement to become defined if no error condition exists.

11. When a character storage unit becomes defined, all associated character storage units become defined.

    When a numeric storage unit becomes defined, all associated numeric storage units of the same type become defined, except that variables associated with the variable in an **ASSIGN** statement become undefined when the **ASSIGN** statement is executed. When an entity of type double precision becomes defined, all totally associated entities of double precision real type become defined.

    A nonpointer scalar object of type nondefault integer, real other than default or double precision, nondefault logical, nondefault complex, nondefault character of any length, or nonsequence type occupies a single unspecified storage unit that is different for each case. A pointer that is distinct from other pointers in at least one of type, kind, and rank occupies a single unspecified storage unit. When an unspecified storage unit becomes defined, all associated unspecified storage units become defined.

When a default complex entity becomes defined, all partially associated default real entities become defined.

12. When both parts of a default complex entity become defined as a result of partially associated default real or default complex entities becoming defined, the default complex entity becomes defined.

13. When all components of a numeric sequence structure or character sequence structure become defined as a result of partially associated objects becoming defined, the structure becomes defined.

14. Execution of an **ALLOCATE** or **DEALLOCATE** statement with a **STAT=** specifier causes the variable specified by the **STAT=** specifier to become defined.

15. Allocation of a zero-sized array causes the array to become defined.

16. Invocation of a procedure causes any automatic object of zero size in that procedure to become defined.

17. Execution of a pointer assignment statement that associates a pointer with a target that is defined causes the pointer to become defined.

Events Causing Undefinition

Events that cause a variable to become undefined are:

1. When a variable of a given type becomes defined, all associated variables of different type become undefined. However, when a variable of type default real is partially associated with a variable of type default complex, the complex variable does not become undefined when the real variable becomes defined and the real variable does not become undefined when the complex variable becomes defined. When a variable of type default complex is partially associated with another variable of type default complex, definition of one does not cause the other to become undefined.

2. Execution of an **ASSIGN** statement causes the variable in the statement to become undefined as an integer. Variables that are associated with the variable also become undefined.

3. If the evaluation of a function may cause an argument of the function or a variable in a module or in a common block to become defined, and if a reference to the function appears in an expression in which the value of the function is not needed to determine the value of the expression, the argument or variable becomes undefined when the expression is evaluated.

4. The execution of a **RETURN** statement or **END** statement within a subprogram causes all variables local to its scoping unit or local to the current instance of its scoping unit for a recursive invocation to become undefined except for the following:

   a. Variables with the **SAVE** attribute.

   b. Variables in blank common.

   c. Variables in a named common block that appears in the subprogram and appears in at least one other scoping unit that is making either a direct or indirect reference to the subprogram.

   d. Variables accessed from the host scoping unit.

   e. Variables accessed from a module that is also referenced directly or indirectly by at least one other scoping unit that is making either a direct or indirect reference to the subprogram.

   f. Variables in a named common block that are initially defined and that have not been subsequently defined or redefined.

5. When an error condition or end-of-file condition occurs during execution of an input statement, all of the variables specified by the input list or namelist-group of the statement become undefined.

6. When an error condition, end-of-file condition, or end-of-record condition occurs during execution of an input/output statement and the statement contains any implied-**DO** lists, all of the implied-**DO** variables in the statement become undefined.

7. Execution of a defined assignment statement may leave all or part of the variable that precedes the equal sign undefined.

8. Execution of a direct access input statement that specifies a record that has not been written previously causes all of the variables specified by the input list of the statement to become undefined.

9. Execution of an **INQUIRE** statement may cause the **NAME=**, **RECL=**, and **NEXTREC=** variables to become undefined.

10. When a character storage unit becomes undefined, all associated character storage units become undefined.

   When a numeric storage unit becomes undefined, all associated numeric storage units become undefined unless the undefinition is a result of defining an associated numeric storage unit of different type (see (1) above).

   When an entity of double precision real type becomes undefined, all totally associated entities of double precision real type become undefined.

When an unspecified storage unit becomes undefined, all associated unspecified storage units become undefined.

11. A reference to a procedure causes part of a dummy argument to become undefined if the corresponding part of the actual argument is defined with a value that is a statement label value.

12. When an allocatable array is deallocated, it becomes undefined. Successful execution of an **ALLOCATE** statement causes the allocated array to become undefined.

13. Execution of an **INQUIRE** statement causes all inquiry specifier variables to become undefined if an error condition exists, except for the variable in the **IOSTAT=** specifier, if any.

14. When a procedure is invoked:

    a. An optional dummy argument that is not associated with an actual argument is undefined.

    b. A dummy argument with **INTENT(OUT)** is undefined.

    c. An actual argument associated with a dummy argument with **INTENT(OUT)** becomes undefined.

    d. A subobject of a dummy argument is undefined if the corresponding subobject of the actual argument is undefined.

    e. The function result variable is undefined.

15. When the association status of a pointer becomes undefined or disassociated, the pointer becomes undefined.

Allocation Status

The allocation status of an allocatable array is one of the following during program execution:

1. Not currently allocated, which means that the array has never been allocated or that the last operation on it was a deallocation.

2. Currently allocated, which means that the array has been allocated by an **ALLOCATE** statement and has not been subsequently deallocated.

3. Undefined, which means that the array does not have the **SAVE** attribute and was currently allocated when execution of a **RETURN** or **END** statement resulted in no executing scoping units having access to it.

If the allocation status of an allocatable array is currently allocated, the array may be referenced and defined. An allocatable array that is not currently allocated must not be referenced or defined. If the allocation status of an allocatable array is undefined, the array must not be referenced, defined, allocated, or deallocated.

Chapter 4. Array Concepts

Fortran 90 provides a set of features, commonly referred to as array language, that let programmers manipulate arrays. This chapter provides background information on arrays and array language:

Related Information: Many statements in "Statements", starting on page 179, have special features and rules for arrays. This chapter makes frequent use of the statement "DIMENSION" on page 224.

A number of new intrinsic functions are especially for arrays. These new functions are mainly those classified as "Transformational Intrinsic Functions" on page 360.

Arrays

An array is an ordered sequence of scalar data. All the elements of an array have the same type and type parameters.

A *whole array* is denoted by the name of the array:

```
! In this declaration, the array is given a type and dimension
REAL, DIMENSION(3) :: A
```

```
! In these expressions, each element is evaluated in each expression
PRINT *, A, A+5, COS(A)
```

A whole array is either a named constant or variable.

Bounds of a Dimension

Each dimension in an array has an upper and lower bound, which determine the range of values that can be used as subscripts for that dimension. A dimension bound can be positive, negative, or zero.

If any lower bound is greater than the corresponding upper bound, the array is a *zero-sized* array, which has no elements but still has the properties of an array. The lower and upper bounds of such a dimension are one and zero, respectively.

When the bounds are specified in array declarators:

- The lower bound is a specification expression. If it is omitted, the default value is 1.
- The upper bound is a specification expression or asterisk (*), and has no default value.

Related Information: "Specification Expressions" on page 67, "LBOUND (ARRAY, DIM)" on page 385, "UBOUND (ARRAY, DIM)" on page 411.

Extent of a Dimension

The *extent* of a dimension is the number of elements in that dimension, computed as the value of the upper bound minus the value of the lower bound, plus one.

```
INTEGER, DIMENSION :: X(5)      ! Extent = 5
REAL :: Y(2:4,3:6)              ! Extent in 1st dimension = 3
                               ! Extent in 2nd dimension = 4
```

The minimum extent is zero, in a dimension where the lower bound is greater than the upper bound.

Different array declarators that are associated by common, equivalence, or argument association can have different ranks and extents.

Rank, Shape, and Size of an Array

The *rank* of an array is the number of dimensions it has:

```
INTEGER, DIMENSION (10) :: A      ! Rank = 1
REAL, DIMENSION (-5:5,100) :: B   ! Rank = 2
```

An array can have from one to seven dimensions.

A scalar is considered to have rank zero.

The *shape* of an array is derived from its rank and extents. It can be represented as a rank-one array where each element is the extent of the corresponding dimension:

```
INTEGER, DIMENSION (10,10) :: A          ! Shape = (/ 10, 10 /)
REAL, DIMENSION (-5:4,1:10,10:19) :: B    ! Shape = (/ 10, 10, 10 /)
```

The *size* of an array is the number of elements in it, equal to the product of the extents of all dimensions:

```
INTEGER A(5)           ! Size = 5
REAL B(-1:0,1:3,4)     ! Size = 2 * 3 * 4 = 24
```

Related Information: These examples show only simple arrays where all bounds are constants. For instructions on calculating the values of these properties for more complicated kinds of arrays, see the following sections.

Related intrinsic functions are "SHAPE (SOURCE)" on page 404, and "SIZE (ARRAY, DIM)" on page 405. The rank of an array A is SIZE(SHAPE(A)).

Array Declarators

An array declarator declares the shape of an array.

You must declare every named array, and no scoping unit can have more than one array declarator for the same name. An array declarator can appear in the following statements: **COMMON**, **DIMENSION**, **ALLOCATABLE**, **POINTER**, **TARGET** and type declaration.

For example:

```
DIMENSION :: A(1:5)          ! Declarator is "(1:5)"
REAL, DIMENSION(1,1:5) :: B  ! Declarator is "(1,1:5)"
INTEGER C(10)                ! Declarator is "(10)"
```

The form of an array declarator is:

```
►►──(──array_spec──)──────────────────────────────────►◄
```

array_spec is an array specification. It is a list of dimension declarators, each of which establishes the lower and upper bounds of an array, or specifies that one or both will be set at run time. Each dimension requires one dimension declarator. An array can have from one to seven dimensions.

An *array_spec* is one of:

> *explicit_shape_spec_list*
> *assumed_shape_spec_list*
> *deferred_shape_spec_list*
> *assumed_size_spec*

Each *array_spec* declares a different kind of array, as explained in the following sections.

Explicit-shape Arrays

Explicit-shape arrays are arrays where the bounds are explicitly specified for each dimension.

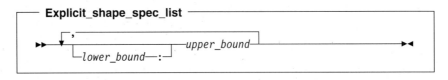

lower_bound, upper_bound
          are specification expressions

If any bound is not constant, the array must be declared inside a subprogram and the nonconstant bounds are determined on entry to the subprogram. If a lower bound is omitted, its default value is one.

The rank is the number of specified upper bounds. The shape of an explicit-shape dummy argument can differ from that of the corresponding actual argument.

The size is determined by the specified bounds.

Examples of Explicit-shape Arrays

```
INTEGER A,B,C(1:10,-5:5)   ! All bounds are constant
A=8; B=3
CALL SUB1(A,B,C)
END

SUBROUTINE SUB1(X,Y,Z)
  INTEGER X,Y,Z(X,Y)        ! Some bounds are not constant
END SUBROUTINE
```

Automatic Arrays

An automatic array is an explicit-shape array that is declared in a subprogram, is not a dummy argument, and has at least one bound that is a nonconstant specification expression. The bounds are evaluated on entry to the subprogram and remain unchanged during execution of the subprogram.

```
INTEGER X
COMMON X
X = 10
CALL SUB1(5)
END

SUBROUTINE SUB1(Y)
  INTEGER X
  COMMON X
  INTEGER Y
  REAL Z (X:20, 1:Y)   ! Automatic array.  Here the bounds are made available
                       ! through dummy arguments and common blocks, although
                       ! Z itself is not a dummy argument.
END SUBROUTINE
```

Related Information: For general information about automatic data objects, see "Automatic Objects" on page 22.

Adjustable Arrays

An *adjustable* array is an explicit-shape array that is declared in a subprogram and has at least one bound that is a nonconstant specification expression. An adjustable array must be a dummy argument.

```
SUBROUTINE SUB1(X, Y)
INTEGER X, Y(X*3)   ! Adjustable array.  Here the bounds depend on a
                    ! dummy argument, and the array name is also passed in.
END SUBROUTINE
```

Assumed-shape Arrays

Assumed-shape arrays are dummy argument arrays where the extent of each dimension is taken from the associated actual arguments. Because the names of assumed-shape arrays are dummy arguments, they must be declared inside subprograms.

Assumed_shape_spec_list

lower_bound   is a specification expression

Each lower bound defaults to one, or may be explicitly specified. Each upper bound is set on entry to the subprogram to the specified lower bound (not the lower bound of the actual argument array) plus the extent of the dimension minus one.

The extent of any dimension is the extent of the corresponding dimension of the associated actual argument.

The rank is the number of colons in the *assumed_shape_spec_list*.

The shape is assumed from the associated actual argument array.

The size is determined on entry to the subprogram where it is declared, and equals the size of the associated argument array.

Note: Subprograms that have assumed-shape arrays as dummy arguments must have explicit interfaces.

Examples of Assumed-shape Arrays

```
INTERFACE
  SUBROUTINE SUB1(B)
    INTEGER B(1:,:,10:)
  END SUBROUTINE
END INTERFACE

INTEGER A(10,11:20,30)
CALL SUB1 (A)
END

SUBROUTINE SUB1(B)
INTEGER B(1:,:,10:)
! Inside the subroutine, B is associated with A.
! It has the same extents as A but different bounds (1:10,1:10,10:39).
END SUBROUTINE
```

Deferred-shape Arrays

Deferred-shape arrays are allocatable arrays or array pointers, where the bounds can be defined or redefined during execution of the program.

```
┌── Deferred_shape_spec_list ──────────────────────────────┐
│        ┌─ , ─┐                                            │
►►──────┴─ : ─┴──────────────────────────────────────────────►◄
```

The extent of each dimension (and the related properties of bounds, shape, and size) are undefined until the array is allocated or the pointer is associated with an array that is defined. Before that point, no part of the array may be defined, or referenced except as an argument to an appropriate inquiry function. At that point, an array pointer assumes the properties of the target array and the properties of an allocatable array are specified in an **ALLOCATE** statement.

The rank is the number of colons in the *deferred_shape_spec_list*.

Although a *deferred_shape_spec_list* may sometimes appear identical to an *assumed_shape_spec_list*, deferred-shape arrays and assumed-shape arrays are not the same. A deferred-shape array must have either the **POINTER** attribute or the **ALLOCATABLE** attribute, while an assumed-shape array must be a dummy argument that does not have the **POINTER** attribute. The bounds of a deferred-shape array, and the actual storage associated with it, can be changed at any time by reallocating the array or by associating the pointer with a different array, while these properties remain the same for an assumed-shape array during the execution of the containing subprogram.

Related Information: "Allocation Status" on page 38, "Pointer Assignment" on page 84, "ALLOCATABLE" on page 184, "ALLOCATED (ARRAY)" on page 367, "ASSOCIATED (POINTER, TARGET)" on page 368.

Allocatable Arrays

A deferred-shape array that has the **ALLOCATABLE** attribute is referred to as an *allocatable array*. Its bounds and shape are determined when storage is allocated for it by an **ALLOCATE** statement.

```
INTEGER, ALLOCATABLE, DIMENSION(:,:,:) :: A

ALLOCATE(A(10,-4:5,20)) ! Bounds of A are now defined (1:10,-4:5,1:20)
DEALLOCATE(A)
ALLOCATE(A(5,5,5))     ! Change the bounds of A
```

- minimize storage used

FORTRAN 77 source

```
integer a(1000),b(1000),c(1000)
C 1000 is the maximum size
write (6,*) "Enter the size of the arrays:"
read (5,*) n
   ⋮
do i=1,n
  a(i)=b(i)+c(i)
end do
end
```

Fortran 90 source

```
integer, allocatable, dimension(:) :: a,b,c
write (6,*) "Enter the size of the arrays:"
read (5,*) n
allocate (a(n),b(n),c(n))
   ⋮
a=b+c
end
```

Array Pointers

An array with the **POINTER** attribute is referred to as an array pointer. Its bounds and shape are determined when it is associated with a target through pointer assignment or execution of an **ALLOCATE** statement. It can appear in a type declaration, **POINTER**, or **DIMENSION** statement.

```
REAL, POINTER, DIMENSION(:,:) :: B
REAL, TARGET, DIMENSION(5,10) :: C, D(10:10)

B => C              ! Bounds of B are now defined (1:5,1:10)
B => D              ! B now has different bounds and is associated
                    !   with different storage
ALLOCATE(B(5,5))    ! Change bounds and storage association again
END
```

Assumed-size Arrays

Assumed-size arrays are dummy argument arrays where the size is inherited from the associated actual array, but the rank and extents may differ. They can only be declared inside subprograms.

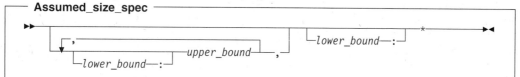

lower_bound, upper_bound
> are specification expressions

If any bound is not constant, the array must be declared inside a subprogram and the nonconstant bounds are determined on entry to the subprogram. If a lower bound is omitted, its default value is one.

The last dimension has no upper bound and is designated instead by an asterisk. You must ensure that references to elements do not go past the end of the actual array.

The rank equals one plus the number of *upper_bound* specifications in its declaration, which may be different from the rank of the actual array it is associated with.

The size is assumed from the actual argument that is associated with the assumed-size dummy argument array:

- If the actual argument is a noncharacter array, the size of the assumed-size array is that of the actual array.
- If the actual argument is an array element from a noncharacter array, and if the size remaining in the array beginning at this element is **S**, then the size of the dummy argument array is **S**. Array elements are processed in array element order.
- If the actual argument is a character array, array element, or array element substring, and assuming that:
  - **A** is the starting offset, in characters, into the character array
  - **T** is the total length, in characters, of the original array.
  - **S** is the length, in characters, of an element in the dummy argument array.

then the size of the dummy argument array is **MAX(INT(T - A + 1) / S, 0)**.

For example:

```
CHARACTER(10) A(10)
CHARACTER(1) B(30)
CALL SUB1(A)            ! Size of dummy argument array is 10
CALL SUB1(A(4))         ! Size of dummy argument array is 6
CALL SUB1(A(6)(5:10))   ! Size of dummy argument array is 3 because there are
                        !   just under 4 elements remaining in A
CALL SUB1(B(12))        ! Size of dummy argument array is 1, because the remainder
                        !   of B can hold just one CHARACTER(10) element

END

SUBROUTINE SUB1(ARRAY)
  CHARACTER(10) ARRAY(*)

  ...
END SUBROUTINE
```

Examples of Assumed-size Arrays

```
INTEGER X(3,2)
DO I = 1,3
   DO J = 1,2
      X(I,J) = I * J      ! The elements of X are 1, 2, 3, 2, 4, 6
   END DO
END DO
PRINT *,SHAPE(X)          ! The shape is (/ 3, 2 /)
PRINT *,X(1,:)            ! The first row is (/ 1, 2 /)
CALL SUB1(X)
CALL SUB2(X)
END

SUBROUTINE SUB1(Y)
  INTEGER Y(2,*)          ! The dimensions of y are the reverse of x above
  PRINT *, SIZE(Y,1)      ! We can examine the size of the first dimension
                          ! but not the last one.
  PRINT *, Y(:,1)         ! We can print out vectors from the first
  PRINT *, Y(:,2)         ! dimension, but not the last one.
END SUBROUTINE

SUBROUTINE SUB2(Y)
  INTEGER Y(*)            ! Y has a different rank than X above.
  PRINT *, Y(6)           ! We have to know (or compute) the position of
                          ! the last element.  Nothing prevents us from
                          ! subscripting beyond the end.

END SUBROUTINE
```

Notes:

1. An assumed-size array cannot be used as a whole array in an executable construct unless it is an actual argument in a subprogram reference that does not require the shape:

```
! A is an assumed-size array.
PRINT *, UBOUND(A,1) ! OK - only examines upper bound of first dimension.
PRINT *, LBOUND(A)   ! OK - only examines lower bound of each dimension.
! However, 'B=UBOUND(A)' or 'A=5' would reference the upper bound of
! the last dimension and are not allowed.  SIZE(A) and SHAPE(A) are
! also not allowed.
```

2. If a section of an assumed-size array has a subscript triplet as its last section subscript, the upper bound must be specified. (Array sections and subscript triplets are explained in a subsequent section.)

```
! A is a 2-dimensional assumed-size array
PRINT *, A(:, 6)      ! Triplet with no upper bound is not last dimension.
PRINT *, A(1, 1:10)   ! Triplet in last dimension has upper bound of 10.
PRINT *, A(5, 5:9:2)  ! Triplet in last dimension has upper bound of 9.
```

Array Elements

Array elements are the scalar data that make up an array. Each element inherits the type, type parameters, and **INTENT**, **PARAMETER**, and **TARGET** attributes from its parent array. The **POINTER** attribute is not inherited.

You identify an array element by an *array element designator*, whose form is:

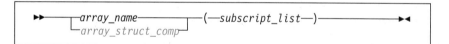

array_name is the name of an array

array_struct_comp is a structure component whose right-most *comp_name* is an array

subscript is an integer scalar expression

Notes

- The number of subscripts must equal the number of dimensions in the array.
- If *array_struct_comp* is present, each part of the structure component except the right-most must have rank zero (that is, must not be an array name or an array section).

- The value of each subscript expression must not be less than the lower bound or greater than the upper bound for the corresponding dimension.

The *subscript value* depends on the value of each subscript expression and on the dimensions of the array. It determines which element of the array is identified by the array element designator.

Related Information: "Structure Components" on page 31, "Array Sections and Structure Components" on page 57.

Array Element Order

The elements of an array are arranged in storage in a sequence known as the *array element order*, in which the subscripts change most rapidly in the first dimension, and subsequently in the remaining dimensions.

For example, an array declared as A(2, 3, 2) has the following elements:

```
Position of Array Element              Array Element Order
-------------------------              -------------------
        A(1,1,1)                               1
        A(2,1,1)                               2
        A(1,2,1)                               3
        A(2,2,1)                               4
        A(1,3,1)                               5
        A(2,3,1)                               6
        A(1,1,2)                               7
        A(2,1,2)                               8
        A(1,2,2)                               9
        A(2,2,2)                              10
        A(1,3,2)                              11
        A(2,3,2)                              12
```

Array Sections

An array section is a selected portion of an array. It is an array subobject that designates a set of elements from an array, or a specified substring or derived-type component from each of those elements. An array section is also an array.

Note: This introductory section describes the simple case, where structure components are not involved. "Array Sections and Structure Components" on page 57 explains the additional rules for specifying array sections that are also structure components.

```
►►──── array_name ─(─ section_subscript_list ─)──────────────────►

►─────────────────────────────────────────────────────────────►◄
          └─ substring_range ─┘

section_subscript:
├──┬─ subscript ──────────┬──────────────────────────────────────┤
   ├─ subscript_triplet ─┤
   └─ vector_subscript ──┘
```

section_subscript designates some set of elements along a particular dimension. It can be composed of a combination of the following:

subscript is a scalar integer expression, explained in "Array Elements" on page 51.

subscript_triplet, vector subscript designate a (possibly empty) sequence of subscripts in a given dimension. For details, see "Subscript Triplets" on page 54 and "Vector Subscripts" on page 56.

Note: At least one of the dimensions must be a subscript triplet or vector subscript, so that an array section is distinct from an array element:

```
INTEGER, DIMENSION(5,5,5) :: A
A(1,2,3) = 100
A(1,3,3) = 101
PRINT *, A(1,2,3)      ! A single array element, 100.
PRINT *, A(1,2:2,3)    ! A one-element array section, (/ 100 /)
PRINT *, A(1,2:3,3)    ! A two-element array section, (/ 100, 101 /)
```

substring_range

```
►►─(─┬──────────┬─:─┬──────────┬─)──────────────────►◄
     └─ int_expr1 ─┘   └─ int_expr2 ─┘
```

int_expr1 and *int_expr2* are scalar integer expressions called substring expressions, defined in "Character Substrings" on page 27. They specify the left-most and right-most character positions, respectively, of a substring of each element in the array section. If an optional *substring_range* is present, the section must be from an array of character objects.

An array section is formed from the array elements specified by the sequences of values from the individual subscripts, subscript triplets, and vector subscripts, arranged in column-major order.

For example, if `SECTION = A( 1:3, (/ 5,6,5 /), 4 )`:

> The sequence of numbers for the first dimension is 1, 2, 3.
> The sequence of numbers for the second dimension is 5, 6, 5.
> The subscript for the third dimension is the constant 4.

The section is made up of the following elements of A, in this order:

```
A(1,5,4)  |                             |   SECTION(1,1)
A(2,5,4)  |----- First column -----|        SECTION(2,1)
A(3,5,4)  |                             |   SECTION(3,1)
A(1,6,4)    |                           |   SECTION(1,2)
A(2,6,4)    |----- Second column ----|      SECTION(2,2)
A(3,6,4)    |                           |   SECTION(3,2)
A(1,5,4)      |                         |   SECTION(1,3)
A(2,5,4)      |----- Third column -----|      SECTION(2,3)
A(3,5,4)      |                         |   SECTION(3,3)
```

Some examples of array sections include:

```
INTEGER, DIMENSION(10,20) :: A

! These references to array sections require loops or multiple
! statements in FORTRAN 77.
PRINT *, A(1:5,1)                    ! Contiguous sequence of elements
PRINT *, A(1:20:2,10)                ! Noncontiguous sequence of elements
PRINT *, A(:,5)                      ! An entire column
PRINT *, A( (/1,10,5/), (/7,3,1/) )  ! A 3x3 assortment of elements
```

Related Information: "Structure Components" on page 31.

Subscript Triplets

A subscript triplet consists of two subscripts and a stride, and defines a sequence of numbers corresponding to array element positions along a single dimension.

subscript1, subscript2 are subscripts that designate the first and last values in the sequence of indices for a dimension.

If the first subscript is omitted, the lower array bound of that dimension is used. If the second subscript is omitted, the upper array bound of that dimension is used. (The second subscript is mandatory for the last dimension when specifying sections of an assumed-size array.)

stride is a scalar integer expression that specifies how many subscript positions to count to reach the next selected element. If the stride is omitted, it has a value of 1.

The stride must have a nonzero value:

- A positive stride specifies a sequence of integers that begins with the first subscript and proceeds in increments of the stride to the largest integer that is not greater than the second subscript. If the first subscript is greater than the second, the sequence is empty.
- When the stride is negative, the sequence begins at the first subscript and continues in increments specified by the stride to the smallest integer equal to or greater than the second subscript. If the second subscript is greater than the first, the sequence is empty.

Calculations of values in the sequence use the same steps as shown in "Executing a DO Statement" on page 94.

A subscript in a subscript triplet does not have to be within the declared bounds for that dimension if all the values used in selecting the array elements for the array section are within the declared bounds:

```
INTEGER A(9)
PRINT *, A(1:9:2)  ! Count from 1 to 9 by 2s: 1, 3, 5, 7, 9.
PRINT *, A(1:10:2) ! Count from 1 to 10 by 2s: 1, 3, 5, 7, 9.
                   ! No element past A(9) is specified.
```

Examples of Subscript Triplets

```
REAL, DIMENSION(10) :: A
INTEGER, DIMENSION(10,10) :: B
CHARACTER(10) STRING(1:100)

PRINT *, A(:)                 ! Print all elements of array.
PRINT *, A(:5)                ! Print elements 1 through 5.
PRINT *, A(3:)                ! Print elements 3 through 10.

PRINT *, STRING(50:100)       ! Print all characters in
                              ! elements 50 through 100.

! The following statement is equivalent to A(2:10:2) = A(1:9:2)
A(2::2) = A(:9:2)             ! LHS = A(2), A(4), A(6), A(8), A(10)
                              ! RHS = A(1), A(3), A(5), A(7), A(9)
                              ! The statement assigns the odd-numbered
                              ! elements to the even-numbered elements.

! The following statement is equivalent to PRINT *, B(1:4:3,1:7:6)
PRINT *, B(:4:3,:7:6)         ! Print B(1,1), B(4,1), B(1,7), B(4,7)

PRINT *, A(10:1:-1)           ! Print elements in reverse order.

PRINT *, A(10:1:1)            ! These two are
PRINT *, A(1:10:-1)           ! both zero-sized.
END
```

Vector Subscripts

A vector subscript is an integer array expression of rank one, designating a sequence of subscripts that correspond to the values of the elements of the expression.

The sequence does not have to be in order, and may contain duplicate values:

```
INTEGER A(10), B(3), C(3)
PRINT *, A( (/ 10,9,8 /) ) ! Last 3 elements in reverse order
B = A( (/ 1,2,2 /) )       ! B(1) = A(1), B(2) = A(2), B(3) = A(2) also
END
```

An array section with a vector subscript in which two or more elements of the vector subscript have the same value is called a many-one section. Such a section must not:

- Appear on the left side of the equal sign in an assignment statement
- Be initialized through a **DATA** statement
- Be used as an input item in a **READ** statement

- An array section used as an internal file must not have a vector subscript.
- If you pass an array section with a vector subscript as an actual argument, the associated dummy argument must not be defined or redefined.
- An array section with a vector subscript must not be the target in a pointer assignment statement.

```
! We can use the whole array VECTOR as a vector subscript for A and B
INTEGER, DIMENSION(3) :: VECTOR= (/ 1,3,2 /), A, B
INTEGER, DIMENSION(4) :: C = (/ 1,2,4,8 /)

A(VECTOR) = B            ! A(1) = B(1), A(3) = B(2), A(2) = B(3)
A = B( (/ 3,2,1 /) )     ! A(1) = B(3), A(2) = B(2), A(3) = B(1)
PRINT *, C(VECTOR(1:2))  ! Prints C(1), C(3)
END
```

Array Sections and Substring Ranges

For an array section with a substring range, each element in the result is the designated character substring of the corresponding element of the array section. The rightmost array name or component name must be of type character.

```
PROGRAM SUBSTRING
TYPE DERIVED
   CHARACTER(10) STRING(5)        ! Each structure has 5 strings of 10 chars.
END TYPE DERIVED

TYPE (DERIVED) VAR, ARRAY(3,3)    ! A variable and an array of derived type.

VAR%STRING(:)(1:3) = 'abc'        ! Assign to chars 1-3 of elements 1-5.
VAR%STRING(3:)(4:6) = '123'       ! Assign to chars 4-6 of elements 3-5.

ARRAY(1:3,2)%STRING(3)(5:10) = 'hello'
                                  ! Assign to chars 5-10 of the third element in
                                  ! ARRAY(1,2)%STRING, ARRAY(2,2)%STRING, and
END                               ! ARRAY(3,2)%STRING
```

Array Sections and Structure Components

To understand how array sections and structure components overlap, you should already be familiar with the syntax for "Structure Components" on page 31.

What we defined at the beginning of this section as an array section is really only a subset of the possible array sections. An array name or array name with a *section_subscript_list* can be a subobject of a structure component:

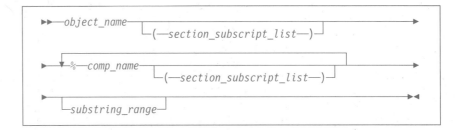

object_name   is the name of an object of derived type

section_subscript_list, substring_range
            are the same as defined under "Array Sections" on page 53

comp_name   is the name of a derived-type component

Notes

- The type of the last component determines the type of the array.
- Only one part of the structure component may have nonzero rank. Either the right-most *comp_name* must have a *section_subscript_list* with nonzero rank, or another part must have nonzero rank.
- Any parts to the right of the part with nonzero rank must not have the **POINTER** attribute.

```
TYPE BUILDING_T
  LOGICAL RESIDENTIAL
END TYPE BUILDING_T

TYPE STREET_T
  TYPE (BUILDING_T) ADDRESS(500)
END TYPE STREET_T

TYPE CITY_T
  TYPE (STREET_T) STREET(100,100)
END TYPE CITY_T

TYPE (CITY_T) PARIS
TYPE (STREET_T) S
TYPE (BUILDING_T) RESTAURANT

! LHS is not an array section, no subscript triplets or vector subscripts.
PARIS%STREET(10,20) = S

! None of the parts are array sections, but the entire construct
!   is a section because STREET has a nonzero rank and is not
!   the right-most part.
PARIS%STREET%ADDRESS(100) = BUILDING_T(.TRUE.)
```

```
! STREET(50:100,10) is an array section, making the LHS an array section
!   with rank=2, shape=(/51,10/).
! ADDRESS(123) must not be an array section because only one can appear
!   in a reference to a structure component.
PARIS%STREET(50:100,10)%ADDRESS(123)%RESIDENTIAL = .TRUE.
END
```

Rank and Shape of Array Sections

For an array section that is not a subobject of a structure component, the rank is the number of subscript triplets and vector subscripts in the *section_subscript_list*. The number of elements in the shape array is the same as the number of subscript triplets and vector subscripts, and each element in the shape array is the number of integer values in the sequence designated by the corresponding subscript triplet or vector subscript.

For an array section that is a subobject of a structure component, the rank and shape are the same as those of the part of the component that is an array name or array section.

```
DIMENSION :: ARR1(10,20,100)

TYPE STRUCT2_T
  LOGICAL SCALAR_COMPONENT
END TYPE

TYPE STRUCT_T
  TYPE (STRUCT2_T), DIMENSION(10,20,100) :: SECTION
END TYPE

TYPE (STRUCT_T) STRUCT

! One triplet + one vector subscript, rank = 2.
! Triplet designates an extent of 10, vector subscript designates
!   an extent of 3, thus shape = (/ 10,3 /).
ARR1(:, (/ 1,3,4 /), 10) = 0

! One triplet, rank = 1.
! Triplet designates 5 values, thus shape = (/ 5 /).
STRUCT%SECTION(1,10,1:5)%SCALAR_COMPONENT = .TRUE.

! Here SECTION is the part of the component that is an array,
!   so rank = 3 and shape = (/ 10,20,100 /), the same as SECTION.
STRUCT%SECTION%SCALAR_COMPONENT = .TRUE.
```

Array Constructors

An array constructor is a sequence of specified scalar values. It constructs a rank-one array whose element values are those specified in the sequence.

```
►►──(──/──ac_value_list──/──)──────────────────────────►◄
```

ac_value is an expression or implied-**DO** list that provides values for array elements. Each *ac_value* in the array constructor must have the same type and type parameters.

If *ac_value* is:

- A scalar expression, its value specifies an element of the array constructor.
- An array expression, the values of the elements of the expression, in array element order, specify the corresponding sequence of elements of the array constructor.
- An implied-**DO** list, it is expanded to form an *ac_value* sequence under the control of the *ac_do_variable*, as in the **DO** construct.

The data type of the array constructor is the same as the data type of the *ac_value_list* expressions. If every expression in an array constructor is a constant expression, the array constructor is a constant expression.

You can construct arrays of rank greater than one using an intrinsic function. See "RESHAPE (SOURCE, SHAPE, PAD, ORDER)" on page 401 for details.

```
INTEGER, DIMENSION(5) :: A, B, C, D(2,2)

A = (/ 1,2,3,4,5 /)            ! Assign values to all elements in A
A(3:5) = (/ 0,1,0 /)           ! Assign values to some elements

C = MERGE (A, B, (/ T,F,T,T,F /)) ! Construct temporary logical mask

! The array constructor produces a rank-one array, which
!   is turned into a 2x2 array that can be assigned to D.
D = RESHAPE( SOURCE = (/ 1,2,1,2 /), SHAPE = (/ 2,2 /) )

! Here, the constructor linearizes the elements of D in
!   array-element order into a one-dimensional result.
PRINT *, A( (/ D /) )
```

Implied-DO List for an Array Constructor

Implied-**DO** loops in array constructors help to create a regular or cyclic sequence of values, to avoid specifying each element individually.

A zero-sized array of rank one is formed if the sequence of values generated by the loop is empty.

implied_do_variable is a named scalar integer variable. In a nonexecutable statement, the type must be integer. Loop processing follows the same rules as for an implied-**DO** in "DATA" on page 216, and uses integer or real arithmetic depending on the type of the implied-**DO** variable.

The variable has the scope of the implied-**DO**, and it must not have the same name as another implied-**DO** variable in a containing array constructor implied-**DO**:

```
M = 0
PRINT *, (/ (M, M=1, 10) /) ! Array constructor implied-DO
PRINT *, M                  ! M still 0 afterwards

PRINT *, (M, M=1, 10)       ! Non-array-constructor implied-DO
PRINT *, M                  ! This one goes to 11

PRINT *, (/ ((M, M=1, 5), N=1, 3) /)
! The result is a 15-element, one-dimensional array.
! The inner loop cannot use N as its variable.
```

expr1, expr2, and *expr3* are integer scalar expressions

```
PRINT *, (/ (I, I = 1, 3) /)
! Sequence is (1, 2, 3)

PRINT *, (/ (I, I = 1, 10, 2) /)
! Sequence is (1, 3, 5, 7, 9)

PRINT *, (/ (I, I+1, I+2, I = 1, 3) /)
! Sequence is (1, 2, 3, 2, 3, 4, 3, 4, 5)

PRINT *, (/ ( (I, I = 1, 3), J = 1, 3 ) /)
! Sequence is (1, 2, 3, 1, 2, 3, 1, 2, 3)

PRINT *, (/ ( (I, I = 1, J), J = 1, 3 ) /)
! Sequence is (1, 1, 2, 1, 2, 3)
```

```
PRINT *, (/2,3,(I, I+1, I = 5, 8)/)
! Sequence is (2, 3, 5, 6, 6, 7, 7, 8, 8, 9).
! The values in the implied-DO loop before
!   I=5 are calculated for each iteration of the loop.
```

Expressions Involving Arrays

Arrays can be used in the same kinds of expressions and operations as scalars. Intrinsic operations, assignments, or elemental procedures can be applied to one or more arrays.

In expressions involving two or more array operands, the arrays must have the same shape so that the corresponding elements of each array can be assigned to or be evaluated. Arrays with the same shape are *conformable*. In a context where a conformable array is expected, you can also use a scalar value: it is conformable with any array, such that each array element has the value of the scalar.

For example:

```
INTEGER, DIMENSION(5,5) :: A,B,C
REAL, DIMENSION(10) :: X,Y

! Here are some operations on arrays
A = B + C       ! Add corresponding elements of both arrays.
A = -B          ! Assign the negative of each element of B.
A = MAX(A,B,C)  ! A(i,j) = MAX( A(i,j), B(i,j), C(i,j) )
X = SIN(Y)      ! Calculate the sine of each element.

! These operations show how scalars are conformable with arrays
A = A + 5       ! Add 5 to each element.
A = 10          ! Assign 10 to each element.
A = MAX(B, C, 5)  ! A(i,j) = MAX( B(i,j), C(i,j), 5 )

END
```

Related Information: "Elemental Intrinsic Procedures" on page 359, "Intrinsic Assignment" on page 78.

"WHERE" on page 351 shows a way to assign values to some elements in an array but not others.

Chapter 5. Expressions and Assignment

This chapter describes the rules for formation, interpretation, and evaluation of expressions and assignment statements:

Related Information

- "Defined Operators" on page 118
- "Defined Assignment" on page 119

Introduction

An expression is a data reference or a computation, and is formed from operands, operators, and parentheses. An expression, when evaluated, produces a value, which has a type, shape, and possibly type parameters.

An *operand* is either a scalar or an array. An *operator* is either intrinsic or defined. A unary operation has the form:

> *operator operand*

A binary operation has the form:

> *operand*₁ *operator operand*₂

where the two operands are shape-conforming. If one operand is an array and the other is a scalar, the scalar is treated as an array of the same shape as the array, and every element of the array has the value of the scalar.

Any expression contained in parentheses is treated as a data entity. Parentheses can be used to specify an explicit interpretation of an expression. They can also be used to restrict the alternative forms of the expression, which can help control the magnitude and accuracy of intermediate values during evaluation of the expression. For example, the two expressions

```
(I*J)/K
I*(J/K)
```

are mathematically equivalent, but may produce different computational values as a result of evaluation.

Primary

A *primary* is the simplest form of an expression. It can be one of the following:

- A data object
- An array constructor
- A structure constructor
- A function reference
- An expression enclosed in parentheses

A primary that is a data object must not be an assumed-size array.

Examples of Primaries

```
12.3              ! Constant
'ABCDEFG'(2:3)    ! Subobject of a constant
VAR               ! Variable name
(/7.0,8.0/)       ! Array constructor
EMP(6,'SMITH')    ! Structure constructor
SIN(X)            ! Function reference
(T-1)             ! Expression in parentheses
```

Type, Parameters, and Shape

The type, type parameters, and shape of a primary are determined as follows:

- A data object or function reference acquires the type, type parameters, and shape of the object or function reference, respectively. The type, parameters, and shape of a generic function reference are determined by the type, parameters, and ranks of its actual arguments.
- A structure constructor is a scalar and its type is that of the constructor name.
- An array constructor has a shape determined by the number of constructor expressions, and its type and parameters are determined by those of the constructor expressions.
- A parenthesized expression acquires the type, parameters, and shape of the expression.

If a pointer appears as one of the following, the associated target is referenced:

- a primary in an operation
- as the expression of a parenthesized primary
- as the only primary on the right-hand side of an intrinsic assignment statement

The type, parameters, and shape of the primary are those of the target. If the pointer is not associated with a target, it can appear only as an actual argument in a procedure reference whose corresponding dummy argument is a pointer, or as the target in a pointer assignment statement.

Given the operation *[expr1] op expr2*, the shape of the operation is the shape of *expr2* if *op* is unary or if *expr1* is a scalar. Otherwise, the shape of the operation is that of *expr1*.

The type and shape of an expression are determined by the operators and by the types and shapes of the expression's primaries. The type of the expression can be intrinsic or derived. An expression of intrinsic type has a kind parameter and, if it is of type character, it also has a length parameter.

Constant Expressions

A *constant expression* is an expression in which each operation is intrinsic and each primary is one of the following:

- A constant or subobject of a constant.
- An array constructor where each element and the bounds and strides of each implied-**DO** are expressions whose primaries are either constant expressions or implied-**DO** variables.
- A structure constructor where each component is a constant expression.
- An elemental intrinsic function reference where each argument is a constant expression.
- A transformational intrinsic function reference where each argument is a constant expression.
- A reference to an array inquiry function (except **ALLOCATED**), a numeric inquiry function, the **BIT_SIZE** function, the **LEN** function, or the **KIND** function. Each argument is either a constant expression or it is a variable whose properties inquired about are not assumed, not defined by an expression that is not a constant expression, and not definable by an **ALLOCATE** or pointer assignment statement.
- A constant expression enclosed in parentheses.

Any subscript or substring expression within the expression must be a constant expression.

Examples of Constant Expressions

```
-48.9
name('Pat','Doe')
TRIM('ABC    ')
(MOD(9,4)**3.5)
```

Initialization Expressions

An *initialization expression* is a constant expression. Rules for constant expressions also apply to initialization expressions, except that items that form primaries are constrained by the following rules:

- The exponentiation operation can only have an integer power.
- A primary that is an elemental intrinsic function reference must be of type integer or character, where each argument is an initialization expression of type integer or character.
- Only one of the following transformational functions can be referenced: **REPEAT, RESHAPE, SELECTED_INT_KIND, SELECTED_REAL_KIND, TRANSFER**, or **TRIM**. Each argument must be an initialization expression.

If an initialization expression includes a reference to an inquiry function for a type parameter or an array bound of an object specified in the same specification part, the type parameter or array bound must be specified in a prior specification of the specification part. The prior specification can be to the left of the inquiry function in the same statement.

Examples of Initialization Expressions

```
3.4**3
KIND(57438)
(/'desk','lamp'/)
'ab'//'cd'//'ef'
```

Restricted Expressions

A *restricted expression* is an expression in which each operation is intrinsic and each primary is:

- A constant or subobject of a constant.
- A variable that is a dummy argument that has neither the **OPTIONAL** nor the **INTENT(OUT)** attribute, or a subobject of such a variable.
- A variable that is in a common block or a subobject of such a variable.
- A variable accessible by use association or host association, or a subobject of such a variable.
- An array constructor where each element and the bounds and strides of each implied-**DO** are expressions whose primaries are either restricted expressions or implied-**DO** variables.

- A structure constructor where each component is a restricted expression.
- An elemental intrinsic function reference of type integer or character where each argument is a restricted expression of type integer or character.
- An intrinsic function reference permitted in an initialization expression, where each argument is a restricted expression.
- A reference to one of the transformational functions: **REPEAT**, **RESHAPE**, **SELECTED_INT_KIND**, **SELECTED_REAL_KIND**, **TRANSFER**, or **TRIM**, where each argument is a restricted expression of type integer or character.
- A reference to an array inquiry function (except **ALLOCATED**), the bit inquiry function **BIT_SIZE**, the character inquiry function **LEN**, the kind inquiry function **KIND**, or a numeric inquiry function. Each argument is either a restricted expression, or it is a variable whose properties inquired about are not dependent on the upper bound of the last dimension of an assumed-size array, not defined by an expression that is not a restricted expression, or not definable by an **ALLOCATE** statement or by a pointer assignment statement.
- A restricted expression enclosed in parentheses.

Any subscript or substring expression must be a restricted expression.

Specification Expressions

A *specification expression* is a scalar, integer, restricted expression.

A variable in a specification expression must have its type and type parameters, if any, specified by a previous declaration in the same scoping unit, or by the implicit typing rules in effect for the scoping unit, or by host or use association. If a variable in a specification expression is typed by the implicit typing rules, its appearance in any subsequent type declaration statement must confirm the implied type and type parameters.

If a specification expression includes a reference to an inquiry function for a type parameter or an array bound of an entity specified in the same specification part, the type parameter or array bound must be specified in a prior specification of the specification part. If a specification expression includes a reference to the value of an element of an array specified in the same specification part, the array bounds must be specified in a prior declaration. The prior specification can be to the left of the inquiry function in the same statement.

Examples of Specification Expressions

```
LBOUND(C,2)+6    ! C is an assumed-shape dummy array
ABS(I)*J         ! I and J are scalar integer variables
276/NN(4)        ! NN is accessible through host association
```

Operators and Expressions

This section presents the expression levels in the order of evaluation precedence, from least to most.

General

The general form of an expression (*general_expr*) is:

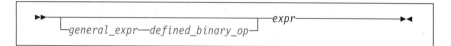

defined_binary_op

        is a defined binary operator. See "Extended Intrinsic and Defined Operations" on page 75.

expr   is one of the kinds of expressions defined below

There are four kinds of intrinsic expressions: arithmetic, character, relational, and logical.

Arithmetic

An arithmetic expression (*arith_expr*), when evaluated, produces a numeric value. The form of *arith_expr* is:

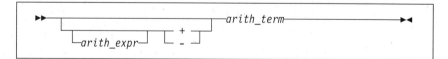

The form of *arith_term* is:

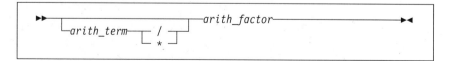

The form of *arith_factor* is:

```
►►──arith_primary─────────────────────────────────────►◄
              └─ ** ──arith_factor─┘
```

An *arith_primary* is a primary of arithmetic type.

The following table shows the available arithmetic operators and the precedence each takes within an arithmetic expression.

Arithmetic Operator	Representation	Precedence
**	Exponentiation	First
*	Multiplication	Second
/	Division	Second
+	Addition or identity	Third
-	Subtraction or negation	Third

The processor evaluates the terms from left to right when evaluating an arithmetic expression containing two or more addition or subtraction operators. For example, 2+3+4 is evaluated as (2+3)+4.

The factors are evaluated from left to right when evaluating a term containing two or more multiplication or division operators. For example, 2*3*4 is evaluated as (2*3)*4.

The primaries are combined from right to left when evaluating a factor containing two or more exponentiation operators. For example, 2**3**4 is evaluated as 2**(3**4).

The precedence of the operators determines the order of evaluation when the processor is evaluating an arithmetic expression containing two or more operators having different precedence. For example, in the expression -A**3, the exponentiation operator (**) has precedence over the negation operator (-). Therefore, the operands of the exponentiation operator are combined to form an expression that is used as the operand of the negation operator. Thus, -A**3 is evaluated as -(A**3).

Note that expressions containing two consecutive arithmetic operators, such as A**-B or A*-B, are not allowed. You can use expressions such as A**(-B) and A*(-B).

If an expression specifies the division of an integer by an integer, the result is rounded to an integer closer to zero. For example, (-7)/3 has the value -2.

Examples of Arithmetic Expressions

Arithmetic Expression	Fully Parenthesized Equivalent
-b**2/2.0	-((b**2)/2.0)
i**j**2	i**(j**2)
a/b**2 - c	(a/(b**2)) - c

Data Type of an Arithmetic Expression

Because the identity and negation operators operate on a single operand, the type of the resulting value is the same as the type of the operand.

The type of the result of the operation x_1 op x_2 can be determined from the following table (I - integer, R - real, Z - complex):

Type of x_1	Type of x_2	Type of Operation Result
I	I, R, Z	I, R, Z
R	I, R, Z	R, R, Z
Z	I, R, Z	Z, Z, Z

The resulting kind type parameter of a binary arithmetic operation is determined as follows:

- given one integer operand and one real/complex operand, the kind type parameter of the result is that of the real/complex operand.
- given both operands are of the same type and have the same kind type parameter (or real and complex operands with the same kind), the kind type parameter of the result remains the same.
- given either two integer operands or two real/complex operands, the kind type parameter of the result is that of the operand with the greater decimal exponent range.

Character

A character expression, when evaluated, produces a result of type character. The form of *char_expr* is:

```
►►──┬─────────────────┬──char_primary────────────────►◄
     └─char_expr──//──┘
```

char_primary is a primary of type character.

The only character operator is //, representing concatenation.

In a character expression containing one or more concatenation operators, the primaries are joined to form one string whose length is equal to the sum of the lengths of the individual primaries. For example, `'AB'//'CD'//'EF'` evaluates to `'ABCDEF'`, a string six characters in length.

Parentheses have no effect on the value of a character expression.

A character expression can involve concatenation of an operand whose length was declared with an asterisk in parentheses (indicating inherited length), if the inherited-length character string is used to declare:

- A dummy argument specified in a **FUNCTION**, **SUBROUTINE**, or **ENTRY** statement. The length of the dummy argument assumes the length of the associated actual argument on invocation.
- A named constant. It takes on the length of the constant value.
- The length of an external function result. The calling scoping unit must not declare the function name with an asterisk. On invocation, the length of the function result assumes this defined length. .

Example of a Character Expression

```
CHARACTER(7)  FIRSTNAME,LASTNAME
FIRSTNAME='Martha'
LASTNAME='Edwards'
PRINT *, LASTNAME//', '//FIRSTNAME       ! Output:'Edwards, Martha'
END
```

Relational

A relational expression (*rel_expr*), when evaluated, produces a result of type logical. A relational expression can appear wherever a logical expression can appear. A relational expression can be an arithmetic relational expression or a character relational expression.

Arithmetic Relational Expressions

An arithmetic relational expression compares the values of two arithmetic expressions. Its form is:

$$\blacktriangleright\!\blacktriangleright\!-\!arith\_expr1\!-\!relational\_operator\!-\!arith\_expr2\!-\!\longrightarrow\!\blacktriangleright\!\blacktriangleleft$$

arith_expr1 and *arith_expr2*

>   are each an arithmetic expression. Complex expressions can only be specified if *relational_operator* is **.EQ.**, **.NE.**, ==, or /=.

relational_operator

>   is any of:

Relational Operator	Representing
.LT. or <	Less than
.LE. or <=	Less than or equal to
.EQ. or ==	Equal to
.NE. or /=	Not equal to
.GT. or >	Greater than
.GE. or >=	Greater than or equal to

An arithmetic relational expression is interpreted as having the logical value .true. if the values of the operands satisfy the relation specified by the operator. If the operands do not satisfy the specified relation, the expression has the logical value .false..

If the types or kind type parameters of the expressions differ, their values are converted to the type and kind type parameter of the expression (*arith_expr1* + *arith_expr2*) before evaluation.

Example of an Arithmetic Relational Expression

```
IF (NODAYS .GT. 365) YEARTYPE = 'leapyear'
```

Character Relational Expressions

A character relational expression compares the values of two character expressions that have the same kind type parameter. Its form is:

```
►►──char_expr1──relational_operator──char_expr2───────────►◄
```

char_expr1 and *char_expr2*
> are each a character expression

relational_operator
> is any of the relational operators described under "Arithmetic Relational Expressions" on page 72

For all relational operators, the collating sequence is used to interpret a character relational expression. The character expression whose value is lower in the collating sequence is less than the other expression. The character expressions are evaluated one character at a time from left to right. You can also use the intrinsic functions (**LGE**, **LGT**, **LLE**, and **LLT**) to compare character strings in the order specified by the ASCII collating sequence. For all relational operators, if the operands are of unequal length, the shorter is extended on the right with blanks. If both *char_expr1* and *char_expr2* are of zero length, they are evaluated as equal.

Example of a Character Relational Expression

```
IF (CHARIN .GT. '0' .AND. CHARIN .LE. '9') CHAR_TYPE = 'digit'
```

Logical

A logical expression (*log_expr*), when evaluated, produces a result of type logical. The form of a logical expression is:

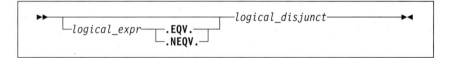

The form of a *logical_disjunct* is:

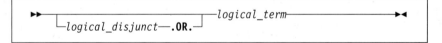

The form of a *logical_term* is:

```
►►─┬─────────────────────┬─logical_factor──────────────────►◄
   └─logical_term─.AND.──┘
```

The form of a *logical_factor* is:

```
►►─┬───────┬─logical_primary───────────────────────────────►◄
   └─.NOT.─┘
```

logical_primary is a primary of type logical.

The logical operators are:

Logical Operator	Representing	Precedence
.NOT.	Logical negation	First (highest)
.AND.	Logical conjunction	Second
.OR.	Logical inclusive disjunction	Third
.EQV.	Logical equivalence	Fourth (lowest)
.NEQV.	Logical nonequivalence	Fourth (lowest)

The precedence of the operators determines the order of evaluation when a logical expression containing two or more operators having different precedence is evaluated. For example, evaluation of the expression A.OR.B.AND.C is the same as evaluation of the expression A.OR.(B.AND.C).

Value of a Logical Expression

Given that x1 and x2 represent logical values, use the following tables to determine the values of logical expressions:

x1	.NOT. x1
True	False
False	True

x1	x2	.AND.	.OR.	.EQV.	.NEQV.
False	False	False	False	True	False
False	True	False	True	False	True

x1	x2	.AND.	.OR.	.EQV.	.NEQV.
True	False	False	True	False	True
True	True	True	True	True	False

For unary logical operations, the kind type parameter of the expression is that of the operand.

For binary logical operations with operands that have different kind type parameters, the kind type parameter of the expression is processor-dependent. For binary logical operations with operands that have the same kind type parameter, the expression has the same kind type parameter.

Primary

The form of a primary expression is:

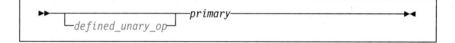

defined_unary_op
> is a defined unary operator. See "Extended Intrinsic and Defined Operations".

Extended Intrinsic and Defined Operations

A defined operation is either a defined unary operation or a defined binary operation. It is defined by a function and a generic interface block (see "Interface Blocks" on page 112). A defined operation is not an intrinsic operation, although an intrinsic operator can be extended in a defined operation. For example, to add two objects of derived type, you can extend the meaning of the intrinsic binary operator for addition (+).

The operand of a unary intrinsic operation that is extended must not have a type that is required by the intrinsic operator. Either or both of the operands of a binary intrinsic operator that is extended must not have the types or ranks that are required by the intrinsic operator.

The defined operator of a defined operation must be defined in a generic interface.

A defined operator is an extended intrinsic operator or has the form:

A defined operator must not contain more than 31 letters and must not be the same as any intrinsic operator or logical literal constant.

See "Generic Interface Blocks" on page 116 for details on defining and extending operators in an interface block.

Evaluating Expressions

Precedence of Operators

An expression can contain more than one kind of operator. When it does, the expression is evaluated from left to right, according to the following precedence among operators:

1. Defined unary
2. Arithmetic
3. Character
4. Relational
5. Logical
6. Defined binary

For example, the logical expression

```
L .OR. A + B .GE. C
```

where L is of type logical, and A, B, and C are of type real, is evaluated the same as the logical expression below:

```
L .OR. ((A + B) .GE. C)
```

An extended intrinsic operator maintains its precedence. That is, the operator does not have the precedence of a defined unary operator or a defined binary operator.

Summary of Interpretation Rules

The order in which primaries that contain operators are combined is:

1. Use of parentheses
2. Precedence of the operators
3. Right-to-left interpretation of exponentiations in a factor
4. Left-to-right interpretation of multiplications and divisions in a term
5. Left-to-right interpretation of additions and subtractions in an arithmetic expression

6. Left-to-right interpretation of concatenations in a character expression
7. Left-to-right interpretation of conjunctions in a logical term
8. Left-to-right interpretation of disjunctions in a logical disjunct
9. Left-to-right interpretation of logical equivalences in a logical expression

Evaluation of Expressions

Arithmetic, character, relational, and logical expressions are evaluated according to the following rules:

- A variable or function must be defined at the time it is used. You must define an integer operand with an integer value, not a statement label value. All referenced characters in a character data object or referenced array elements in an array or array section must be defined at the time the reference is made. All components of a structure must be defined when a structure is referenced. A pointer must be associated with a defined target.

  Execution of an array element reference, array section reference, and substring reference requires the evaluation of its subscript, section subscript and substring expressions. Evaluation of any array element subscript, section subscript, substring expression, or the bounds and stride of any array constructor implied-**DO** is not affected, nor does it affect, the type of the containing expression. See "Expressions Involving Arrays" on page 62.

  You cannot use any constant integer operation or floating-point operation whose result is not mathematically defined in an executable program. If such expressions are nonconstant and are executed, they are detected at run time. (Examples are dividing by zero and raising a zero-valued primary to a zero-valued or negative-valued power.) As well, you cannot raise a negative-valued primary of type real to a real power.

- A processor does not need to evaluate each operand of an expression if the value of the expression can be determined otherwise. For example, a logical expression may not need to be completely evaluated to determine its value. Consider the following logical expression (assume that LFCT is a function of type logical):

  A .LT. B .OR. LFCT(Z)

  If A is less than B, the processor may not need the function reference to be evaluated to determine that this expression is true.

- The invocation of a function in a statement must not affect, or be affected by, the evaluation of any other entity within the statement in which the function reference appears. When the value of an expression is true, invocation of a function reference in the expression of a logical **IF** statement or a **WHERE** statement can affect entities in the statement that is executed. If a function reference causes definition or undefinition of an actual argument of the function, that argument or any associated entities must not appear elsewhere in the same statement. For example, you cannot use the statements:

```
A(I) = FUNC1(I)
Y = FUNC2(X) + X
```

if the reference to FUNC1 defines I or the reference to FUNC2 defines X.

The data type of an expression in which a function reference appears does not affect, nor is it affected by, the evaluation of the actual arguments of the function.

- An argument to a statement function reference must not be altered by evaluating that reference.

Intrinsic Assignment

Assignment statements are executable statements that define or redefine variables based on the result of expression evaluation.

A defined assignment is not intrinsic, and is defined by a subroutine and an interface block. See "Defined Assignment" on page 119.

The general form of an intrinsic assignment is:

$$\blacktriangleright\!\blacktriangleright\!-variable\!-\ =\ -expression\!-\!\!\!\!\!\blacktriangleright\!\blacktriangleleft$$

The shapes of *variable* and *expression* must conform. *variable* must be an array if *expression* is an array (see "Expressions Involving Arrays" on page 62). If *expression* is a scalar and *variable* is an array, *expression* is treated as an array of the same shape as *variable* with every array element having the same value as the scalar value of *expression*. *variable* must not be a many-one array section (see "Vector Subscripts" on page 56 for details), and neither *variable* nor *expression* can be an assumed-size array. The types of *variable* and *expression* must conform as follows:

Type of *variable*	Type of *expression*
Numeric	Numeric
Logical	Logical
Character	Character
Derived type	Derived type (same as *variable*)

In numeric assignment statements, *variable* and *expression* can specify different numeric types and different kind type parameters. For logical assignment statements, the kind type parameters can differ. For character assignment statements, the length type parameters can differ, although the kind type parameters must be the same.

If the length of a character variable is greater than the length of a character expression, the character expression is extended on the right with blanks until the lengths are equal. If the length of the character variable is less than the character expression, the character expression is truncated on the right to match the length of the character variable.

If *variable* is a pointer, it must be associated with a definable target that has type, type parameters and shape that conform with those of *expression*. The value of *expression* is then assigned to the target associated with *variable*.

Both *variable* and *expression* can contain references to any portion of *variable*.

An assignment statement causes the evaluation of *expression* and all expressions within *variable* before assignment, the possible conversion of *expression* to the type and type parameters of *variable*, and the definition of *variable* with the resulting value. No value is assigned to *variable* if it is a zero-length character object or a zero-sized array.

A derived-type assignment statement is an intrinsic assignment statement if there is no accessible defined assignment for objects of this derived type. The derived type expression must be of the same derived type as the variable. (See "Determining Type for Derived Types" on page 30 for the rules that determine when two structures are of the same derived type.) Assignment is performed as if each component of the expression is assigned (or pointer assigned) to the corresponding component of the variable. Pointer assignment is executed for pointer components and intrinsic assignment is performed for nonpointer components.

When *variable* is a subobject, the assignment does not affect the definition status or value of other parts of the object.

Arithmetic Conversion

For numeric intrinsic assignment, the value of *expression* may be converted to the type and kind type parameter of *variable*, as specified in the following table:

Type of *variable*	Value Assigned
Integer	INT(*expression*,KIND=KIND(*variable*))
Real	REAL(*expression*,KIND=KIND(*variable*))
Complex	CMPLX(*expression*,KIND=KIND(*variable*))

Character Assignment

Only as much of the character expression as is necessary to define the character variable needs to be evaluated. For example:

```
CHARACTER SCOTT*4, DICK*8
SCOTT = DICK
```

This assignment of DICK to SCOTT requires that you have previously defined the substring DICK(1:4). You do not have to previously define the rest of DICK (DICK(5:8)).

Examples of Intrinsic Assignment

```
INTEGER I(10)
LOGICAL INSIDE
REAL R,RMIN,RMAX
REAL :: A=2.3,B=4.5,C=6.7
TYPE PERSON
   INTEGER(4) P_AGE
   CHARACTER(20) P_NAME
END TYPE
TYPE (PERSON) EMP1, EMP2
CHARACTER(10) :: CH = 'ABCDEFGHIJ'

I = 5                        ! All elements of I assigned value of 5

RMIN = 28.5 ; RMAX = 29.5
R = (-B + SQRT(B**2 - 4.0*A*C))/(2.0*A)
INSIDE = (R .GE. RMIN) .AND. (R .LE. RMAX)

CH(2:4) = CH(3:5)                ! CH is now 'ACDEEFGHIJ'

EMP1 = PERSON(45, 'Frank Jones')
EMP2 = EMP1

! EMP2%P_AGE is assigned EMP1%P_AGE using arithmetic assignment
! EMP2%P_NAME is assigned EMP1%P_NAME using character assignment

END
```

WHERE Construct

The **WHERE** construct masks the evaluation of array expressions and array assignment.

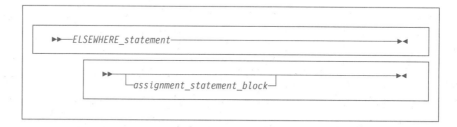

WHERE_statement
> See "WHERE" on page 351 for syntax details

END_WHERE_statement
> See "END (Construct)" on page 237 for syntax details

ELSEWHERE_block

ELSEWHERE statement
> See "ELSEWHERE" on page 234 for syntax details

The logical array expression determines the mask.

In each *assignment_statement*, the *mask_expr* and the variable being defined must be arrays of the same shape, and *assignment_statement* cannot be a defined assignment.

When an assignment statement in a **WHERE** statement is executed, the expression of the assignment statement is evaluated for all the elements where *mask_expr* is true and the result is assigned to the corresponding elements of the variable in the assignment statement, according to the rules of intrinsic assignment. When a **WHERE** construct is executed, *mask_expr* is evaluated. Each assignment statement in the **WHERE** block is evaluated, in sequence, as if it were

```
WHERE (mask_expr) assignment_statement
```

and then each assignment statement in the **ELSEWHERE** block is evaluated, in sequence, as if it were

```
WHERE (.NOT. mask_expr) assignment_statement
```

If a nonelemental function reference occurs in the expression or variable of an assignment statement, the function is evaluated without any masked control by *mask_expr*; that is, all of its argument expressions are fully evaluated and the function is fully evaluated. If the result is an array and the reference is not within the argument list of a nonelemental function, elements corresponding to true values in *mask_expr* (false in the *mask_expr* after **ELSEWHERE**) are selected for use in evaluating each expression.

If an elemental intrinsic operation or function reference occurs in the expression or variable of an assignment statement and is not within the argument list of a nonelemental function reference, the operation is performed or the function is evaluated only for the elements corresponding to true values in *mask_expr* (false values after **ELSEWHERE**).

If an array constructor appears in an assignment statement, the array constructor is evaluated without any masked control by *mask_expr* and then the assignment statement is evaluated.

In a masked array assignment, only a **WHERE** statement or a **WHERE** construct statement can be a branch target statement. The value of *mask_expr*, evaluated at the beginning of the masked array assignment, governs the masking in the execution of the masked array assignment; subsequent changes to entities in *mask_expr* have no effect on the masking. The execution of a function reference in the mask expression of a **WHERE** statement is permitted to affect entities in the assignment statement. Execution of an **END WHERE** has no effect.

Examples of the WHERE Construct

```fortran
REAL, DIMENSION(10) :: A,B,C,D
WHERE (A>0.0)
  A = LOG(A)            ! Only the positive elements of A
                        !   are used in the LOG calculation.
  B = A                 ! The mask uses the original array A
                        !   instead of the new array A.
  C = A / SUM( LOG(A) ) ! A is evaluated by LOG, but
                        !   the resulting array is an
                        !   argument to a non-elemental
                        !   function, all elements in A will
                        !   be used in evaluating SUM.
END WHERE

WHERE(D>0.0)
  C = CSHIFT(A,1)       ! CSHIFT applies to all elements in array A,
                        ! and the array element values of D determine
                        ! which CSHIFT expression determines the
                        ! corresponding element values of C.
ELSEWHERE
  C = CSHIFT(A,2)
ENDWHERE
END
```

Pointer Assignment

The pointer assignment statement causes a pointer to become associated with a target or causes the pointer's association status to become disassociated or undefined.

target   is a variable or expression. It must have the same type, type parameters and rank as *pointer_object*.

pointer_object must have the **POINTER** attribute.

A target that is an expression must yield a value that has the **POINTER** attribute. A target that is a variable must have the **TARGET** attribute (or be a subobject of such an object) or the **POINTER** attribute. A target must not be an array section with a vector subscript, nor can it be a whole assumed-size array.

The size, bounds, and shape of the target of a disassociated array pointer are undefined. No part of such an array can be defined or referenced, although the array can be the argument of an intrinsic inquiry function that is inquiring about association status, argument presence, or a property of the type or type parameters.

Any previous association between *pointer_object* and a target is broken. If *target* is not a pointer, *pointer_object* becomes associated with *target*. If *target* is itself an associated pointer, *pointer_object* is associated with the target of *target*. If *target* is a pointer with an association status of disassociated or undefined, *pointer_object* acquires the same status.

Pointer assignment for a pointer structure component can also occur via execution of a derived-type intrinsic assignment statement or a defined assignment statement.

During pointer assignment of an array pointer, the lower bound of each dimension is the result of the **LBOUND** intrinsic function applied to the corresponding dimension of the target. For an array section or array expression that is not a whole array or a structure component, the lower bound is 1. The upper bound of each dimension is the result of the **UBOUND** intrinsic function applied to the corresponding dimension of the target.

Related Information: See "ALLOCATE" on page 186 for an alternative form of associating a pointer with a target.

See "Pointers as Dummy Arguments" on page 136 for details on using pointers in procedure references.

Examples of Pointer Assignment

```
TYPE T
  INTEGER, POINTER :: COMP_PTR
ENDTYPE T
TYPE(T) T_VAR
INTEGER, POINTER :: P,Q,R
INTEGER, POINTER :: ARR(:)
INTEGER, TARGET :: MYVAR
INTEGER, TARGET :: DARG(1:5)
P => MYVAR              ! P points to MYVAR
Q => P                 ! Q points to MYVAR
NULLIFY (R)            ! R is disassociated
Q => R                 ! Q is disassociated
T_VAR = T(P)           ! T_VAR%COMP_PTR points to MYVAR
ARR => DARG(1:3)
END
```

Chapter 6. Control

This chapter describes:

You can control your program's execution sequence by constructs containing statement blocks and other executable statements that can alter the normal execution sequence, as defined under "Order of Statements and Execution Sequence" on page 18. The construct descriptions in this chapter do not provide detailed syntax of any construct statements; rather, references are made to the "Statements" section.

If a construct is contained in another construct, it must be wholly contained (nested) within that construct. If a statement specifies a construct name, it belongs to that construct; otherwise, it belongs to the innermost construct in which it appears.

Statement Blocks

A *statement block* consists of a sequence of zero or more executable statements, executable constructs, **FORMAT** statements, and **DATA** statements that are embedded in another executable construct and are treated as a single unit.

Within an executable program, it is not permitted to transfer control from outside of the statement block to within it. It is permitted to transfer control within the statement block, or from within the statement block to outside the block. For example, in a statement block, you can have a statement with a statement label and a **GO TO** statement using that label.

IF Construct

The **IF** construct selects no more than one of its statement blocks for execution.

```
►►──Block_IF_statement───────────────────────────────►◄

     ►►──statement_block──────────────────────────►◄

  ►►─────────────────────────────────────────────►◄
       └─►─ELSE_IF_block─┘

  ►►───────────────────────────────────────────────►◄
       └─ELSE_block─┘

  ►►──END_IF_statement────────────────────────────►◄
```

Block_IF_statement
> See "IF (Block)" on page 265 for syntax details.

END_IF_statement
> See "END (Construct)" on page 237 for syntax details.

ELSE_IF_block

```
►►──ELSE_IF_statement──────────────────────────────►◄

     ►►──statement_block──────────────────────────►◄
```

ELSE_IF_statement
> See "ELSE IF" on page 233 for syntax details.

ELSE_block

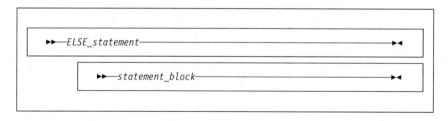

ELSE_statement
>   See "ELSE" on page 232 for syntax details.

The scalar logical expressions in an **IF** construct (that is, the block **IF** and **ELSE IF** statements) are evaluated in the order of their appearance until a true value, an **ELSE** statement, or an **END IF** statement is found:

- If a true value or an **ELSE** statement is found, the statement block immediately following executes, and the **IF** construct is complete. The scalar logical expressions in any remaining **ELSE IF** statements or **ELSE** statements of the **IF** construct are not evaluated.
- If an **END IF** statement is found, no statement blocks execute, and the **IF** construct is complete.

If the **IF** construct name is specified, it must appear on the **IF** statement and **END IF** statement, and optionally on any **ELSE IF** or **ELSE** statements.

Examples

```
! Get a record (containing a command) from the terminal

   DO
      WHICHC: IF (CMD .EQ. 'RETRY') THEN       ! named IF construct
          IF (LIMIT .GT. FIVE) THEN            ! nested IF construct
!             Print retry limit exceeded
              CALL STOP
          ELSE
              CALL RETRY
          END IF
      ELSE IF (CMD .EQ. 'STOP') THEN WHICHC    ! ELSE IF blocks
          CALL STOP
      ELSE IF (CMD .EQ. 'ABORT') THEN
          CALL ABORT
      ELSE WHICHC                              ! ELSE block
!         Print unrecognized command
      END IF WHICHC
   END DO
   END
```

CASE Construct

The **CASE** construct has a concise syntax for selecting, at most, one of a number of statement blocks for execution. The case selector of each **CASE** statement is compared to the expression of the **SELECT CASE** statement.

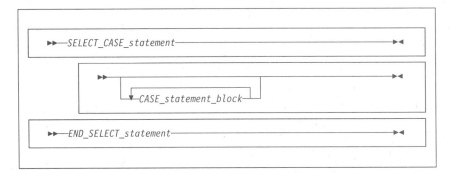

SELECT_CASE_statement
>   defines the case expression that is to be evaluated. See "SELECT CASE" on page 330 for syntax details.

END_SELECT_statement
>   terminates the **CASE** construct. See "END (Construct)" on page 237 for syntax details.

CASE_statement_block

CASE_statement
>   defines the case selector, which is a value, set of values, or default case, for which the subsequent statement block is executed. See "CASE" on page 196 for syntax details.

In the construct, each case value must be of the same type as the case expression. The kind type parameters must also be the same for character expressions, although the length type parameter can differ.

The **CASE** construct executes as follows:

1. The case expression is evaluated. The resulting value is the case index.
2. The case index is compared to the *case_selector* of each **CASE** statement.
3. If a match occurs, the statement block associated with that **CASE** statement is executed. No statement block is executed if no match occurs. (See "CASE" on page 196 for details on determining a match.)
4. Execution of the construct is complete and control is transferred to the statement after the **END SELECT** statement.

A **CASE** construct contains zero or more **CASE** statements that can each specify a value range, although the value ranges specified by the **CASE** statements cannot overlap.

A default *case_selector* can be specified by one of the **CASE** statements. A default *CASE_statement_block* can appear anywhere in the **CASE** construct; it can appear at the beginning or end, or among the other blocks.

If a construct name is specified, it must appear on the **SELECT CASE** statement and **END SELECT** statement, and optionally on any **CASE** statements.

You can only branch to the **END SELECT** statement from within the **CASE** construct. A **CASE** statement cannot be a branch target.

Examples

```
      ZERO: SELECT CASE(N)

      CASE DEFAULT ZERO
          OTHER: SELECT CASE(N) ! start of CASE construct OTHER
              CASE(:-1)
                  SIGNUM = -1     ! this statement executed when n≤-1
              CASE(1:) OTHER
                  SIGNUM = 1
          END SELECT OTHER        ! end of CASE construct OTHER
      CASE (0)
          SIGNUM = 0

      END SELECT ZERO
      END
```

DO Construct

The **DO** construct specifies the repeated execution of a statement block. Such a repeated block is called a *loop*.

The iteration count of a loop can be determined at the beginning of execution of the **DO** construct, unless it is indefinite.

You can curtail a specific iteration with the **CYCLE** statement, and the **EXIT** statement terminates the loop.

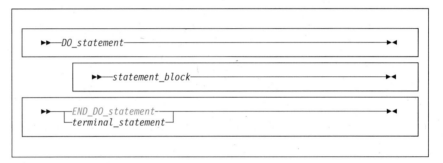

DO_statement
> See "DO" on page 225 for syntax details

END_DO_statement
> See "END (Construct)" on page 237 for syntax details

terminal_statement
> is a statement that terminates the **DO** construct. See the description below.

If you specify a **DO** construct name on the **DO** statement, you must terminate the construct with an **END DO** statement with the same construct name. Conversely, if you do not specify a **DO** construct name on the **DO** statement, and you terminate the **DO** construct with an **END DO** statement, you must not have a **DO** construct name on the **END DO** statement.

The Terminal Statement

The terminal statement must follow the **DO** statement and must be an executable statement. See "Introduction" on page 180 for a listing of statements that can be used as the terminal statement. If the terminal statement of a **DO** construct is a logical **IF** statement, it can contain any executable statement except those statements to which the restrictions on the logical **IF** statement apply.

If you specify a statement label in the **DO** statement, you must terminate the **DO** construct with a statement that is labeled with that statement label.

You can terminate a labeled **DO** statement with an **END DO** statement that is labeled with that statement label, but you cannot terminate it with an unlabeled **END DO** statement. If you do not specify a label in the **DO** statement, you must terminate the **DO** construct with an **END DO** statement.

Nested, labeled **DO** and **DO WHILE** constructs can share the same terminal statement if the terminal statement is labeled, and if it is not an **END DO** statement.

Range of a DO Construct

The range of a **DO** construct consists of all the executable statements following the **DO** statement, up to and including the terminal statement. In addition to the rules governing the range of constructs, you can only transfer control to a shared terminal statement from the innermost sharing **DO** construct.

Active and Inactive DO Constructs

A **DO** construct is either active or inactive. Initially inactive, a **DO** construct becomes active only when its **DO** statement is executed. Once active, the **DO** construct becomes inactive only when:

- Its iteration count becomes zero.
- A **RETURN** statement occurs within the range of the **DO** construct.
- Control transfers to a statement in the same scoping unit but outside the range of the **DO** construct.
- A subroutine invoked from within the **DO** construct returns, through an alternate return specifier, to a statement that is outside the range of the **DO** construct.
- An **EXIT** statement that belongs to the **DO** construct executes.
- An **EXIT** statement or a **CYCLE** statement that is within the range of the **DO** construct, but belongs to an outer **DO** or **DO WHILE** construct, executes.
- A **STOP** statement executes or the program stops for any other reason.

When a **DO** construct becomes inactive, the **DO** variable retains the last value assigned to it.

Executing a DO Statement

An infinite **DO** loops indefinitely.

If the loop is not an infinite **DO**, the **DO** statement includes an initial parameter, a terminal parameter, and an optional increment.

1. The initial parameter, m_1, the terminal parameter, m_2, and the increment, m_3, are established by evaluating the **DO** statement expressions (*a_expr1*, *a_expr2*, and *a_expr3*, respectively). Evaluation includes, if necessary, conversion to the type of the **DO** variable according to the rules for arithmetic conversion (see "Arithmetic Conversion" on page 79). If you do not specify *a_expr3*, m_3 has a value of 1. m_3 must not have a value of zero.

2. The **DO** variable becomes defined with the value of the initial parameter (m_1).

3. The iteration count is established, determined by the expression:

   ```
   MAX (INT ( (m₂ - m₁ + m₃) / m₃), 0)
   ```

   Note that the iteration count is 0 whenever:

   ```
   m₁ > m₂ and m₃ > 0, or
   m₁ < m₂ and m₃ < 0
   ```

The iteration count cannot be calculated if the **DO** variable is missing. This is referred to as an infinite **DO** construct.

At the completion of the **DO** statement, loop control processing begins.

Loop Control Processing

Loop control processing determines if further execution of the range of the **DO** construct is required. The iteration count is tested. If the count is not zero, the first statement in the range of the **DO** construct begins execution. If the iteration count is zero, the **DO** construct becomes inactive. If, as a result, all of the **DO** constructs sharing the terminal statement of this **DO** construct are inactive, normal execution continues with the execution of the next executable statement following the terminal statement. However, if some of the **DO** constructs sharing the terminal statement are active, execution continues with incrementation processing of the innermost active **DO** construct.

Execution of the Range

Statements that are part of the statement block are in the range of the **DO** construct. They are executed until the terminal statement is reached. Except by incrementation processing, you cannot redefine the **DO** variable nor can it become undefined during execution of the range of the **DO** construct.

Terminal Statement Execution

Execution of the terminal statement occurs as a result of the normal execution sequence, or as a result of transfer of control, subject to the restriction that you cannot transfer control into the range of a **DO** construct from outside the range.

Unless execution of the terminal statement results in a transfer of control, execution continues with incrementation processing.

Incrementation Processing

1. The **DO** variable, the iteration count, and the increment of the active **DO** construct whose **DO** statement was most recently executed, are selected for processing.
2. The value of the **DO** variable is increased by the value of m_3.
3. The iteration count is decreased by 1.
4. Execution continues with loop control processing of the same **DO** construct whose iteration count was decremented.

Migration Tip

- Use **EXIT**, **CYCLE**, and infinite **DO** statements instead of a **GOTO** statement.

FORTRAN 77 source

```
        I = 0
        J = 0
20      CONTINUE
        I = I + 1
        J = J + 1
        PRINT *, I
        IF (I.GT.4) GOTO 10    ! Exiting loop
        IF (J.GT.3) GOTO 20    ! Iterate loop immediately
        I = I + 2
        GOTO 20
10      CONTINUE
        END
```

Fortran 90 source

```
        I = 0 ; J = 0
        J = 0
        DO
          I = I + 1
          J = J + 1
          PRINT *, I
          IF (I.GT.4) EXIT
          IF (J.GT.3) CYCLE
          I = I + 2
        END DO
        END
```

Examples

```
INTEGER :: SUM=0
OUTER: DO
  INNER: DO
    READ (5,*) J
    IF (J.LE.I) THEN
      PRINT *, 'VALUE MUST BE GREATER THAN ', I
      CYCLE INNER
    END IF
    SUM=SUM+J
    IF (SUM.GT.500) EXIT OUTER
    IF (SUM.GT.100) EXIT INNER
  END DO INNER
  SUM=SUM+I
  I=I+10
END DO OUTER
PRINT *, 'SUM =',SUM
END
```

DO WHILE Construct

The **DO WHILE** construct specifies the repeated execution of a statement block for as long as the scalar logical expression specified in the **DO WHILE** statement is true. You can curtail a specific iteration with the **CYCLE** statement, and the **EXIT** statement terminates the loop.

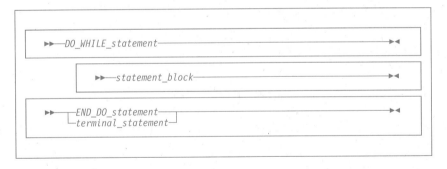

DO_WHILE_statement
> See "DO WHILE" on page 227 for syntax details

END_DO_statement
> See "END (Construct)" on page 237 for syntax details

terminal_stmt is a statement that terminates the **DO WHILE** construct. See "The Terminal Statement" on page 93 for details.

The rules discussed earlier concerning **DO** construct names and ranges, active and inactive **DO** constructs, and terminal statements also apply to the **DO WHILE** construct.

Example

```
I=10
TWO_DIGIT: DO WHILE ((I.GE.10).AND.(I.LE.99))
  J=J+I
  READ (5,*) I
END DO TWO_DIGIT
END
```

Branching

You can also alter the normal execution sequence by *branching*. A branch transfers control from one statement to a labeled branch target statement in the same scoping unit. A branch target statement can be any executable statement except a **CASE**, **ELSE**, or **ELSE IF** statement.

The following statements can be used for branching:

- Assigned **GO TO**

  transfers program control to an executable statement, whose statement label is designated in an **ASSIGN** statement. See "GO TO (Assigned)" on page 260 for syntax details.

- Computed **GO TO**

  transfers control to possibly one of several executable statements. See "GO TO (Computed)" on page 262 for syntax details.

- Unconditional **GO TO**

  transfers control to a specified executable statement. See "GO TO (Unconditional)" on page 263 for syntax details.

- Arithmetic **IF**

  transfers control to one of three executable statements, depending on the evaluation of an arithmetic expression. See "IF (Arithmetic)" on page 264 for syntax details.

The following input/output specifiers can also be used for branching:

- the **END=** end-of-file specifier

  transfers control to a specified executable statement if an endfile record is encountered (and no error occurs) in a **READ** statement.

- the **ERR=** error specifier

transfers control to a specified executable statement in the case of an error. You can specify this specifier in the **BACKSPACE**, **ENDFILE**, **REWIND**, **CLOSE**, **OPEN**, **READ**, **WRITE**, and **INQUIRE** statements.

- the **EOR=** end-or-record specifier

  transfers control to a specified executable statement if an end-of-record condition is encountered (and no error occurs) in a **READ** statement.

Chapter 7. Program Units and Procedures

This chapter describes:

Scope

A program unit consists of a set of nonoverlapping scoping units. A *scoping unit* is that portion of a program unit that has its own scope boundaries. It is one of the following:

- A derived-type definition
- A procedure interface body (not including any derived-type definitions and interface bodies within it)
- A program unit, module subprogram, or internal subprogram (not including derived-type definitions, interface bodies, module subprograms, and internal subprograms).

A *host scoping unit* is the scoping unit that immediately surrounds another scoping unit. For example, in the following diagram, the host scoping unit of the internal function C is the scoping unit of the main program A. Host association is the method by which an internal subprogram, module subprogram, or derived-type definition accesses names from its host.

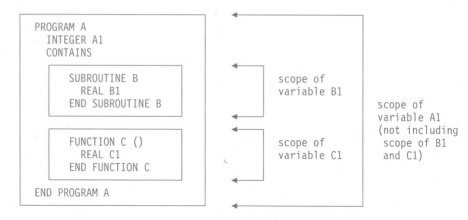

Entities that have scope are:

- A name (see below)
- A label (local entity)
- An external input/output unit number (global entity)
- An operator symbol. Intrinsic operators are global entities, while defined operators are local entities.
- An assignment symbol (global entity)

If the scope is an executable program, the entity is called a *global entity*. If the scope is a scoping unit, the entity is called a *local entity*. If the scope is a statement or part of a statement, the entity is called a *statement entity*.

The Scope of a Name

Global Entity

Global entities are program units, external procedures, and common blocks.

If a name identifies a global entity, it cannot be used to identify any other global entity in the same executable program.

Local Entity

Entities of the following classes are local entities of the scoping unit in which they are defined:

1. Named variables that are not statement entities, module procedures, named constants, derived-type definitions, construct names, generic identifiers, statement functions, internal subprograms, dummy procedures, intrinsic procedures, and namelist group names.

2. Components of a derived-type definition (each derived-type definition has its own class).

A component name has the same scope as the type of which it is a component. It may appear only within a component designator of a structure of that type.

If the derived type is defined in a module and contains the **PRIVATE** statement, the type and its components are accessible in any of the defining module's subprograms by host association. If the accessing scoping unit accesses this type by use association, that scoping unit (and any scoping unit that accesses the entities of that scoping unit by host association) can access the derived-type definition but not its components.

3. Argument keywords (in a separate class for each procedure with an explicit interface).

A dummy argument name in an internal procedure, module procedure, or a procedure interface block has a scope as an argument keyword of the scoping unit of its host. As an argument keyword, it may appear only in a procedure reference for the procedure of which it is a dummy argument. If the procedure or procedure interface block is accessible in another scoping unit by use association or host association, the argument keyword is accessible for procedure references for that procedure in that scoping unit.

In a scoping unit, a name that identifies a local entity of one class may be used to identify a local entity of another class. Such a name must not be used to identify another local entity of the same class, except in the case of generic names. A name that identifies a global entity in a scoping unit cannot be used to identify a local entity of Class 1 in that scoping unit, except for a common block name or the name of an external function.

A common block name in a scoping unit can be the name of any local entity other than a named constant or intrinsic procedure. The name is recognized as the common block entity only when the name is delimited by slashes in a **COMMON** or **SAVE** statement. If it is not, the name identifies the local entity. An intrinsic procedure name can be the name of a common block in a scoping unit that does not reference the intrinsic procedure. In this case, the intrinsic procedure name is not accessible.

An external function name can also be the function result name. This is the only way that an external function name can also be a local entity.

If a scoping unit contains a local entity of Class 1 with the same name as an intrinsic procedure, the intrinsic procedure is not accessible in that scoping unit.

An interface block generic name can be the same as any of the procedure names in the interface block, or the same as any accessible generic name. It can be the same as any generic intrinsic procedure. See "Resolution of Procedure References" on page 138 for more details.

Statement Entity

The following items are statement entities:

- Name of a statement function dummy argument.

    SCOPE: Scope of the statement in which it appears.

- Name of a variable that appears as the **DO** variable of an implied-**DO** in a **DATA** statement or array constructor.

    SCOPE: Scope of the implied-**DO** list.

Except for a common block name or scalar variable name, the name of a global entity or local entity of class 1 that is accessible in the scoping unit of a statement must not be the name of a statement entity of that statement. Within the scope of a statement entity, another statement entity must not have the same name.

If the name of a global or local entity accessible in the scoping unit of a statement is the same as the name of a statement entity in that statement, the name is interpreted within the scope of the statement entity as that of the statement entity. Elsewhere in the scoping unit, including parts of the statement outside the scope of the statement entity, the name is interpreted as that of the global or local entity.

If a statement entity has the same name as an accessible name that denotes a variable, constant, or function, the statement entity has the same type and type parameters as the variable, constant or function. Otherwise, the type of the statement entity is determined through the implicit typing rules in effect. If the statement entity is the **DO** variable of an implied-**DO** in a **DATA** statement, the variable cannot have the same name as an accessible named constant.

Association

Association exists if the same data can be identified with different names in the same scoping unit, or with the same name or different names in different scoping units of the same executable program.

Host Association

Host association allows an internal subprogram, module subprogram, or derived-type definition to access named entities that exist in its host. Accessed entities have the same attributes and are known by the same name (if available) as they are in the host. The entities are objects, derived-type definitions, namelist groups, statement functions, interface blocks and procedures.

A name that is specified with the **EXTERNAL** attribute is a global name. Any entity in the host scoping unit that has this name as its nongeneric name is inaccessible by that name and by host association.

The following list of entities are local within a scoping unit when declared or initialized in that scoping unit:

- A variable name in a **COMMON** statement or initialized in a **DATA** statement
- An array name in a **DIMENSION** statement or an **ALLOCATABLE** statement
- A name of a derived type
- An object name in a type declaration, **EQUIVALENCE**, **POINTER**, **SAVE**, or **TARGET** statement
- A named constant in a **PARAMETER** statement
- A namelist group name in a **NAMELIST** statement
- A generic interface name or a defined operator
- An intrinsic procedure name in an **INTRINSIC** statement
- A function name in a **FUNCTION** statement, statement function statement, or type declaration statement
- A result name in a **FUNCTION** statement or an **ENTRY** statement
- A subroutine name in a **SUBROUTINE** statement
- An entry name in an **ENTRY** statement
- A dummy argument name in a **FUNCTION**, **SUBROUTINE**, **ENTRY** or statement function statement
- The name of a named construct

Entities that are local to a subprogram are not accessible in the host scoping unit.

A local entity must not be referenced or defined before the **DATA** statement when:

1. An entity is local to a scoping unit only because it is initialized in a **DATA** statement, and
2. An entity in the host has the same name as this local entity.

If a derived-type name of a host is inaccessible, structures of that type or subobjects of such structures are still accessible.

If a subprogram gains access to a pointer by host association, the pointer association that exists at the time the subprogram is invoked remains current within the subprogram. This pointer association can be changed within the subprogram. The pointer association remains current when the procedure finishes executing, except when this causes the pointer to become undefined, in which case the association status of the host-associated pointer becomes undefined.

An interface body does not access named entities through host association, although it can access entities by use association.

The host scoping unit of an internal or module subprogram can contain the same use-associated entities.

Example of Host Association

```
SUBROUTINE MYSUB
TYPE DATES                     ! Define DATES
  INTEGER START
  INTEGER END
END TYPE DATES
CONTAINS
  INTEGER FUNCTION MYFUNC(PNAME)
  TYPE PLANTS
    TYPE (DATES) LIFESPAN    ! Host association of DATES
      CHARACTER(10) SPECIES
      INTEGER PHOTOPER
    END TYPE PLANTS
  END FUNCTION MYFUNC
END SUBROUTINE MYSUB
```

Use Association

Use association occurs when a scoping unit accesses the entities of a module with the **USE** statement. Use-associated entities can be renamed for use in the local scoping unit. The association is in effect for the duration of the executable program. See "USE" on page 348 for details.

```
MODULE M
  CONTAINS
  SUBROUTINE PRINTCHAR(X)
    CHARACTER(20) X
    PRINT *, X
  END SUBROUTINE
END MODULE

PROGRAM MAIN
USE M                          ! Accesses public entities of module M
CHARACTER(20) :: NAME='George'
CALL PRINTCHAR(NAME)           ! Calls PRINTCHAR from module M
END
```

Pointer Association

A target that is associated with a pointer can be referenced by a reference to the pointer. This is called *pointer association*.

A pointer always has an association status:

Associated

- The **ALLOCATE** statement successfully allocates the pointer, which has not been subsequently disassociated or undefined.

  ```
  ALLOCATE (P(3))
  ```

- The pointer is pointer-assigned to a target that is currently associated or has the **TARGET** attribute and, if allocatable, is currently allocated.

  ```
  P => T
  ```

Disassociated

- The pointer is nullified by a **NULLIFY** statement.

  ```
  NULLIFY (P)
  ```

- The pointer is deallocated.

  ```
  DEALLOCATE (P)
  ```

- The pointer is pointer-assigned to a disassociated pointer.

  ```
  NULLIFY (Q); P => Q
  ```

Undefined

- Initially
- If its target was never allocated.
- If its target was deallocated other than through the pointer.

  ```
  POINTER P(:), Q(:)
  ALLOCATE (P(3))
  Q => P
  DEALLOCATE (Q)    ! Deallocate target of P through Q.
                    ! P is now undefined.
  END
  ```

- If the execution of a **RETURN** or **END** statement causes the pointer's target to become undefined.
- After the execution of a **RETURN** or **END** statement in a procedure where the pointer was declared or accessed, except for objects described in item 4 under "Events Causing Undefinition" on page 36.

Definition Status and Association Status

The definition status of a pointer is that of its target. If a pointer is associated with a definable target, the definition status of the pointer can be defined or undefined according to the rules for a variable.

If the association status of a pointer is disassociated or undefined, the pointer must not be referenced or deallocated. Whatever its association status, a pointer can always be nullified, allocated or pointer-assigned. When a pointer is allocated, its definition status is undefined. When a pointer is pointer-assigned, its association and definition status are determined by its target. So, if a pointer becomes associated with a target that is defined, the pointer becomes defined.

Program Units, Procedures and Subprograms

A program unit is a sequence of one or more lines, organized as statements, comments, and **INCLUDE** lines. Specifically, a program unit can be:

- The main program
- A module
- A block data program unit
- An external function subprogram
- An external subroutine subprogram

An executable program is a collection of program units consisting of one main program, and any number of external subprograms, modules, and block data program units.

A subprogram can be invoked by a main program or by another subprogram to perform a particular activity. When a procedure is invoked, the referenced subprogram is executed.

An external or module subprogram can contain multiple **ENTRY** statements. The subprogram defines a procedure for the **SUBROUTINE** or **FUNCTION** statement, as well as one procedure for each **ENTRY** statement.

An external procedure is defined either by an external subprogram or by a program unit in a programming language other than Fortran.

Names of main programs, external procedures, block data program units, and modules are global entities. Names of internal and module procedures are local entities.

Internal Procedures

External subprograms, module subprograms, and main programs can have internal subprograms, whether the internal subprograms are functions or subroutines, as long as the internal subprograms follow the **CONTAINS** statement.

An internal procedure is defined by an internal subprogram. Internal subprograms cannot appear in other internal subprograms. A module procedure is defined by a module subprogram or an entry in a module subprogram.

Internal procedures and module procedures are the same as external procedures except that:

- The name of the internal procedure or module procedure is not a global entity
- An internal subprogram must not contain an **ENTRY** statement
- The internal procedure name must not be argument associated with a dummy procedure
- The internal subprogram or module subprogram has access to host entities by host association

FORTRAN 77 source

```
PROGRAM MAIN
  INTEGER A
  A=58
  CALL SUB(A)
C A MUST BE PASSED
END

SUBROUTINE SUB(A)
  INTEGER A,B,C    ! A must be redeclared
  C=A+B
END SUBROUTINE
```

Fortran 90 source

```
PROGRAM MAIN
  INTEGER :: A=58
  CALL SUB
  CONTAINS
  SUBROUTINE SUB
    INTEGER B,C
    C=A+B            ! A is accessible via host association
  END SUBROUTINE
END
```

Interface Concepts

The interface of a procedure determines the form of the procedure reference. The interface consists of:

- The characteristics of the procedure
- The name of the procedure
- The name and characteristics of each dummy argument
- The generic identifiers of the procedure, if any

The characteristics of a procedure consist of:

- Distinguishing the procedure as a subroutine or a function
- Distinguishing each dummy argument either as a data object, dummy procedure, or alternate return specifier

  The characteristics of a dummy data object are its type, type parameters (if any), shape, intent, whether it is optional, whether it is a pointer, and whether it is a target. Any dependence on other objects for type parameter or array bound determinations is a characteristic. If a shape, size, or character length is assumed, it is a characteristic.

The characteristics of a dummy procedure are the explicitness of its interface, its procedure characteristics (if the interface is explicit), and whether it is optional.

- If the procedure is a function, specifying the characteristics of the result value: its type, type parameters (if any), rank, and whether it is a pointer. For nonpointer array results, its shape is a characteristic. Any dependence on other objects for type parameters or array bound determinations is a characteristic. If the length of a character object is assumed, this is a characteristic.

If a procedure is accessible in a scoping unit, it has an interface that is either explicit or implicit in that scoping unit. The rules are:

Entity	Interface
Dummy procedure	Explicit in a scoping unit if an interface block exists or is accessible Implicit in all other cases
External subprogram	Explicit in a scoping unit other than its own if an interface block exists or is accessible Implicit in all other cases
Recursive procedure with a result clause	Explicit in the subprogram's own scoping unit
Module procedure	Always explicit
Internal procedure	Always explicit
Generic procedure	Always explicit
Intrinsic procedure	Always explicit
Statement function	Always implicit

Internal subprograms cannot appear in an interface block.

A procedure must not have more than one accessible interface in a scoping unit.

The interface of a statement function cannot be specified in an interface block.

Explicit Interface

A procedure must have an explicit interface if:

1. A reference to the procedure appears

   - with an argument keyword
   - as a defined assignment (for subroutines only)
   - in an expression as a defined operator (for functions only)
   - as a reference by its generic name

2. The procedure has

   - an optional dummy argument
   - an array-valued result (for functions only)
   - a dummy argument that is a pointer, target, or an assumed-shape array
   - a result whose length type parameter is neither assumed nor constant (for character functions only)
   - a pointer result (for functions only)

Implicit Interface

A procedure has an implicit interface if its interface is not fully known; that is, it has no explicit interface.

Interface Blocks

The *interface block* provides a means of specifying an explicit interface for external procedures and dummy procedures. You can also use an interface block to define generic identifiers. An *interface body* in an interface block specifies the explicit specific interface for an existing external procedure or dummy procedure.

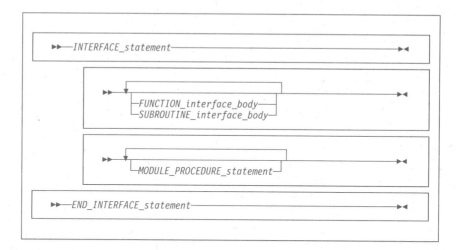

INTERFACE_statement
See "INTERFACE" on page 281 for syntax details

END_INTERFACE_statement
See "END INTERFACE" on page 239 for syntax details

MODULE_PROCEDURE_statement
See "MODULE PROCEDURE" on page 290 for syntax details

FUNCTION_interface_body

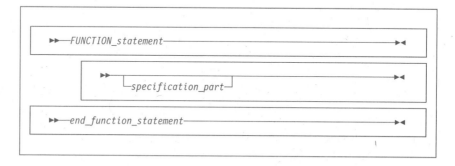

SUBROUTINE_interface_body

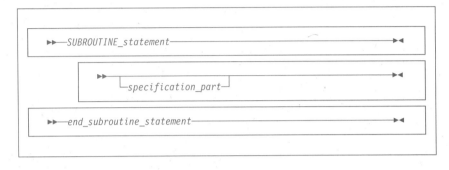

FUNCTION_statement, SUBROUTINE_statement
> For syntax details, see "FUNCTION" on page 257 and "SUBROUTINE" on page 336.

specification_part
> is a sequence of statements from the statement groups numbered **2** through **8**, (except for **3**) in "Order of Statements and Execution Sequence" on page 18.

end_function_statement, end_subroutine_statement
> For syntax details of both statements, see "END" on page 235.

In an interface body, you specify all the characteristics of the procedure. The characteristics must be consistent with those specified in the subprogram definition, except that dummy argument names may be different. The *specification_part* of an interface body can contain statements that specify attributes or define values for data objects that do not determine characteristics of the procedure. Such specification statements have no effect on the interface. Interface blocks do not specify the characteristics of module procedures, whose characteristics are defined in the module subprogram definitions.

An interface body cannot contain **ENTRY** statements, **DATA** statements, **FORMAT** statements, statement function statements, or executable statements. You can specify an entry interface by using the entry name as the procedure name in an interface body.

An interface body does not access named entities by host association. It is treated as if it had a host with the default implicit rules. See "How Type Is Determined" on page 33 for a discussion of the implicit rules.

An interface block can be generic or nongeneric. A generic interface block must specify a generic specification in the **INTERFACE** statement, while a nongeneric interface block must not specify such a generic specification. See "INTERFACE" on page 281 for details.

The interface bodies within a nongeneric interface block can contain interfaces for both subroutines and functions.

A generic name specifies a single name to reference all of the procedures in the interface block. At most, one specific procedure is invoked each time there is a procedure reference with a generic name.

The **MODULE PROCEDURE** statement is allowed only if the interface block has a generic specification and is contained in a scoping unit where each procedure name is accessible as a module procedure.

Example of an Interface

```
MODULE M
 CONTAINS
 SUBROUTINE S1(IARG)
   IARG = 1
 END SUBROUTINE S1
 SUBROUTINE S2(RARG)
   RARG = 1.1
 END SUBROUTINE S2
 SUBROUTINE S3(LARG)
   LOGICAL LARG
   LARG = .TRUE.
 END SUBROUTINE S3
END

USE M
INTERFACE SS
  SUBROUTINE SS1(IARG,JARG)
  END SUBROUTINE
  MODULE PROCEDURE S1,S2,S3
END INTERFACE
CALL SS(II)                ! Calls subroutine S1 from M
CALL SS(I,J)               ! Calls subroutine SS1
END

SUBROUTINE SS1(IARG,JARG)
  IARG = 2
  JARG = 3
END SUBROUTINE
```

You can always reference a procedure through its specific interface. If a generic interface exists for a procedure, the procedure can also be referenced through the generic interface.

Within an interface body, if a dummy argument is intended to be a dummy procedure, it must have the **EXTERNAL** attribute or there must be an interface for the dummy argument.

Generic Interface Blocks

A generic interface block must specify a generic name, defined operator, or defined assignment in an **INTERFACE** statement. The generic name is a single name with which to reference all of the procedures specified in the interface block. It can be the same as any accessible generic name, or any of the procedure names in the interface block.

If two or more generic interfaces that are accessible in a scoping unit have the same local name, they are interpreted as a single generic interface.

Generic Procedure References That Are Unambiguous

Whenever a generic procedure reference is made, only one specific procedure is invoked. The following rules ensure that a generic reference is unambiguous.

If two procedures in the same scoping unit both define assignment or both have the same defined operator and the same number of arguments, you must specify a dummy argument that corresponds by position in the argument list to a dummy argument of the other that has a different type, kind type parameter, or rank.

Within a scoping unit, two procedures that have the same generic name must both be subroutines or both be functions. Also, at least one of them must have a nonoptional dummy argument that both:

1. Corresponds by position in the argument list to a dummy argument that is either not present in the argument list of the other subprogram, or is present with a different type, kind type parameter, or rank.
2. Corresponds by argument keyword to a dummy argument not present in the other argument list, or present with a different type, kind type parameter, or rank.

When an interface block extends an intrinsic procedure (see the next section), the above rules apply as if the intrinsic procedure consisted of a collection of specific procedures, one procedure for each allowed set of arguments.

Example of a Generic Interface Block

```
PROGRAM MAIN
INTERFACE A
  FUNCTION AI(X)
    INTEGER AI, X
  END FUNCTION AI
END INTERFACE
INTERFACE A
  FUNCTION AR(X)
    REAL AR, X
  END FUNCTION AR
END INTERFACE
INTERFACE FUNC
  FUNCTION FUNC1(I, EXT)      ! Here, EXT is a procedure
    INTEGER I
    EXTERNAL EXT
  END FUNCTION FUNC1
  FUNCTION FUNC2(EXT, I)
    INTEGER I
    REAL EXT                  ! Here, EXT is a variable
  END FUNCTION FUNC2
END INTERFACE
EXTERNAL MYFUNC
IRESULT=A(INTVAL)             ! Call to function AI
RRESULT=A(REALVAL)            ! Call to function AR
RESULT=FUNC(1,MYFUNC)         ! Call to function FUNC1
END PROGRAM MAIN
```

Extending Intrinsic Procedures with Generic Interface Blocks

A generic intrinsic procedure can be extended or redefined. An extended intrinsic procedure supplements the existing specific intrinsic procedures. A redefined intrinsic procedure replaces an existing specific intrinsic procedure.

When a generic name is the same as a generic intrinsic procedure name and the name has the **INTRINSIC** attribute (or appears in an intrinsic context), the generic interface extends the generic intrinsic procedure.

When a generic name is the same as a generic intrinsic procedure name and the name does not have the **INTRINSIC** attribute (nor appears in an intrinsic context), the generic interface can redefine the generic intrinsic procedure.

A generic interface name cannot be the same as a specific intrinsic procedure name if the name has the **INTRINSIC** attribute (or appears in an intrinsic context).

Example of Extending and Redefining Intrinsic Procedures

```
PROGRAM MAIN
INTRINSIC MAX
INTERFACE MAX                  ! Extension to intrinsic MAX
  FUNCTION MAXCHAR(STRING)
    CHARACTER(50) STRING
  END FUNCTION MAXCHAR
END INTERFACE
INTERFACE ABS                  ! Redefines generic ABS as ABS does
  FUNCTION MYABS(ARG)          ! not appear in an
    REAL(8) MYABS, ARG         ! INTRINSIC statement
  END FUNCTION MYABS
END INTERFACE
REAL(8) DARG, DANS
REAL(4) RANS
INTEGER IANS,IARG
CHARACTER(50) NAME
DANS = ABS(DARG)               ! Calls external MYABS
IANS = ABS(IARG)               ! Calls intrinsic IABS
DANS = DABS(DARG)              ! Calls intrinsic DABS
IANS = MAX(NAME)               ! Calls external MAXCHAR
RANS = MAX(1.0,2.0)            ! Calls intrinsic AMAX1
END PROGRAM MAIN
```

Defined Operators

A defined operator is a user-defined unary or binary operator, or an extended intrinsic operator (see "Extended Intrinsic and Defined Operations" on page 75). A defined operator must be defined by both a function and a generic interface block.

1. To define the unary operation *op* x_1:

   a. A function or entry must exist that specifies exactly one dummy argument, d_1.
   b. The *generic_spec* in an **INTERFACE** statement specifies **OPERATOR** *(op)*.
   c. The type of x_1 is the same as the type of the dummy argument d_1.
   d. The type parameters, if any, of x_1 must match those of d_1.
   e. The rank of x_1 (and its shape if it is an array) must match that of d_1.

2. To define the binary operation x_1 *op* x_2:

   a. The function is specified with a **FUNCTION** or **ENTRY** statement that specifies two dummy arguments, d_1 and d_2.
   b. The *generic_spec* in an **INTERFACE** block specifies **OPERATOR** *(op)*.
   c. The types of x_1 and x_2 are the same as those of the dummy arguments d_1 and d_2, respectively.

d. The type parameters, if any, of x_1 and x_2 match those of d_1 and d_2, respectively.

e. The ranks of x_1 and x_2 (and their shapes if either or both are arrays) match those of d_1 and d_2, respectively.

3. If *op* is an intrinsic operator, the types or ranks of either x_1 or x_2 are not those required for an intrinsic operation.

4. The *generic_spec* must not specify **OPERATOR** for functions with no arguments or for functions with more than two arguments.

5. Each argument must be nonoptional.

6. The arguments must be specified with **INTENT(IN)**.

7. Each function specified in the interface block cannot have a result of assumed character length.

8. If the operator specified is an intrinsic operator, the number of function arguments must be consistent with the intrinsic uses of that operator.

9. A given defined operator can, as with generic names, apply to more than one function, in which case it is generic just like generic procedure names. For intrinsic operator symbols, the generic properties include the intrinsic operations they represent.

Example of a Defined Operator

```
INTERFACE OPERATOR (.DETERMINANT.)
  FUNCTION IDETERMINANT (ARRAY)
    INTEGER, INTENT(IN), DIMENSION (:,:) :: ARRAY
    INTEGER IDETERMINANT
  END FUNCTION
END INTERFACE
END
```

Defined Assignment

A defined assignment is treated as a reference to a subroutine, with the left-hand side as the first argument and the right-hand side enclosed in parentheses as the second argument.

1. To define the defined assignment $x_1 = x_2$:

   a. The subroutine is specified with a **SUBROUTINE** or **ENTRY** statement that specifies two dummy arguments, d_1 and d_2.

   b. The *generic_spec* of an interface block specifies **ASSIGNMENT (=)**.

   c. The types of x_1 and x_2 are the same as those of the dummy arguments d_1 and d_2, respectively.

   d. The type parameters, if any, of x_1 and x_2 match those of d_1 and d_2, respectively.

e. The ranks of x_1 and x_2 (and their shapes if either or both are arrays) must match those of d_1 and d_2, respectively.

2. **ASSIGNMENT** must only be used for subroutines with exactly two arguments.

3. Each argument must be nonoptional.

4. The first argument must have **INTENT(OUT)** or **INTENT(INOUT)**, and the second argument must have **INTENT(IN)**.

5. The types of the arguments must not be both numeric, both logical, or both character with the same kind parameter.

6. The **ASSIGNMENT** generic specification specifies that the assignment operation is extended or redefined if both sides of the equal sign are of the same derived type.

Example of Defined Assignment

```
INTERFACE ASSIGNMENT(=)
  SUBROUTINE BIT_TO_NUMERIC (N,B)
    INTEGER, INTENT(OUT) :: N
    LOGICAL, INTENT(IN), DIMENSION(:) :: B
  END SUBROUTINE
END INTERFACE
```

Main Program

A main program is the program unit that receives control from the system when the executable program is invoked at run time.

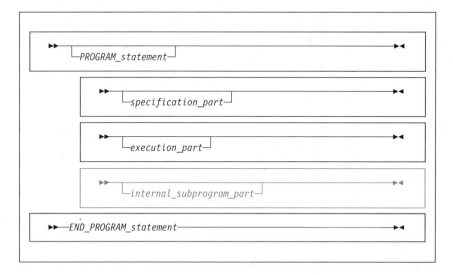

PROGRAM_statement
> See "PROGRAM" on page 312 for syntax details

specification_part
> is a sequence of statements from the statement groups numbered **2** through **9** in "Order of Statements and Execution Sequence" on page 18

execution_part
> is a sequence of statements from the statement groups numbered **3**, **9**, and **10** in "Order of Statements and Execution Sequence" on page 18, and which must begin with a statement from statement group **10**

internal_subprogram_part
> See "Internal Procedures" on page 109 for details

END_PROGRAM_statement
> See "END" on page 235 for syntax details

A main program cannot contain an **ENTRY** statement, nor can it specify an automatic object.

A main program cannot reference itself, directly or indirectly.

Modules

A module contains specifications and definitions that can be accessed from other program units. These definitions include data object definitions, namelist groups, derived-type definitions, procedure interface blocks and procedure definitions.

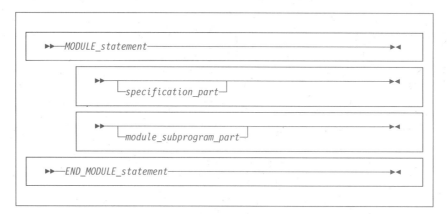

MODULE_statement
> See "MODULE" on page 288 for syntax details

specification_part
> is a sequence of statements from the statement groups numbered **2** through **9** in "Order of Statements and Execution Sequence" on page 18

module_subprogram_part:

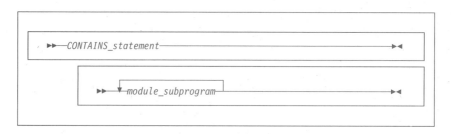

CONTAINS_statement
> See "CONTAINS" on page 212 for syntax details

END_MODULE_statement
> See "END" on page 235 for syntax details

A module subprogram is contained in a module but is not an internal subprogram. Module subprograms must follow a **CONTAINS** statement, and can contain internal procedures. A module procedure is defined by a module subprogram or an entry in a module subprogram.

Executable statements within a module can only be specified in module subprograms.

The declaration of a module function name of type character cannot have an asterisk as a length specification.

specification_part cannot contain statement function statements, **ENTRY** statements, or **FORMAT** statements, although these statements can appear in the specification part of a module subprogram.

Automatic objects cannot appear in the scope of a module.

An accessible module procedure can be invoked by another subprogram in the module or by any scoping unit outside the module through use association (that is, by using the **USE** statement). See "USE" on page 348 for details.

A module is a host to any module procedures or derived-type definitions it contains, which can access entities in the scope of the module through host association.

A module procedure can be used as an actual argument associated with a dummy procedure argument.

The name of a module procedure is local to the scope of the module and cannot be the same as the name of any entity in the module, except for a common block name.

- Eliminate common blocks, and **INCLUDE** directives
- Use modules to hold global data and procedures to ensure consistency of definitions

FORTRAN 77 source

```
      COMMON /BLOCK/A, B, C, NAME, NUMBER
      REAL A, B, C
      A = 3
      CALL CALLUP(D)
      PRINT *, NAME, NUMBER
      END

      SUBROUTINE CALLUP (PARM)
        COMMON /BLOCK/A, B, C, NAME, NUMBER
        REAL A, B, C
        ...
        NAME = 3
        NUMBER = 4
      END
```

Fortran 90 source

```
      MODULE FUNCS
        REAL A, B, C              ! Common block no longer needed
        INTEGER NAME, NUMBER      ! Global data
        CONTAINS
            SUBROUTINE CALLUP (PARM)
              ...
              NAME = 3
              NUMBER = 4
            END SUBROUTINE
      END MODULE FUNCS

      PROGRAM MAIN
      USE FUNCS
      A = 3
      CALL CALLUP(D)
      PRINT *, NAME, NUMBER
      END
```

Example of a Module

```
MODULE M
  INTEGER SOME_DATA
  CONTAINS
    SUBROUTINE SUB()                      ! Module subprogram
      INTEGER STMTFNC
      STMTFNC(I) = I + 1
      SOME_DATA = STMTFNC(5) + INNER(3)
      CONTAINS
        INTEGER FUNCTION INNER(IARG)      ! Internal subprogram
          INNER = IARG * 2
        END FUNCTION
    END SUBROUTINE SUB
END MODULE

PROGRAM MAIN
  USE M                                   ! Main program accesses
  CALL SUB()                              !   module M
END PROGRAM
```

Block Data Program Unit

A block data program unit provides initial values for objects in named common blocks.

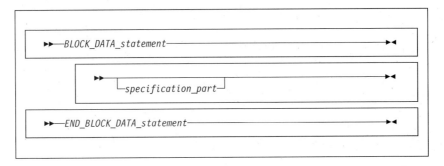

BLOCK_DATA_statement
> See "BLOCK DATA" on page 193 for syntax details

specification_part
> is a sequence of statements from the statement groups numbered **2** through **9** (except for **3**) in "Order of Statements and Execution Sequence" on page 18

END_BLOCK_DATA_statement
> See "END" on page 235 for syntax details

In *specification_part*, you can specify type declaration, **USE**, **IMPLICIT**, **COMMON**, **DATA**, and **EQUIVALENCE** statements, derived-type definitions, and the allowable attribute specification statements. The only attributes that can be specified include **PARAMETER**, **DIMENSION**, **INTRINSIC**, **POINTER**, **SAVE**, and **TARGET**.

You can have more than one block data program unit in an executable program, but only one can be unnamed. You can also initialize multiple named common blocks in a block data program unit.

Restrictions on common blocks in block data program units are:

- All items in a named common block must appear in the **COMMON** statement, even if they are not all initialized.
- The same named common block must not be referenced in two different block data program units.
- Only nonpointer objects in named common blocks can be initialized in block data program units.
- Objects in blank common blocks cannot be initialized.

Example of a Block Data Program Unit

```
PROGRAM MAIN
  COMMON /L3/ C, X(10)
  COMMON /L4/ Y(5)
END PROGRAM

BLOCK DATA BDATA
  COMMON /L3/ C, X(10)
  DATA C, X /1.0, 10*2.0/    ! Initializing common block L3
END BLOCK DATA

BLOCK DATA                        ! An unnamed block data program unit
  PARAMETER (Z=10)
  DIMENSION Y(5)
  COMMON /L4/ Y
  DATA Y /5*Z/
END BLOCK DATA
```

Function and Subroutine Subprograms

A subprogram is either a function or a subroutine, and is either an internal, external, or module subprogram. You can also specify a function in a statement function statement. An external subprogram is a program unit.

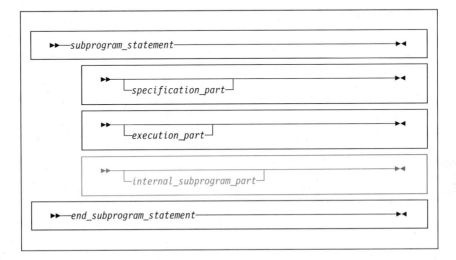

subprogram_statement
> See "FUNCTION" on page 257 or "SUBROUTINE" on page 336 for syntax details

specification_part
> is a sequence of statements from the statement groups numbered **2** through **9** in "Order of Statements and Execution Sequence" on page 18

execution_part
> is a sequence of statements from the statement groups numbered **3**, **9**, and **10** in "Order of Statements and Execution Sequence" on page 18, and which must begin with a statement from statement group **10**

internal_subprogram_part
> See "Internal Procedures" on page 109 for details

end_subprogram_statement
> See "END" on page 235 for syntax details on the **END** statement for functions and subroutines

An internal subprogram is declared *after* the **CONTAINS** statement in the main program, a module subprogram, or an external subprogram, but *before* the

END statement of the host program. The name of an internal subprogram must not be defined in the specification section in the host scoping unit.

An external procedure has global scope with respect to the executable program. In the calling program unit, you can specify the interface to an external procedure in an interface block or you can define the external procedure name with the **EXTERNAL** attribute.

A subprogram can contain any statement except **PROGRAM, BLOCK DATA** and **MODULE** statements. An internal subprogram cannot contain an **ENTRY** statement or an internal subprogram.

Procedure References

There are two types of procedure references:

- A subroutine is invoked by execution of a **CALL** statement (see "CALL" on page 194 for details) or defined assignment statement.
- A function is invoked during evaluation of a function reference or defined operation.

Function Reference

A function reference is used as a primary in an expression:

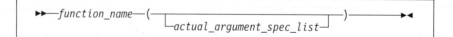

Executing a function reference results in the following order of events:

1. Actual arguments that are expressions are evaluated.
2. Actual arguments are associated with their corresponding dummy arguments.
3. Control transfers to the specified function.
4. The function is executed.
5. The value (or status or target, for pointer functions) of the function result variable is available to the referencing expression.

Execution of a function reference must not alter the value of any other data item within the statement in which the function reference appears. Invocation of a function reference in the logical expression of a logical **IF** statement or **WHERE** statement can affect entities in the statement that is executed when the value of the expression is true.

Examples of Subprograms and Procedure References

```
PROGRAM MAIN
REAL QUAD,X2,X1,X0,A,C3
QUAD=0; A=X1*X2
X2 = 2.0
X1 = SIN(4.5)                    ! Reference to intrinsic function
X0 = 1.0
CALL Q(X2,X1,X0,QUAD)            ! Reference to external subroutine
C3 = CUBE()                      ! Reference to internal function
CONTAINS
   REAL FUNCTION CUBE()          ! Internal function
     CUBE = A**3
   END FUNCTION CUBE
END

SUBROUTINE Q(A,B,C,QUAD)         ! External subroutine
   REAL A,B,C,QUAD
   QUAD = (-B + SQRT(B**2-4*A*C)) / (2*A)
END SUBROUTINE Q
```

Intrinsic Procedures

An intrinsic procedure is a procedure already defined by the processor. See "Intrinsic Procedures" on page 359 for details.

You can reference some intrinsic procedures by a generic name, some by a specific name, and some by both:

A generic intrinsic function does not require a specific argument type and usually produces a result of the same type as that of the argument, with some exceptions. Generic names simplify references to intrinsic procedures because the same procedure name can be used with more than one type of argument; the type and kind type parameter of the arguments determine which specific function is used.

A specific intrinsic function requires a specific argument type and produces a result of a specific type.

A specific intrinsic function name can be passed as an actual argument. If a specific intrinsic function has the same name as a generic intrinsic function, the specific name is referenced. All references to a dummy procedure that are associated with a specific intrinsic procedure must use arguments that are consistent with the interface of the intrinsic procedure.

Whether or not you can pass the name of an intrinsic procedure as an argument depends on the procedure. You can use the specific name of an intrinsic procedure that has been specified with the **INTRINSIC** attribute as an actual argument in a procedure reference.

- An **IMPLICIT** statement does not change the type of an intrinsic function.

- If an intrinsic name is specified with the **INTRINSIC** attribute, the name is always recognized as an intrinsic procedure.

Conflicts between Intrinsic Procedure Names and Other Names

Because intrinsic procedure names are recognized, when a data object is declared with the same name as an intrinsic procedure, the intrinsic procedure is inaccessible.

A generic interface block can extend or redefine a generic intrinsic function, as described in "Interface Blocks" on page 112. If the function already has the **INTRINSIC** attribute, it is extended; otherwise, it can be redefined.

Arguments

Actual Argument Specification

```
►►─────┬──────────────────┬──argument──────────────────────►◄
       └─arg_keyword─ = ─┘
```

arg_keyword   is a dummy argument name in the explicit interface of the procedure being invoked

argument   is an actual argument

An actual argument appears in the argument list of a procedure reference. An actual argument in a procedure reference can be one of the following:

- An expression
- A variable
- A procedure name
- An alternate return specifier (if the actual argument is in a **CALL** statement), having the form *stmt_label*, where *stmt_label* is the statement label of an executable statement in the same scoping unit as the **CALL** statement.

An actual argument specified in a statement function reference must be a scalar object.

A procedure name cannot be the name of an internal procedure, statement function, or the generic name of a procedure.

Argument Keywords

Argument keywords allow you to specify actual arguments in a different order than the dummy arguments. With argument keywords, any actual arguments that correspond to optional dummy arguments can be omitted; that is, dummy arguments that merely serve as placeholders are not necessary.

Each argument keyword must be the name of a dummy argument in the explicit interface of the procedure being referenced. An argument keyword must not appear in an argument list of a procedure that has an implicit interface.

In the argument list, if an actual argument is specified with an argument keyword, the subsequent actual arguments in the list must also be specified with argument keywords.

An argument keyword cannot be specified for label parameters. Label parameters must appear before referencing the argument keywords in that procedure reference.

Example of Argument Keywords

```
INTEGER MYARRAY(1:10)
INTERFACE
  SUBROUTINE SORT(ARRAY, DESCENDING, ARRAY_SIZE)
    INTEGER ARRAY_SIZE, ARRAY(ARRAY_SIZE)
    LOGICAL, OPTIONAL :: DESCENDING
  END SUBROUTINE
END INTERFACE
CALL SORT(MYARRAY, ARRAY_SIZE=10)  ! No actual argument corresponds to the
                                   ! optional dummy argument DESCENDING
END

SUBROUTINE SORT(ARRAY, DESCENDING, ARRAY_SIZE)
  INTEGER ARRAY_SIZE, ARRAY(ARRAY_SIZE)
  LOGICAL, OPTIONAL :: DESCENDING
  IF (PRESENT(DESCENDING)) THEN
    ⋮
END SUBROUTINE
```

Dummy Arguments

A dummy argument is specified in a statement function statement, **FUNCTION** statement, **SUBROUTINE** statement, or **ENTRY** statement. Dummy arguments in statement functions, function subprograms, interface bodies, and subroutine subprograms indicate the types of actual arguments and whether each argument is a scalar value, array, procedure, or statement label. A dummy argument in an external, module, or internal subprogram definition, or in an interface body, is classified as one of the following:

- A variable name
- A procedure name
- An asterisk (in subroutines only, to indicate an alternate return point)

A dummy argument in a statement function definition is classified as a variable name.

A given name can appear only once in a dummy argument list.

The name of a variable that appears as a dummy argument in a statement function statement has a scope of the statement in which it appears. It has the type that it would have if it were the name of a variable in the scoping unit that includes the statement function. It cannot have the same name as an accessible array.

Argument Association

Actual arguments are associated with dummy arguments when a function or subroutine is referenced. In a procedure reference, the actual argument list identifies the correspondence between the actual arguments provided in the list and the dummy arguments of the subprogram.

When there is no argument keyword, an actual argument is associated with the dummy argument that occupies the corresponding position in the dummy argument list. The first actual argument becomes associated with the first dummy argument, the second actual argument with the second dummy argument, and so forth. Each actual argument must be associated with a dummy argument.

When a keyword is present, the actual argument is associated with the dummy argument whose name is the same as the argument keyword. In the scoping unit that contains the procedure reference, the names of the dummy arguments must exist in an accessible explicit interface.

Argument association within a subprogram terminates upon execution of a **RETURN** or **END** statement in the subprogram. There is no retention of argument association between one reference of a subprogram and the next reference of the subprogram.

Actual arguments must agree in type and type parameters with their corresponding dummy arguments (and in shape if the dummy arguments are pointers or assumed-shape), except for two cases: a subroutine name has no type and must be associated with a dummy procedure name that is a subroutine, and an alternate return specifier has no type and must be associated with an asterisk.

Argument association can be carried through more than one level of procedure reference.

If a subprogram reference causes a dummy argument in the referenced subprogram to become associated with another dummy argument in the referenced subprogram, neither dummy argument can become defined, redefined, or undefined during that subprogram. For example, if a subroutine definition is:

```
SUBROUTINE XYZ (A,B)
```

and it is referenced by:

```
CALL XYZ (C,C)
```

the dummy arguments A and B each become associated with the same actual argument C and, therefore, with each other. Neither A nor B can be defined, redefined, or undefined during the execution of subroutine XYZ or by any procedures referenced by XYZ.

If a dummy argument becomes associated with an entity in a common block or an entity accessible through use or host association, the value of the entity must only be altered through the use of the dummy argument name, while the entity is associated with the dummy argument. If any part of a data object is defined through a dummy argument, the data object can be referenced only through that dummy argument, either before or after the definition occurs. These restrictions also apply to pointer targets.

Intent of Dummy Arguments

With the **INTENT** attribute, you can explicitly specify the intended use of a dummy argument. Use of this attribute may improve optimization of the program's calling procedure when an explicit interface exists. For example, a processor implementation may pass **INTENT(IN)** variables by value to reduce overhead costs. Also, the explicitness of argument intent may provide more opportunities for error checking. See "INTENT" on page 279 for syntax details.

Optional Dummy Arguments

The **OPTIONAL** attribute specifies that a dummy argument need not be associated with an actual argument in a reference to a procedure. Some advantages of the **OPTIONAL** attribute include:

- The use of optional dummy arguments to override default behavior. For an example, see "Example of Argument Keywords" on page 131.

- Additional flexibility in procedure references. For example, a procedure could include optional arguments for error handlers or return codes, but you can select which procedure references would supply the corresponding actual arguments.

See "OPTIONAL" on page 300 for details about syntax and rules.

Length of Character Arguments

If the length of a character dummy argument is a nonconstant specification expression, the object is a dummy argument with a runtime length. If an object that is not a dummy argument has a runtime length, it is an automatic object. See "Automatic Objects" on page 22 for details.

If a dummy argument has a length specifier of an asterisk in parentheses, the length of the dummy argument is "inherited" from the actual argument. The length is inherited because it is specified outside the program unit containing the dummy argument. If the associated actual argument is an array name, the length inherited by the dummy argument is the length of an array element in the associated actual argument array.

Variables as Dummy Arguments

A dummy argument that is a variable must be associated with an actual argument that is a variable with the same type and kind type parameter.

If the actual argument is scalar, the corresponding dummy argument must be scalar, unless the actual argument is an element of an array that is not an assumed-shape or pointer array (or a substring of such an element). If the procedure is referenced by a generic name or as a defined operator or defined assignment, the ranks of the actual arguments and corresponding dummy arguments must agree. A scalar dummy argument can be associated only with a scalar actual argument.

If a scalar dummy argument is of type character, its length must be less than or equal to the length of the actual argument. The dummy argument is associated with the leftmost characters of the actual argument. If the character dummy argument is an array, the length restriction applies to the entire array rather than each array element. That is, the lengths of associated array elements can vary, although the whole dummy argument array cannot be longer than the whole actual argument array.

If the dummy argument is an assumed-shape array, the actual argument must not be an assumed-size array or a scalar (including a designator for an array element or an array element substring).

If the dummy argument is an explicit-shape or assumed-size array, and if the actual argument is a noncharacter array, the size of the dummy argument must not exceed the size of the actual argument array. Each actual array element is associated with the corresponding dummy array element. If the actual argument is a noncharacter array element with a subscript value of as, the size of the dummy argument array must not exceed the size of the actual argument array + 1 - as. The dummy argument array element with a subscript value of ds becomes associated with the actual argument array element that has a subscript value of as + ds - 1.

If an actual argument is a character array, character array element, or character substring, and begins at a character storage unit acu of an array, character storage unit dcu of an associated dummy argument array becomes associated with character storage unit acu+dcu-1 of the actual array argument.

You can define a dummy argument that is a variable name within a subprogram if the associated actual argument is a variable. You must not redefine a dummy argument that is a variable name within a subprogram if the associated actual argument is not definable.

If the actual argument is an array section with a vector subscript, the associated dummy argument cannot be defined.

If a nonpointer dummy argument is associated with a pointer actual argument, the actual argument must be currently associated with a target, to which the dummy argument becomes argument associated.

If both the dummy and actual arguments are targets (and the actual argument is not an array section with a vector subscript), the dummy and actual arguments must have the same shape.

If the dummy argument is neither a target nor a pointer, any pointers associated with the actual argument do not become associated with the corresponding dummy argument on invocation of the procedure.

If both the dummy and actual arguments are targets (and the actual argument is not an array section with a vector subscript):

1. Any pointers associated with the actual argument become associated with the corresponding dummy argument on invocation of the procedure.
2. When execution of the procedure completes, any pointers associated with the dummy argument remain associated with the actual argument.

If the dummy argument is a target and the corresponding actual argument is not a target or is an array section with a vector subscript, any pointers associated with the dummy argument become undefined when execution of the procedure completes. When execution of a procedure completes, any pointer that remains defined and that is associated with a dummy target argument remains associated with the corresponding actual argument if the actual argument is a target.

Pointers as Dummy Arguments

If a dummy argument is a pointer, the actual argument must be a pointer and their types, type parameters, and ranks must match. The actual argument reference is to the pointer itself, not to its target. When the procedure is invoked:

- The dummy argument acquires the pointer association status of the actual argument.
- If the actual argument is associated, the dummy argument is associated with the same target.

The association status can change during execution of the procedure. When the procedure finishes executing, the dummy argument's association status becomes undefined, if it is associated.

Procedures as Dummy Arguments

A dummy argument that is identified as a procedure is called a dummy procedure. It can only be associated with an actual argument that is a specific intrinsic procedure, module procedure, external procedure, or another dummy procedure. See "Intrinsic Procedures" on page 359 for details on which intrinsic procedures can be passed as actual arguments.

The dummy procedure and corresponding actual argument must both be functions or both be subroutines. Dummy arguments of the actual procedure argument must match those of the dummy procedure argument. If they are functions, they must match in type, type parameters, rank, shape (if they are nonpointer arrays), and whether they are pointers. If the length of a function result is assumed, this is a characteristic of the result. If the function result specifies a type parameter or array bound that is not a constant expression, the dependence on the entities in the expression is a characteristic of the result.

Dummy procedures that are subroutines are treated as if they have a type that is different from the intrinsic data types, derived types, and alternate return specifiers. Such dummy arguments only match actual arguments that are subroutines or dummy procedures.

Internal subprograms cannot be associated with a dummy procedure argument.

Examples of Procedures as Dummy Arguments

```
PROGRAM MYPROG
INTERFACE
  SUBROUTINE SUB (ARG1)
    EXTERNAL ARG1
    INTEGER ARG1
  END SUBROUTINE SUB
END INTERFACE

EXTERNAL IFUNC, RFUNC
REAL RFUNC

CALL SUB (IFUNC)    ! Valid reference
CALL SUB (RFUNC)    ! Invalid reference
!
! The first reference to SUB is valid because IFUNC becomes an
! implicitly declared integer, which then matches the explicit
! interface. The second reference is invalid because RFUNC is
! explicitly declared real, which does not match the explicit
! interface.
END PROGRAM

SUBROUTINE ROOTS
  EXTERNAL NEG
  X = QUAD(A,B,C,NEG)
  RETURN
END

FUNCTION QUAD(A,B,C,FUNCT)
  INTEGER FUNCT
  VAL = FUNCT(A,B,C)
  RETURN
END

FUNCTION NEG(A,B,C)
  RETURN
END
```

Asterisks as Dummy Arguments

A dummy argument that is an asterisk can only appear in the dummy argument list of a **SUBROUTINE** statement or an **ENTRY** statement in a subroutine subprogram. The corresponding actual argument must be an alternate return specifier, which indicates the statement label of a statement in the same scope as the **CALL** statement, to which control is returned.

Example of an Alternate Return Specifier

```
   CALL SUB(*10)
   STOP                       ! STOP is never executed
10 PRINT *, 'RETURN 1'
   CONTAINS
     SUBROUTINE SUB(*)
        ⋮
       RETURN 1               ! Control returns to statement with label 10
     END SUBROUTINE
   END
```

Resolution of Procedure References

The subprogram name in a procedure reference is either established to be generic, established to be only specific, or not established.

A subprogram name is established to be generic in a scoping unit if one or more of the following is true:

- The scoping unit has an interface block with that name.
- The name of the subprogram is the same as the name of a generic intrinsic procedure that is specified in the scoping unit with the **INTRINSIC** attribute.
- The scoping unit accesses the generic name from a module through use association.
- There are no declarations of the subprogram name in the scoping unit, but the name is established to be generic in the host scoping unit.

A subprogram name is established to be only specific in a scoping unit when it has not been established to be generic and one of the following is true:

- An interface body in the scoping unit has the same name.
- There is a statement function, module procedure, or an internal subprogram in the scoping unit that has the same name.
- The name of the subprogram is the same as the name of a specific intrinsic procedure that is specified with the **INTRINSIC** attribute in the scoping unit.
- The scoping unit contains an **EXTERNAL** statement with the subprogram name.
- The scoping unit accesses the specific name from a module through use association.
- There are no declarations of the subprogram name in the scoping unit, but the name is established to be specific in the host scoping unit.

When a subprogram name is neither established to be generic nor specific, it is not established.

Rules for Resolving Procedure References to Names

The following rules are used to resolve a procedure reference to a name established to be generic:

1. If there is an interface block with that name in the scoping unit or accessible through use association, and the reference is consistent with one of the specific interfaces of that interface block, the reference is to the specific procedure associated with the specific interface.
2. If Rule 1 does not apply, the reference is to an intrinsic procedure if the procedure name in the scoping unit is specified with the **INTRINSIC** attribute or accesses a module entity whose name is specified with the **INTRINSIC** attribute, and the reference is consistent with the interface of that intrinsic procedure.
3. If neither Rule 1 nor Rule 2 apply, but the name is established to be generic in the host scoping unit, the name is resolved by applying Rule 1 and Rule 2 to the host scoping unit. For this rule to apply, there must be agreement between the host scoping unit and the scoping unit of which the name is either a function or a subroutine.
4. If Rule 1, Rule 2 and Rule 3 do not apply, the reference must be to the generic intrinsic procedure with that name.

The following rules are used to resolve a procedure reference to a name established to be only specific:

1. If the scoping unit is a subprogram, and it contains either an interface body with that name or the name has the **EXTERNAL** attribute, and if the name is a dummy argument of that subprogram, the dummy argument is a dummy procedure. The reference is to that dummy procedure.
2. If Rule 1 does not apply, and the scoping unit contains either an interface body with that name or the name has the **EXTERNAL** attribute, the reference is to an external subprogram.
3. In the scoping unit, if a statement function or internal subprogram has that name, the reference is to that procedure.
4. In the scoping unit, if the name has the **INTRINSIC** attribute, the reference is to the intrinsic procedure with that name.
5. The scoping unit contains a reference to a name that is the name of a module procedure that is accessed through use association. Because of possible renaming in the **USE** statement, the name of the reference may differ from the original procedure name.
6. If none of these rules apply, the reference is resolved by applying these rules to the host scoping unit.

The following rules are used to resolve a procedure reference to a name that is not established:

1. If the scoping unit is a subprogram and if the name is the name of a dummy argument of that subprogram, the dummy argument is a dummy procedure. The reference is to that dummy procedure.
2. If Rule 1 does not apply, and the name is the name of an intrinsic procedure, the reference is to that intrinsic procedure. For this rule to apply, there must be agreement between the intrinsic procedure definition and the reference that the name is either a function or subroutine.
3. If neither Rule 1 nor 2 apply, the reference is to the external procedure with that name.

Recursion

A procedure that can reference itself, directly or indirectly, is called a recursive procedure. Such a procedure can reference itself indefinitely until a specific condition is met. For example, you can determine the factorial of the positive integer N as follows:

```
INTEGER N, RESULT, FACTORIAL
READ (5,*) N
IF (N.GE.0) THEN
  RESULT = FACTORIAL(N)
END IF
CONTAINS
  RECURSIVE FUNCTION FACTORIAL (N) RESULT (RES)
    INTEGER RES
    IF (N.EQ.0) THEN
      RES = 1
    ELSE
      RES = N * FACTORIAL(N-1)
    END IF
  END FUNCTION FACTORIAL
END
```

For details on syntax and rules, see "FUNCTION" on page 257, "SUBROUTINE" on page 336, or "ENTRY" on page 243.

Chapter 8. Input/Output Concepts

This chapter describes:

Records

A record is a sequence of characters or a sequence of values. The three kinds of records are formatted, unformatted, and endfile.

Formatted Records

A formatted record is a sequence of characters that the processor can represent, although a processor may not allow some control characters to appear in a formatted record. The length of the record (which can be zero) is measured in characters and depends primarily on the number of characters put into the record when it is written; the length may depend on the processor and the external medium. Only formatted input/output statements can read or write formatted records.

You can create formatted records by means other than Fortran.

Unformatted Records

An unformatted record is a sequence of values in an internal representation that can contain both character and noncharacter data or can contain no data. The values are in their internal form and are not converted in any way when read or written.

Endfile Records

If it exists, an endfile record is the last record of a file. It has no length. It can be written explicitly by an **ENDFILE** statement. It can be written implicitly to a file connected for sequential access when the last data transfer statement was a **WRITE** statement, no intervening file positioning statement referring to the file has been executed, and

- A **REWIND** or **BACKSPACE** statement references the unit to which the file is connected, or
- The file is closed, either explicitly by a **CLOSE** statement, implicitly by a program termination not caused by an error condition, or implicitly by another **OPEN** statement for the same unit.

Files

A file is a sequence of records. The two kinds of files are external and internal. Access to an external file can be sequential or direct.

External Files

An external file is associated with an input/output device, such as a disk, tape, or terminal.

An external file is said to exist for an executable program if it is available to the program for reading or writing, or was created within the program. Creating an external file causes it to exist. Deleting an external file ends its existence. An external file can exist without containing any records.

The position of an external file is usually established by the preceding input/output operation. An external file can be positioned to:

- The initial point, which is the position just before the first record.

- The terminal point, which is the position just after the last record.

- The current record, when the file is positioned within a record. Otherwise, there is no current record.

- The preceding record, which is the record just before the current record. If there is no current record, the preceding record is the record just before the current file position. A preceding record does not exist when the file is positioned at its initial point or within the first record of the file.

- The next record, which is the record just after the current record. If there is no current record, the next record is the record just after the current position. The next record does not exist when the file is positioned at the terminal point or within the last record of the file.

- An indeterminate position after an error.

External File Access Modes: Sequential or Direct

The two methods of accessing the records of an external file are sequential and direct. The method is determined when the file is connected to a unit.

A file connected for sequential access contains records in the order they were written. The records must be either all formatted or all unformatted; the last record of the file must be an endfile record. The records must not be read or written by direct access input/output statements during the time the file is connected for sequential access.

The records of a file connected for direct access can be read or written in any order. The records must be either all formatted or all unformatted; the last record of the file can be an endfile record if the file was previously connected for sequential access. In this case, the endfile record is not considered a part of the file when it is connected for direct access. The records must not be read or written using sequential access, list-directed formatting, namelist formatting, or a nonadvancing input/output statement.

Each record in a file connected for direct access has a record number that identifies its order in the file. The record number is an integer value that must be specified when the record is read or written. Records are numbered sequentially. The first record is number 1. Records need not be read or written in the order of their record numbers. For example, records 9, 5, and 11 can be written in that order without writing the intermediate records.

All records in a file connected for direct access must have the same length, which is specified in the **OPEN** statement when the file is connected (see "OPEN" on page 295).

Records in a file connected for direct access cannot be deleted, but they can be rewritten with a new value. A record cannot be read unless it has first been written.

Internal Files

An internal file is a character variable that is not an array section with a vector subscript. An internal file always exists.

If an internal file is a scalar character variable, the file consists of one record with a length equal to that of the scalar variable. If an internal file is a character array, each element of the array is a record of the file, with each record having the same length.

Reading and writing records are accomplished by sequential access formatted input/output statements. **READ** and **WRITE** are the only input/output statements that can specify an internal file.

If a **WRITE** statement writes less than an entire record, blanks fill the remainder of the record.

On input, blanks are treated in the same way as for an external file opened with **BLANK=NULL** specified. Records are padded with blanks as required.

A scalar character variable that is a record of an internal file can become defined or undefined by means other than an output statement. For example, you can define it by a character assignment statement.

Units

A unit is a means of referring to an external file. Programs refer to external files by the unit numbers indicated by unit specifiers in input/output statements. See page 315 for the form of a unit specifier.

Connection of a Unit

The association of a unit with an external file is called a connection. A connection must occur before the records of the file can be read or written.

There are two ways to connect a file to a unit:

- Preconnection
- Explicit connection, using the **OPEN** statement (see page 295)

Preconnection

Preconnection occurs once the program begins executing. Preconnected units can be specified in input/output statements without the prior execution of an **OPEN** statement.

Disconnection

The **CLOSE** statement disconnects a file from a unit. The file can be connected again within the same program to the same unit or to a different unit, and the unit can be connected again within the same program to the same file or a different file.

Executing Data Transfer Statements

The **READ** statement obtains data from an external or internal file and places it in internal storage. Values are transferred from the file to the data items specified by the input list, if one is specified.

The **WRITE** statement places data obtained from internal storage into an external or internal file. The **PRINT** statement places data obtained from internal storage into an external file. Values are transferred to the file from the data items specified by the output list and format specification, if you specify them. Execution of a **WRITE** or **PRINT** statement for a file that does not exist creates the file, unless an error occurs.

If the output list is omitted in a **PRINT** statement, a blank record is transmitted to the output device unless the **FORMAT** statement referred to contains as its first specification a character string edit descriptor or a slash edit descriptor. In this case, the records indicated by these specifications are transmitted to the output device.

Zero-sized arrays and implied-**DO** lists with iteration counts of zero are ignored when determining the next item to be processed. Zero-length character items are not ignored.

If an input/output item is a pointer, data is transferred between the file and the associated target.

During advancing input from a file whose **PAD=** specifier has the value **NO**, the input list and format specification must not require more characters from the record than the record contains. If the **PAD=** specifier has the value **YES** or if the input file is an internal file, blank characters are supplied if the input list and format specification require more characters from the record than the record contains.

During nonadvancing input from a file whose **PAD=** specifier has the value **NO**, an end-of-record condition occurs if the input list and format specification require more characters from the record than the record contains. If the **PAD=** specifier has the value **YES**, an end-of-record condition occurs and blank characters are supplied if an input item and its corresponding data edit descriptor require more characters from the record than the record contains.

Advancing and Nonadvancing Input/Output

Advancing input/output positions the file after the last record that is read or written, unless an error condition is encountered.

Nonadvancing input/output can position the file at a character position within the current record. With nonadvancing input/output, you can read or write a record of the file by a sequence of input/output statements that each access a portion of the record. You can also read variable-length records and inquire about their lengths.

```
! Reads digits using nonadvancing input

    INTEGER COUNT
    CHARACTER(1) DIGIT
    OPEN (7)
    DO
     READ (7,FMT="(A1)",ADVANCE="NO",EOR=100) DIGIT
       COUNT = COUNT + 1
     IF ((ICHAR(DIGIT).LT.ICHAR('0')).OR.(ICHAR(DIGIT).GT.ICHAR('9'))) THEN
       PRINT *,"Invalid character ", DIGIT, " at record position ",COUNT
       STOP
     END IF
    END DO
100 PRINT *,"Number of digits in record = ", COUNT
    END
```

File Position Before and After Data Transfer

For an explicit connection (by an **OPEN** statement) for sequential input/output that specifies the **POSITION=** specifier, the file position can be explicitly positioned at the beginning, at the end, or where the position is on opening.

A file that did not exist previously is positioned at its initial point. If the **OPEN** statement does not specify the **POSITION=** specifier and the file existed previously, the default value is **ASIS**; that is, the file position remains unchanged.

A **REWIND** statement can be used to position a file at its beginning.

The positioning of a file prior to data transfer depends on the method of access:

- Sequential access for an external file:
  - For advancing input, the file is positioned at the beginning of the next record. This record becomes the current record.
  - For advancing output, a new record is created and becomes the last record of the file.
- Sequential access for an internal file: the file is positioned at the beginning of the first record of the file. This record becomes the current record.
- Direct access: the file is positioned at the beginning of the record specified by the record specifier. This record becomes the current record.

After advancing input/output data transfer, the file is positioned:

- Beyond the endfile record if an end-of-file condition exists as a result of reading an endfile record.
- Beyond the last record read or written if no error or end-of-file condition exists. That last record becomes the preceding record. A record written on a file connected for sequential access becomes the last record of the file.

For nonadvancing input, if no error condition or end-of-file condition occurs, but an end-of-record condition occurs, the file is positioned just after the record read. If no error condition, end-of-file condition or end-of-record condition occurs in a nonadvancing input statement, the file position does not change. If no error condition occurs in a nonadvancing output statement, the file position is not changed. In all other cases, the file is positioned just after the record read or written and that record becomes the preceding record.

If a file is positioned beyond the endfile record, a **READ**, **WRITE**, **PRINT**, or **ENDFILE** statement cannot be executed. A **BACKSPACE** or **REWIND** statement can be used to reposition the file.

Error, End-Of-Record, and End-Of-File Conditions

The set of input/output error conditions is processor dependent. If an error condition occurs during execution of an input/output statement, the position of the file becomes indeterminate.

An end-of-record condition occurs when a nonadvancing **READ** statement attempts to transfer data from a position beyond the end of the current record. When an end-of-record condition occurs:

1. If the **PAD=** specifier has the value **YES**, the record is padded with blanks to satisfy the input list item and corresponding data edit descriptor that require more characters than the record contains.
2. Execution of the **READ** statement terminates and any implied-**DO** variables become undefined.
3. The file specified in the input statement is positioned after the current record.

An end-of-file condition occurs when either:

- an endfile record is encountered during the reading of a file connected for sequential access, or
- an attempt is made to read a record beyond the end of an internal file.

An end-of-file condition can occur at the beginning of execution of a **READ** statement or during execution of a formatted **READ** statement when more than one record is required by the interaction of the input list and format.

If an error or end-of-file condition occurs during execution of an input/output statement, execution of the statement terminates and any implied-**DO** variables become undefined. On input, all input list items become undefined.

Program execution is terminated if one of the following conditions occur:

- An error condition occurs during execution of an input/output statement that contains neither an **IOSTAT=** nor an **ERR=** specifier.
- An end-of-file condition occurs during execution of a **READ** statement that contains neither an **IOSTAT=** specifier nor an **END=** specifier.
- an end-of-record condition occurs during execution of a nonadvancing **READ** statement that contains neither an **IOSTAT=** specifier nor an **EOR=** specifier.

Chapter 9. Input/Output Formatting

Formatted **READ**, **WRITE**, and **PRINT** statements use formatting information to direct the editing (conversion) between internal data representations and character representations in formatted records (see "FORMAT" on page 252). This chapter describes the three methods of formatting:

- Format-directed formatting
- List-directed formatting
- Namelist formatting

Format-directed Formatting

In format-directed formatting, editing is controlled by edit descriptors in a format specification. A format specification is specified in a **FORMAT** statement or as the value of a character array or character expression in a data transfer statement.

Data Edit Descriptors

Forms	Use	Page
A **A**w	Edits character values	152
Bw **B**$w.m$	Edits binary values	153
E$w.d$ **E**$w.d$**E**e **D**$w.d$ **EN**$w.d$ **EN**$w.d$**E**e **ES**$w.d$ **ES**$w.d$**E**e	Edits real and complex numbers with exponents	154
F$w.d$	Edits real and complex numbers without exponents	157
G$w.d$ **G**$w.d$**E**e	Edits data fields of any intrinsic type, with the output format adapting to the type of the data and, if the data is of type real, the magnitude of the data	158
Iw **I**$w.m$	Edits integer numbers	160
Lw	Edits logical values	161
Ow **O**$w.m$	Edits octal values	162
Zw **Z**$w.m$	Edits hexadecimal values	163

where:

w	specifies the width of a field, including all blanks
m	specifies the number of digits to be printed
d	specifies the number of digits to the right of the decimal point
e	specifies the number of digits in the exponent field

w, *m*, *d*, and *e* is an unsigned integer literal constant.

You cannot specify kind parameters for *w*, *m*, *d*, or *e*.

Control Edit Descriptors

Forms	Use	Page
/ *r*/	Specifies the end of data transfer on the current record	164
:	Specifies the end of format control if there are no more items in the input/output list	165
BN	Ignores nonleading blanks in numeric input fields	165
BZ	Interprets nonleading blanks in numeric input fields as zeros	165
*k***P**	Specifies a scale factor for real and complex items	167
S **SS**	Specifies plus signs are not to be written	168
SP	Specifies plus signs are to be written	168
T*c*	Specifies the absolute position in a record from which, or to which, the next character is transferred	168
TL*c*	Specifies the relative position (backward from the current position in a record) from which, or to which, the next character is transferred	168
TR*c*	Specifies the relative position (forward from the current position in a record) from which, or to which, the next character is transferred	168
*o***X**	Specifies the relative position (forward from the current position in a record) from which, or to which, the next character is transferred	168

where:

r	is a repeat specifier. It is an unsigned, positive, integer literal constant.

k	specifies the scale factor to be used. It is an optionally signed, integer literal constant.	
c	specifies the character position in a record. It is an unsigned, nonzero, integer literal constant.	
o	is the relative character position in a record. It is an unsigned, nonzero, integer literal constant.	

Kind type parameters cannot be specified for *r*, *k*, *c*, or *o*.

Character String Edit Descriptors

Forms	Use	Page
*n*H*str*	Outputs a character string (str)	166
'*str*' "*str*"	Outputs a character string (*str*)	165

n	is the number of characters in a literal field. It is an unsigned, positive, integer literal constant. Blanks are included in character count. A kind type parameter cannot be specified.

Editing

Editing is performed on fields. A field is the part of a record that is read on input or written on output when format control processes one of the data or character string edit descriptors. The field width is the size of the field in characters.

The **I**, **F**, **E**, **EN**, **ES**, **B**, **O**, **Z**, **D**, and **G** edit descriptors are collectively called numeric edit descriptors. They are used to format integer, real, and complex data. The general rules that apply to these edit descriptors are:

- On input:

  - Leading blanks are not significant. The interpretation of other blanks is controlled by the **BLANK=** specifier in the **OPEN** statement and the **BN** and **BZ** edit descriptors. A field of all blanks is considered to be zero. Plus signs are optional, although they cannot be specified for the **B**, **O**, and **Z** edit descriptors.

  - In **F**, **E**, **EN**, **ES**, **D**, and **G** editing, a decimal point appearing in the input field overrides the portion of an edit descriptor that specifies the decimal point location. The field can have more digits than can be represented internally.

- On output:

- Characters are right-justified inside the field. Leading blanks are supplied if the editing process produces fewer characters than the field width. If the number of characters is greater than the field width, or if an exponent exceeds its specified length, the entire field is filled with asterisks.
- A negative value is prefixed with a minus sign. By default, a positive or zero value is unsigned; it can be prefixed with a plus sign, as controlled by the **S**, **SP**, and **SS** edit descriptors.

> **Note:** In the examples of edit descriptors, a lowercase b in the Output column indicates that a blank appears at that position.

Complex Editing

A complex value is a pair of separate real components. Therefore, complex editing is specified by a pair of edit descriptors. The first edit descriptor edits the real part of the number, and the second edit descriptor edits the imaginary part of the number. The two edit descriptors can be the same or different. One or more control edit descriptors can be placed between the two edit descriptors, but no data edit descriptors can appear between them.

Data Edit Descriptors

A (Character) Editing
Forms:

> **A**
>
> **A**w

The **A** edit descriptor directs the editing of character values. It can correspond to an input/output list item of type character. The kind type parameter of all characters transferred and converted is implied by the corresponding list item.

On input, if w is greater than or equal to the length (call it *len*) of the input list item, the right-most *len* characters are taken from the input field. If the specified field width is less than *len*, the w characters are left-justified, with (*len* - w) trailing blanks added.

On output, if w is greater than *len*, the output field consists of (w - *len*) blanks followed by the *len* characters from the internal representation. If w is less than or equal to *len*, the output field consists of the left-most w characters from the internal representation.

If w is not specified, the width of the character field is the length of the corresponding input/output list item.

B (Binary) Editing

Forms:

B_w_

B_w.m_

The **B** edit descriptor directs editing between values of type integer in internal form and their binary representation. (A binary digit is either 0 or 1.)

_m_ must have a value that is less than or equal to _w_.

On input, _w_ binary digits are edited and form the internal representation for the value of the input list item. The binary digits in the input field correspond to the right-most binary digits of the internal representation of the value assigned to the input list item. _m_ has no effect on input.

The output field for **B**_w_ consists of zero or more leading blanks followed by the internal value in a form identical to the binary digits without leading zeros. Note that a binary constant always consists of at least one digit.

The output field for **B**_w.m_ is the same as for **B**_w_, except that the digit string consists of at least _m_ digits. If necessary, the digit string is padded with leading zeros. The value of _m_ must not exceed the value of _w_. If _m_ is zero and the value of the internal datum is zero, the output field consists of only blank characters, regardless of the sign control in effect.

Asterisks are printed when the output field width is not sufficient to contain the entire output. On input, the **BN** and **BZ** edit descriptors affect the **B** edit descriptor.

Examples of B Editing on Input

Input	Format	Value
111	B3	7
110	B3	6

Examples of B Editing on Output

Value	Format	Output
7	B3	111
6	B5	bb110
17	B6.5	b10001
17	B4.2	****
22	B6.5	b10110
22	B4.2	****

E and D Editing

Forms:

Ew.d
Ew.d **E**e
Dw.d

The **E** and **D** edit descriptors direct editing between real and complex numbers in internal form and their character representations with exponents. An **E** or **D** edit descriptor can correspond to an input/output list item of type real or to either part (real or imaginary) of an input/output list item of type complex.

The form of the input field is the same as for **F** editing. *e* has no effect on input.

The form of the output field for a scale factor of 0 is:

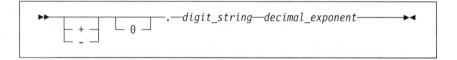

digit_string is a digit string whose length is the *d* most significant digits of the value after rounding.

decimal_exponent

is a decimal exponent of one of the following forms (*z* is a digit):

Edit Descriptor	Absolute Value of Exponent (with scale factor of 0)	Form of Exponent
Ew.d	$|\text{decimal\_exponent}| \leq 99$	$E \pm z_1 z_2$
Ew.d	$99 < |\text{decimal\_exponent}| \leq 999$	$\pm z_1 z_2 z_3$
Ew.d**E**e	$|\text{decimal\_exponent}| \leq (10^e) - 1$	$E \pm z_1 z_2 ... z_e$
Dw.d	$|\text{decimal\_exponent}| \leq 99$	$D \pm z_1 z_2$
Dw.d	$99 < |\text{decimal\_exponent}| \leq 999$	$\pm z_1 z_2 z_3$

The forms **E**w.d and **D**w.d must not be used if $|\text{decimal\_exponent}| > 999$.

The scale factor *k* (see "P (Scale Factor) Editing" on page 167) controls decimal normalization. If $-d < k \leq 0$, the output field contains $|k|$ leading zeros and $d - |k|$ significant digits after the decimal point. If $0 < k < d+2$, the output field contains *k* significant digits to the left of the decimal point and $d-k+1$ significant digits to the right of the decimal point. You cannot use other values of *k*.

See the general information about numeric editing on page 151 for additional information.

Examples of E and D Editing on Input

(Assume **BN** editing is in effect for blank interpretation.)

```
Input      Format      Value
12.34      E8.4        12.34
.1234E2    E8.4        12.34
2.E10      E12.6E1     2.E10
```

Examples of E and D Editing on Output

```
Value      Format      Output

1234.56    E10.3       b0.123E+04
1234.56    D10.3       b0.123D+04
```

EN Editing
Forms:

> **EN**w.d
> **EN**w.d**E**e

The **EN** edit descriptor produces an output field in the form of a real number in engineering notation such that the decimal exponent is divisible by three and the absolute value of the significand is greater than or equal to 1 and less than 1000, except when the output value is zero. The scale factor has no effect on output.

The **EN** edit descriptor can correspond to an input/output list item of type real or to either part (real or imaginary) of an input/output list item of type complex.

The form and interpretation of the input field is the same as for F editing.

The form of the output field is:

yyy   are the 1 to 3 decimal digits representative of the most significant digits of the value of the datum after rounding (*yyy* is an integer such that $1 \leq yyy < 1000$ or, if the output value is zero, *yyy* = 0).

digit_string	are the *d* next most significant digits of the value of the datum after rounding.	
exp	is a decimal exponent, divisible by three, of one of the following forms (z is a digit):	

Edit Descriptor	Absolute Value of Exponent	Form of Exponent
EN*w.d*	|*exp*| ≤ 99	E±$z_1 z_2$
EN*w.d*	99 < |*exp*| ≤ 999	±$z_1 z_2 z_3$
EN*w.d*E*e*	|*exp*| ≤ 10^e−1	E±z_1 ... z_e

For additional information on numeric editing, see "Editing" on page 151.

Examples of EN Editing

```
Value        Format      Output
3.14159      EN12.5      b3.14159E+00
1.41425D+5   EN15.5E4    141.42500E+0003
3.14159D-12  EN15.5E1    ***************
```

ES Editing
Forms:

> **ES*w.d***
> **ES*w.d*E*e***

The **ES** edit descriptor produces an output field in the form of a real number in scientific notation such that the absolute value of the significand is greater than or equal to 1 and less than 10, except when the output value is zero. The scale factor has no effect on output.

The **ES** edit descriptor can correspond to an input/output list item of type real or to either part (real or imaginary) of an input/output list item of type complex.

The form and interpretation of the input field is the same as for F editing.

The form of the output field is:

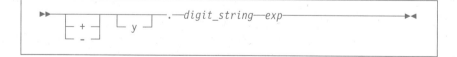

y		is a decimal digit representative of the most significant digit of the value of the datum after rounding.
digit_string		are the *d* next most significant digits of the value of the datum after rounding.
exp		is a decimal exponent having one of the following forms (z is a digit):

Edit Descriptor	Absolute Value of Exponent	Form of Exponent
ES*w.d*	|*exp*| ≤ 99	E± $z_1 z_2$
ES*w.d*	99 < |*exp*| ≤ 999	±$z_1 z_2 z_3$
ES*w.dEe*	|*exp*| ≤ 10^e−1	E±z_1 ... z_e

For additional information on numeric editing, see "Editing" on page 151.

Examples of ES Editing

```
Value        Format      Output
31415.9      ES12.5      b3.14159E+04
14142.5D+3   ES15.5E4    bb1.41425E+0007
31415.9D-22  ES15.5E1    ***************
```

F (Real without Exponent) Editing
Form:

   F*w.d*

The **F** edit descriptor directs editing between real and complex numbers in internal form and their character representations without exponents.

The **F** edit descriptor can correspond to an input/output list item of type real or to either part (real or imaginary) of an input/output list item of type complex.

The input field for the **F** edit descriptor consists of, in order:

1. An optional sign.
2. A string of digits optionally containing a decimal point. If the decimal point is present, it overrides the *d* specified in the edit descriptor. If the decimal point is omitted, the right-most *d* digits of the string are interpreted as following the decimal point, and leading blanks are converted to zeros if necessary.
3. Optionally, an exponent, having one of the following forms:
   - A signed digit string
   - **E** or **D** followed by zero or more blanks and by an optionally signed digit string. **E** and **D** are processed identically.

The output field for the **F** edit descriptor consists of, in order:

1. Blanks, if necessary.
2. A minus sign if the internal value is negative, or an optional plus sign if the internal value is zero or positive.
3. A string of digits that contains a decimal point and represents the magnitude of the internal value, as modified by the scale factor in effect and rounded to *d* fractional digits. See "P (Scale Factor) Editing" on page 167 for more information.

See also the general information about numeric editing on page 151.

Examples of F Editing on Input

(Assume **BN** editing is in effect for blank interpretation.)

```
Input      Format      Value
-100       F6.2        -1.0
2.9        F6.2        2.9
4.E+2      F6.2        400.0
```

Examples of F Editing on Output

```
Value      Format      Output

+1.2       F8.4          bb1.2000
.12345     F8.3          bbbb0.123
```

G (General) Editing
Forms:

> **G**w.d
> **G**w.d**E**e

The **G** edit descriptor can correspond to an input/output list item of any type. Editing of integer data follows the rules of the **I** edit descriptor; editing of real and complex data follows the rules of the **E** or **F** edit descriptors (depending on the magnitude of the value); editing of logical data follows the rules of the **L** edit descriptor; and editing of character data follows the rules of the **A** edit descriptor.

Generalized Real and Complex Editing: The method of representation in the output field depends on the magnitude of the datum being edited. Let N be the magnitude of the internal datum. If $0 < N < 0.1-0.5 \times 10^{-d-1}$ or $N \geq 10^d-0.5$ or N is 0 and d is 0, **G**w.d output editing is the same as k**PE**w.d output editing and **G**w.d**E**e output editing is the same as k**PE**w.d**E**e output editing, where k**P** refers to the scale factor ("P (Scale Factor) Editing" on page 167) currently in effect. If $0.1-0.5 \times 10^{-d-1} \leq N < 10^d-0.5$ or N is identically 0 and d is not zero, the scale factor has no effect, and the value of N determines the editing as follows:

Magnitude of Datum	Equivalent Conversion
$N = 0$	$F(w-n).(d-1),n('b')$ (d must not be 0)
$0.1-0.5 \times 10^{-d-1}$ $\leq N < 1-$ 0.5×10^{-d}	$F(w-n).d,n('b')$
$1-0.5 \times 10^{-d} \leq$ $N < 10-$ $0.5 \times 10^{-d+1}$	$F(w-n).(d-1),n('b')$
$10-0.5 \times 10^{-d+1}$ $\leq N < 100-0.5 \times 10^{-d+2}$	$F(w-n).(d-2),n('b')$
...	...
$10^{d-2}-0.5 \times 10^{-2}$ $\leq N < 10^{d-1}$ -0.5×10^{-1}	$F(w-n).1,n('b')$
$10^{d-1}-0.5 \times 10^{-1}$ $\leq N < 10^d$ -0.5	$F(w-n).0,n('b')$

where b is a blank. n is 4 for **G**w.d and $e+2$ for **G**w.d**E**e.

Note that the scale factor has no effect unless the magnitude of the datum to be edited is outside the range that permits effective use of F editing.

On output, according to FORTRAN 77, the number is converted using either **E** or **F** editing, depending on the number. The field is padded with blanks on the right as necessary. Letting N be the magnitude of the number, editing is as follows:

- If $N<0.1$ or $N \geq 10^d$:
  - **G**w.d editing is the same as **E**w.d editing
  - **G**w.d**E**e editing is the same as **E**w.d**E**e editing.
- If $N \geq 0.1$ and $N<10^d$:

Magnitude of Datum	Equivalent Conversion
$0.1 \leq N < 1$	$F(w\text{-}n).d, n('b')$
$1 \leq N < 10$	$F(w\text{-}n).(d\text{-}1), n('b')$
.	.
.	.
$10^{d\text{-}2} \leq N < 10^{d\text{-}1}$	$F(w\text{-}n).1, n('b')$
$10^{d\text{-}1} \leq N < 10^{d}$	$F(w\text{-}n).0, n('b')$

Note: While FORTRAN 77 does not address how rounding of values affects the output field form, Fortran 90 does. Therefore, some FORTRAN 77 processors may produce a different output form than Fortran 90 processors for certain combinations of values and **G** edit descriptors.

See the general information about numeric editing on page 151.

Examples of G Editing on Output

```
Value      Format      Output
0.0        G10.2       bbb0.0
0.0995     G10.2       bb0.10
99.5       G10.2       bb0.10E+03
```

I (Integer) Editing
Forms:

> I*w*
> I*w.m*

The **I** edit descriptor directs editing between integers in internal form and character representations of integers. The corresponding input/output list item can be of type integer.

w includes the optional sign. *m* must have a value that is less than or equal to *w*.

The input field for the **I** edit descriptor must be an optionally signed digit string, unless it is all blanks. If all blanks, the input field is considered to be zeros.

m is useful on output only. It has no effect on input.

The output field for the **I** edit descriptor consists of, in order:

1. Zero or more leading blanks
2. A minus sign, if the internal value is negative, or an optional plus sign, if the internal value is zero or positive

3. The magnitude in the form of:
   - A digit string without leading zeros if *m* is not specified
   - A digit string of at least *m* digits if *m* is specified and, if necessary, with leading zeros. If the internal value and *m* are both zero, blanks are written.

For additional information about numeric editing, see page 151.

Examples of I Editing on Input

(Assume **BN** editing is in effect for blank interpretation.)

```
Input      Format    Value
-123       I6        -123
123456     I7.5      123456
1234       I4        1234
```

Examples of I Editing on Output

```
Value      Format    Output
-12        I7.6      -000012
12345      I5        12345
```

L (Logical) Editing
Form:

   Lw

The **L** edit descriptor directs editing between logical values in internal form and their character representations. The **L** edit descriptor can correspond to an input/output list item of type logical.

The input field consists of optional blanks, followed by an optional decimal point, followed by a T for true or an F for false. *w* includes blanks. Any characters following the T or F are accepted on input but are ignored; therefore, the strings .TRUE. and .FALSE. are acceptable input forms.

The output field consists of T or F preceded by (*w* - 1) blanks.

Examples of L Editing on Input

```
Input      Format    Value
T          L4        true
.FALSE.    L7        false
```

Examples of L Editing on Output

```
Value      Format      Output
TRUE       L4          bbbT
FALSE      L1          F
```

O (Octal) Editing

Forms:

> O*w*
>
> O*w.m*

The **O** edit descriptor directs editing between values of type integer in internal form and their octal representation. (An octal digit is one of 0-7.)

w includes blanks. *m* must have a value that is less than or equal to *w*.

On input, *w* octal digits are edited and form the internal representation for the value of the input list item. The octal digits in the input field correspond to the right-most octal digits of the internal representation of the value assigned to the input list item. *m* has no effect on input.

The output field for O*w* consists of zero or more leading blanks followed by the internal value in a form identical to the octal digits without leading zeros. Note that an octal constant always consists of at least one digit.

The output field for O*w.m* is the same as for O*w*, except that the digit string consists of at least *m* digits. If necessary, the digit string is padded with leading zeros. The value of *m* must not exceed the value of *w*. If *m* is zero and the value of the internal datum is zero, the output field consists of only blank characters, regardless of the sign control in effect.

Asterisks are printed when the output field width is not sufficient to contain the entire output. On input, the **BN** and **BZ** edit descriptors affect the **O** edit descriptor.

Examples of O Editing on Input

```
Input      Format      Value
123        O3          83
120        O3          80
```

Examples of O Editing on Output

```
Value      Format      Output

80         O5          bb120
83         O2          **
```

Z (Hexadecimal) Editing
Forms:

> *Zw*
> *Zw.m*

The **Z** edit descriptor directs editing between values of type integer in internal form and their hexadecimal representation. (A hexadecimal digit is one of 0-9, A-F, or, if representable, a-f.)

m must have a value that is less than or equal to *w*.

On input, *w* hexadecimal digits are edited and form the internal representation for the value of the input list item. The hexadecimal digits in the input field correspond to the right-most hexadecimal digits of the internal representation of the value assigned to the input list item. *m* has no effect on input.

The output field for **Z***w* consists of zero or more leading blanks followed by the internal value in a form identical to the hexadecimal digits without leading zeros. Note that a hexadecimal constant always consists of at least one digit.

The output field for **Z***w.m* is the same as for **Z***w*, except that the digit string consists of at least *m* digits. If necessary, the digit string is padded with leading zeros. The value of *m* must not exceed the value of *w*. If *m* is zero and the value of the internal datum is zero, the output field consists of only blank characters, regardless of the sign control in effect.

Asterisks are printed when the output field width is not sufficient to contain the entire output. On input, the **BN** and **BZ** edit descriptors affect the **Z** edit descriptor.

Examples of Z Editing on Input

```
Input     Format      Value
0C        Z2          12
7FFF      Z4          32767
```

Examples of Z Editing on Output

Value	Format	Output
12	Z4	bbbC
-1	Z2	**

Control Edit Descriptors

/ (Slash) Editing
Forms:

> /
> r/

The slash edit descriptor indicates the end of data transfer on the current record. The repeat specifier (*r*) has a default value of 1.

When you connect a file for input using sequential access, each slash edit descriptor positions the file at the beginning of the next record.

When you connect a file for output using sequential access, each slash edit descriptor creates a new record and positions the file to write at the start of the new record.

When you connect a file for input or output using direct access, each slash edit descriptor increases the record number by one, and positions the file at the beginning of the record that has that record number.

Examples of Slash Editing on Input

```
500    FORMAT(F6.2 / 2F6.2)
100    FORMAT(3/)
```

: (Colon) Editing
Form:

    :

The colon edit descriptor terminates format control (which is discussed on page 169) if no more items are in the input/output list. If more items are in the input/output list when the colon is encountered, it is ignored.

Example of Colon Editing

```
10      FORMAT(3(:'Array Value',F10.5)/)
```

Apostrophe/Double Quotation Mark Editing (Character-String Edit Descriptor)
Forms:

    'character string'
    "character string"

The apostrophe/double quotation mark edit descriptor specifies a character literal constant in an output format specification. The width of the output field is the length of the character literal constant. See page 26 for additional information on character literal constants.

Examples of Apostrophe/Double Quotation Mark Editing

```
        ITIME=8

        WRITE(*,5) ITIME
5       FORMAT('The value is -- ',I2)          ! The value is -- 8
        WRITE(*,10) ITIME
10      FORMAT(I2,'o''clock')                  ! 8o'clock
        WRITE(*,'(I2,''o''''clock'')') ITIME   ! 8o'clock

        WRITE(*,15) ITIME
15      FORMAT("The value is -- ",I2)          ! The value is -- 8
        WRITE(*,20) ITIME
20      FORMAT(I2,"o'clock")                   ! 8o'clock
        WRITE(*,'(I2,"o''clock")') ITIME       ! 8o'clock
```

BN (Blank Null) and BZ (Blank Zero) Editing
Forms:

    BN
    BZ

The **BN** and **BZ** edit descriptors control the interpretation of nonleading blanks by subsequently processed **I**, **F**, **E**, **EN**, **ES**, **D**, **G**, **B**, **O**, and **Z** edit descriptors. **BN** and **BZ** have effect only on input.

BN specifies that blanks in numeric input fields are to be ignored, and remaining characters are to be interpreted as though right-justified. A field of all blanks has a value of zero.

BZ specifies that nonleading blanks in numeric input fields are to be interpreted as zeros.

The initial setting for blank interpretation is determined by the **BLANK=** specifier of the **OPEN** statement. (See "OPEN" on page 295.) The initial setting is determined as follows:

- If **BLANK=** is not specified, blank interpretation is the same as if **BN** editing was specified.
- If **BLANK=** is specified, blank interpretation is the same as if **BN** editing were specified when the specifier value is **NULL**, or the same as if **BZ** editing were specified when the specifier value is **ZERO**.

The initial setting for blank interpretation takes effect at the start of a formatted **READ** statement and stays in effect until a **BN** or **BZ** edit descriptor is encountered or until format control finishes. Whenever a **BN** or **BZ** edit descriptor is encountered, the new setting stays in effect until another **BN** or **BZ** edit descriptor is encountered, or until format control terminates.

H Editing
Form:

> *n***H** *str*

The **H** edit descriptor specifies a character string (*str*) and its length (*n*) in an output format specification. The string can consist of any of the characters allowed in a character literal constant.

If an **H** edit descriptor occurs within a character literal constant, the constant delimiter character (for example, apostrophe) can be represented within *str* if two such characters are consecutive. Otherwise, another delimiter must be used.

The **H** edit descriptor must not be used on input.

Examples of H Editing

```
50    FORMAT(16HThe value is -- ,I2)
10    FORMAT(I2,7Ho'clock)
      WRITE(*,'(I2,7Ho''clock)') ITIME
```

P (Scale Factor) Editing

Form:

k**P**

The scale factor, k, applies to all subsequently processed **F**, **E**, **EN**, **ES**, **D**, and **G** edit descriptors until another scale factor is encountered or until format control terminates. The value of k is zero at the beginning of each input/output statement. It is an optionally signed integer value representing a power of ten.

On input, when an input field using an **F**, **E**, **EN**, **ES**, **D**, or **G** edit descriptor contains an exponent, the scale factor is ignored. Otherwise, the internal value equals the external value multiplied by $10^{(-k)}$.

On output:

- In **F** editing, the external value equals the internal value multiplied by 10^k.
- In **E** and **D** editing, the external decimal field is multiplied by 10^k. The exponent is then reduced by k.
- In **G** editing, fields are not affected by the scale factor unless they are outside the range that can use **F** editing. If the use of **E** editing is required, the scale factor has the same affect as with **E** output editing.
- In **EN** and **ES** editing, the scale factor has no effect.

Examples of P Editing on Input

```
Input       Format      Value
98.765      3P,F8.6     .98765E-1
98.765      -3P,F8.6    98765.
.98765E+2   3P,F10.5    .98765E+2
```

Examples of P Editing on Output

```
Value       Format      Output

5.67        -3P,F7.2    bbb0.01
12.34       -2P,F6.4    0.1234
12.34       2P,E10.3    b12.34E+00
```

S, SP, and SS (Sign Control) Editing
Forms:

> S
> SP
> SS

The **S**, **SP**, and **SS** edit descriptors control the output of plus signs by all subsequently processed **I**, **F**, **E**, **EN**, **ES**, **D**, and **G** edit descriptors until another **S**, **SP**, or **SS** edit descriptor is encountered or until format control terminates.

S and **SS** specify that plus signs are not to be written. (They produce identical results.) **SP** specifies that plus signs are to be written.

Examples of S, SS, and SP Editing on Output

```
Value      Format      Output
12.3456    S,F8.4      b12.3456
12.3456    SS,F8.4     b12.3456
12.3456    SP,F8.4     +12.3456
```

T, TL, TR, and X (Positional) Editing
Forms:

> T*c*
> TL*c*
> TR*c*
> *o*X

The **T**, **TL**, **TR**, and **X** edit descriptors specify the position where the transfer of the next character to or from a record starts. This position is:

- For **T***c*, the *c*th character position.
- For **TL***c*, *c* characters backward from the current position. If the value of *c* is greater than or equal to the current position, the next character accessed is position one of the record.
- For **TR***c*, *c* characters forward from the current position.
- For *o***X**, *o* characters forward from the current position.

The **TR** and **X** edit descriptors give identical results.

On input, a **TR** or **X** edit descriptor can specify a position beyond the last character of the record if no characters are transferred from that position.

On output, a **T**, **TL**, **TR**, or **X** edit descriptor does not by itself cause characters to be transferred. If characters are transferred to positions at or after the position specified by the edit descriptor, positions skipped and previously unfilled are filled with blanks. The result is the same as if the entire record were initially filled with blanks.

On output, a **T**, **TL**, **TR**, or **X** edit descriptor can result in repositioning so that subsequent editing with other edit descriptors causes character replacement.

Examples of T, TL, and X Editing on Input

```
150   FORMAT(I4,T30,I4)
200   FORMAT(F6.2,5X,5(I4,TL4))
```

Examples of T, TL, TR, and X Editing on Output

```
50    FORMAT('Column 1',5X,'Column 14',TR2,'Column 25')
100   FORMAT('aaaaa',TL2,'bbbbb',5X,'ccccc',T10,'ddddd')
```

Interaction between Input/Output Lists and Format Specifications

The beginning of format-directed formatting initiates format control. Each action of format control depends on the next edit descriptor contained in the format specification and the next item in the input/output list, if one exists.

If an input/output list specifies at least one item, at least one data edit descriptor must exist in the format specification. Note that an empty format specification (parentheses only) can be used only if there are no items in the input/output list or if each item is a zero-sized array. If this is the case and advancing input/output is in effect, one input record is skipped, or one output record containing no characters is written. For nonadvancing input/output, the file position is left unchanged.

A format specification is interpreted from left to right, except when a repeat specification (*r*) is present. A format item preceded by a repeat specification is processed as a list of *r* format specifications or edit descriptors identical to the format specification or edit descriptor without the repeat specification.

One item specified by the input/output list corresponds to each data edit descriptor. A list item of type complex requires the interpretation of two **F**, **E**, **EN**, **ES**, **D**, or **G** edit descriptors. No item specified by the input/output list corresponds to a control edit descriptor or character string edit descriptor. Format control communicates information directly with the record.

Format control operates as follows:

1. If a data edit descriptor is encountered, format control processes an input/output list item, if there is one, or terminates the input/output command if the list is empty. If the list item processed is of type complex, any two edit descriptors are processed.

2. The colon edit descriptor terminates format control if no more items are in the input/output list. If more items are in the input/output list when the colon is encountered, it is ignored.

3. If the end of the format specification is reached, format control terminates if the entire input/output list has been processed, or control reverts to the beginning of the format item terminated by the last preceding right parenthesis. The following items apply when the latter occurs:

   - The reused portion of the format specification must contain at least one data edit descriptor.
   - If reversion is to a parenthesis that is preceded by a repeat specification, the repeat specification is reused.
   - Reversion, of itself, has no effect on the scale factor, on the **S**, **SP**, or **SS** edit descriptors, or on the **BN** or **BZ** edit descriptors.
   - If format control reverts, the file is positioned in a manner identical to the way it is positioned when a slash edit descriptor is processed.

It is important to consider the maximum size record allowed on the input/output medium when defining a Fortran record by a **FORMAT** statement. For example, if a Fortran record is to be printed, the record should not be longer than the printer's line length.

List-directed Formatting

In list-directed formatting, editing is controlled by the types and lengths of the data being read or written. An asterisk format identifier specifies list-directed formatting. For example:

```
REAL TOTAL1, TOTAL2
PRINT *, TOTAL1, TOTAL2
```

List-directed formatting can only be used with sequential files.

The characters in a formatted record processed under list-directed formatting constitute a sequence of values separated by value separators:

- A value has the form of a constant or null value.
- A value separator is a comma, slash, or set of contiguous blanks. A comma or slash can be preceded and followed by one or more blanks.

List-directed Input

Input list items in a list-directed **READ** statement are defined by corresponding values in records. The form of each input value must be acceptable for the type of the input list item. An input value has one of the following forms:

- c
- $r * c$

- *r* *

c is a literal constant of intrinsic type or a non-delimited character constant. *r* is an unsigned, nonzero, integer literal constant. A kind type parameter must not be specified for either *r* or *c*. The constant *c* is interpreted as though it had the same kind type parameter as the corresponding list item.

The *r* * *c* form is equivalent to *r* successive appearances of the constant. The *r* * form is equivalent to *r* successive appearances of the null value.

A null value is represented by one of the following:

- Two successive commas, with zero or more intervening blanks
- A comma followed by a slash, with zero or more intervening blanks
- An initial comma in the record, preceded by zero or more blanks

A character value can be continued in as many records as required. If the next effective item is of type character and:

1. The character constant does not contain the value separators blank, comma, or slash, and
2. The character constant does not cross a record boundary, and
3. The first nonblank character is not a quotation mark or apostrophe, and
4. The leading characters are not numeric followed by an asterisk, and
5. The character constant contains at least one character,

the delimiting apostrophes or quotation marks are not required. If the delimiters are omitted, the character constant is terminated by the first blank, comma, slash, or end-of-record, and apostrophes and double quotation marks within the datum are not to be doubled.

The end of a record:

- Has the same effect as a blank separator unless the blank is within a character literal constant or complex literal constant.
- Does not cause insertion of a blank or any other character in a character value
- Must not separate two apostrophes representing an apostrophe.

Two or more consecutive blanks are treated as a single blank unless the blanks are within a character value.

A null value has no effect on the definition status of the corresponding input list item.

A slash indicates the end of the input list, and list-directed formatting is terminated. If additional items remain in the input list when a slash is encountered, it is as if null values had been specified for those items.

If an object of derived type occurs in an input list, it is treated as if all the structure components were listed in the same order as in the definition of the derived type.

List-directed Output

List-directed **WRITE** and **PRINT** statements produce values in the order they appear in an output list. Values are written in a form that is valid for the data type of each output list item.

Except for complex constants and character constants, the end of a record must not occur within a constant and blanks must not appear within a constant.

Integer values are written using **I** editing.

Real values are written using **E** or **F** editing. (See "E and D Editing" on page 154 or "F (Real without Exponent) Editing" on page 157 for more information.)

Complex constants are enclosed in parentheses with a comma separating the real and imaginary parts, each produced as defined above for real constants. The end of a record can occur between the comma and the imaginary part only if the entire constant is as long as (or longer than) an entire record. The only embedded blanks permitted within a complex constant are between the comma and the end of a record and one blank at the beginning of the next record.

Logical values are written as T for the value true and F for the value false.

Character constants produced for an internal file, or for a file opened without a **DELIM=** specifier or with a **DELIM=** specifier with a value of **NONE**:

1. Are not delimited by apostrophes or quotation marks,
2. Are not separated from each other by value separators,
3. Have each internal apostrophe or double quotation mark represented externally by one apostrophe or double quotation mark, and
4. Have a blank character inserted by the processor for carriage control at the beginning of any record that begins with the continuation of a character constant from the preceding record.

Undelimited character data may not be read back correctly using list-directed input.

Character constants produced for a file opened with a **DELIM=** specifier with a value of **QUOTE** are delimited by double quotation marks, followed by a value separator, and have each internal quote represented on the external medium by two contiguous double quotation marks. Character constants produced for a file opened with a **DELIM=** specifier with a value of **APOSTROPHE** are delimited by apostrophes, followed by a value separator, and have each internal apostrophe represented on the external medium by two contiguous apostrophes.

Slashes (as value separators) and null values are not written.

Arrays are written in column-major order.

You can specify a structure in an output list. On list-directed output, a structure is treated as if all of its components were listed in the same order as they are defined in the derived-type definition.

Except for continuation of delimited character constants, each output record begins with a blank character to provide carriage control when the record is printed.

Namelist Formatting

Namelist formatting can only be used with sequential files.

Namelist Input Data

The form of input for namelist input is:

1. Optional blanks
2. The ampersand (&) character, followed immediately by the namelist group name specified in the **NAMELIST** statement
3. One or more blanks
4. A sequence of zero or more name-value subsequences, separated by value separators
5. A slash to terminate the namelist input

Blanks at the beginning of an input record that continues a delimited character constant are considered part of the constant.

The form of a name-value subsequence in an input record is:

```
▶▶──name── = ──constant_list────────────────────────────▶◀
```

name   is a variable

constant has the following forms:

```
▶▶──┬──────┬──literal_constant──────────────▶◀
     └─r*───┘
```

<table>
<tr><td style="vertical-align: top;">r</td><td>is an unsigned, nonzero, scalar, integer literal constant specifying the number of times the literal_constant is to occur. r cannot specify a kind type parameter.</td></tr>
<tr><td style="vertical-align: top;">literal_constant</td><td>is a scalar literal constant of intrinsic type that cannot specify a kind type parameter, or it is a null value. The constant is treated as if it had the same kind type parameter as the corresponding list item. If literal_constant is of type character, it must be delimited by apostrophes or quotation marks. If literal_constant is of type logical, it can be specified as T or F.</td></tr>
</table>

Any subscripts, strides, and substring range expressions used to qualify *name* must be integer literal constants with no kind type parameter specified.

For information on the type of noncharacter input data, see "List-directed Input" on page 170.

If *name* is neither an array nor an object of derived type, *constant_list* must contain only a single constant.

Variable names specified in the input file must appear in the namelist list, but the order of the input data is not significant. A name that has been made equivalent to *name* cannot be substituted for that name in the namelist list. See "NAMELIST" on page 292 for details on what can appear in a namelist list.

In each name-value subsequence, the name must be the name of a namelist group item with an optional qualification. The name with the optional qualification must not be a zero-sized array, zero-sized array section, or zero-length character string. The optional qualification, if specified, must not contain a vector subscript.

If *name* is an array or array section without vector subscripts, it is expanded into a list of all the elements of the array, in the order that they are stored. If *name* is a structure, it is expanded into a list of ultimate components of intrinsic type, in the order specified in the derived-type definition.

If *name* is an array or structure, the number of constants in *constant_list* must be less than or equal to the number of items specified by the expansion of *name*. If the number of constants is less than the number of items, the remaining items retain their former values.

A null value is specified by:

1. The *r* * form
2. Blanks between two consecutive value separators following an equal sign
3. Zero or more blanks preceding the first value separator and following an equal sign
4. Two consecutive nonblank value separators

A null value has no effect on the definition status of the corresponding input list item. If the namelist group object list item is defined, it retains its previous value; if it is undefined, it remains undefined. A null value must not be used as either the real or imaginary part of a complex constant, but a single null value can represent an entire complex constant.

The end of a record following a value separator, with or without intervening blanks, does not specify a null value.

A slash encountered as a value separator during the execution of a namelist input statement causes termination of execution of that input statement after assignment of the previous value. If there are additional items in the namelist group object being transferred, the effect is as if null values had been supplied for them.

Example of Namelist Input Data: File NMLEXP contains the following data before the **READ** statement is executed:

Character position:

```
            1         2         3
1...+....0....+....0....+....0
```

File contents:
```
 &NAME1
 I=5,
 SMITH%P_AGE=40
 /
```

The above file contains four data records. The program contains the following:
```
TYPE PERSON
  INTEGER P_AGE
  CHARACTER(20) P_NAME
END TYPE PERSON
TYPE(PERSON) SMITH
NAMELIST /NAME1/ I,J,K,SMITH
I=1
J=2
K=3
SMITH=PERSON(20,'John Smith')
OPEN(7,FILE='NMLEXP')
```

```
READ(7,NML=NAME1)
! Only the value of I and P_AGE in SMITH are
! altered (I = 5, SMITH%P_AGE = 40).
! J, K and P_NAME in SMITH remain the same.

END
```

Note: In the previous example, the data items appear in separate data
records. The following example is a file with the same data items, but
they are in one data record:

Character position:

```
        1        2        3        4
1...+....0....+....0....+....0....+....0
```

File contents:

```
 &NAME1 I= 5, SMITH%P_AGE=40 /
```

Namelist Output Data

When output data is written using a namelist list, it is written in a form that can
be read using a namelist list (except for character data that is not delimited).
All variables specified in the namelist list and their values are written out, each
according to its type. Character data is delimited as specified by the **DELIM=**
specifier. The fields for the data are made large enough to contain all the
significant digits. The values of a complete array are written out in
column-major order.

The processor may begin new records, as necessary; there is no minimum
number of output records required.

The namelist group name and namelist item names are output in uppercase.

Character constants produced for a file opened without a **DELIM=** specifier or
with a **DELIM=** specifier with a value of **NONE**:

1. Are not delimited by apostrophes or quotation marks,
2. Are not separated from each other by value separators,
3. Have each internal apostrophe or quotation mark represented externally by
   one apostrophe or quotation mark, and
4. Have a blank character inserted by the processor for carriage control at the
   beginning of any record that begins with the continuation of a character
   constant from the preceding record.

Nondelimited character data that has been written out cannot be read as
character data.

Character constants produced for a file opened with a **DELIM=** specifier with a value of **QUOTE** are delimited by double quotation marks, are preceded and followed by a value separator, and have each internal quotation mark represented on the external medium by two contiguous quotation marks.

Character constants produced for a file opened with a **DELIM=** specifier with a value of **APOSTROPHE** are delimited by apostrophes, are preceded and followed by a value separator, and have each internal apostrophe represented on the external medium by two contiguous apostrophes.

To restrict namelist output records to a given width, specify the **RECL=** specifier (in the **OPEN** statement).

Except for continuation of delimited character constants, each output record begins with a blank character to provide carriage control when the record is printed.

For information on the type of noncharacter output data, see "List-directed Output" on page 172.

Example of Namelist Output Data

```
TYPE PERSON
  INTEGER P_AGE
  CHARACTER(20) P_NAME
END TYPE PERSON
TYPE(PERSON) SMITH

NAMELIST /NL1/ I,J,C,SMITH
CHARACTER(5) :: C='BACON'
INTEGER I,J
I=12046
J=12047
SMITH=PERSON(20,'John Smith')
WRITE(6,NL1)
END
```

After execution of the **WRITE** statement, the output data may appear as follows (depending on the processor):

```
     1         2         3         4
1...+....0....+....0....+....0....+....0
 &NL1
 I=12046, J=12047, C=BACON, SMITH=20, John Smith
 /
```

Part 2. Statements

Introduction

This section provides an alphabetical reference to all Fortran statements. Each statement description is organized to help you readily access the syntax and rules. For more detailed information on the elements that make up statements and the proper contexts for using the statements, each statement section points to related information in the Concepts and Elements section.

The following table lists the executable statements, the *specification_part* statements, and those statements that can be used as the terminal statement of a **DO** or **DO WHILE** construct.

STATEMENT NAME	EXECUTABLE STATEMENT	SPECIFICATION STATEMENT	TERMINAL STATEMENT
ALLOCATABLE		X	
ALLOCATE	X		X
ASSIGN	X		X
BACKSPACE	X		X
BLOCK DATA			
CALL	X		X
CASE	X		
CHARACTER		X	
CLOSE	X		X
COMMON		X	
COMPLEX		X	
CONTAINS			
CONTINUE	X		X
CYCLE	X		
DATA		X	
DEALLOCATE	X		X
Derived Type			
DIMENSION		X	
DO	X		
DO WHILE	X		
DOUBLE PRECISION		X	
ELSE	X		
ELSE IF	X		
ELSEWHERE	X		
END	X		
END BLOCK DATA			
END DO	X		X
END IF	X		
END FUNCTION	X		
END INTERFACE		X	
END MODULE			
END PROGRAM	X		

STATEMENT NAME	EXECUTABLE STATEMENT	SPECIFICATION STATEMENT	TERMINAL STATEMENT
END SELECT	X		
END SUBROUTINE	X		
END TYPE		X	
END WHERE	X		
ENDFILE	X		X
ENTRY		X	
EQUIVALENCE		X	
EXIT	X		
EXTERNAL		X	
FORMAT		X	
FUNCTION			
GO TO (Assigned)	X		
GO TO (Computed)	X		X
GO TO (Unconditional)	X		
IF (Block)	X		
IF (Arithmetic)	X		
IF (Logical)	X		X
IMPLICIT		X	
INQUIRE	X		X
INTEGER		X	
INTENT		X	
INTERFACE		X	
INTRINSIC		X	
LOGICAL		X	
MODULE			
MODULE PROCEDURE		X	
NAMELIST		X	
NULLIFY	X		X
OPEN	X		X
OPTIONAL		X	
PARAMETER		X	
PAUSE	X		X
POINTER		X	
PRINT	X		X
PRIVATE		X	
PROGRAM			
PUBLIC		X	
READ	X		X
REAL		X	
RETURN	X		
REWIND	X		X
SAVE		X	
SELECT CASE	X		
SEQUENCE		X	

STATEMENT NAME	EXECUTABLE STATEMENT	SPECIFICATION STATEMENT	TERMINAL STATEMENT
Statement Function		X	
STOP	X		
SUBROUTINE			
TARGET		X	
TYPE		X	
Type Declaration		X	
USE		X	
WHERE	X		X
WRITE	X		X

Assignment and pointer assignment statements are discussed in "Expressions and Assignment" on page 63. Both statements are executable and can serve as terminal statements.

Attributes

Each attribute has a corresponding attribute specification statement, and the syntax diagram provided for the attribute illustrates this form. An entity can also acquire this attribute from a type declaration statement or, in some cases, through a default setting. For example, entity A, said to have the **PRIVATE** attribute, could have acquired the attribute in any of the following ways:

```
REAL, PRIVATE :: A      ! Type declaration statement

PRIVATE :: A            ! Attribute specification statement

MODULE X
   PRIVATE              ! Default setting
   REAL :: A
END MODULE
```

The following table maps out the compatibility of attributes.

An "X" indicates whether an entity can have the attributes indicated both horizontally and vertically.

	ALLOCATABLE	DIMENSION	EXTERNAL	INTENT	INTRINSIC	OPTIONAL	PARAMETER	POINTER	PRIVATE	PUBLIC	SAVE	TARGET
ALLOCATABLE		X							X	X	X	X
DIMENSION	X			X		X	X	X	X	X	X	X
EXTERNAL						X			X	X		
INTENT		X				X						X
INTRINSIC									X	X		
OPTIONAL		X	X	X				X				X
PARAMETER		X							X	X		
POINTER		X				X			X	X	X	
PRIVATE	X	X	X		X		X	X			X	X
PUBLIC	X	X	X		X		X	X			X	X
SAVE	X	X							X	X	X	X
TARGET	X	X		X		X			X	X	X	

ALLOCATABLE

Purpose

The **ALLOCATABLE** attribute declares allocatable arrays — that is, arrays whose bounds are determined when space is dynamically allocated by execution of an **ALLOCATE** statement.

Format

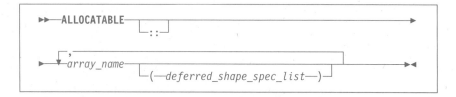

array_name   is the name of an allocatable array

deferred_shape_spec
            is a colon(:), where each colon represents a dimension

Rules

The array cannot be a dummy argument or function result. If the array is specified elsewhere in the scoping unit with the **DIMENSION** attribute, the array specification must be a *deferred_shape_spec*.

```
┌─── Attributes Compatible with the ALLOCATABLE Attribute ───┐
│                                                            │
│   • DIMENSION       • PUBLIC        • TARGET               │
│   • PRIVATE         • SAVE                                 │
│                                                            │
└────────────────────────────────────────────────────────────┘
```

Examples

```
REAL, ALLOCATABLE :: A(:,:)   ! Two-dimensional array A declared
                              ! but no space yet allocated

READ (5,*) I,J
ALLOCATE (A(I,J))
END
```

Related Information

ALLOCATE

Purpose

The **ALLOCATE** statement dynamically provides storage for pointer targets and allocatable arrays.

Format

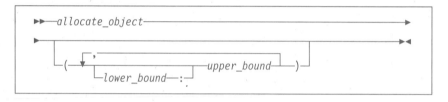

stat_variable   is a scalar integer variable

allocation

allocate_object
> is a variable name or structure component. It must be a pointer or an allocatable array.

lower_bound, upper_bound
> are each scalar integer expressions

Rules

Execution of an **ALLOCATE** statement for a pointer causes the pointer to become associated with the target allocated. For an allocatable array, the array becomes definable.

The number of dimensions specified (i.e., the number of upper bounds in *allocation*) must be equal to the rank of *allocate_object*. When an **ALLOCATE** statement is executed for an array, the values of the bounds are determined at that time. Subsequent redefinition or undefinition of any entities in the bound expressions does not affect the array specification. Any lower bound, if omitted, is assigned a default value of 1. If any lower bound value exceeds the corresponding upper bound value, that dimension has an extent of 0 and *allocate_object* is zero-sized.

A specified bound must not be an expression that contains as a primary an array inquiry function whose argument is an *allocate_object* in the same **ALLOCATE** statement. Similarly, the *stat_variable* must not be allocated within the **ALLOCATE** statement in which it appears.

If the **STAT=** specifier is not present and an error condition occurs during execution of the statement, the program terminates. If the **STAT=** specifier is present, successful execution of the **ALLOCATE** statement causes the *stat_variable* to be assigned the value zero, while an error condition during execution causes the *stat_variable* to be assigned a processor-dependent positive integer value.

Allocating an allocatable array that is already allocated causes an error condition in the **ALLOCATE** statement.

Pointer allocation creates an object that has the **TARGET** attribute. Additional pointers can be associated with this target (or a subobject of it) through pointer assignment. If you reallocate a pointer that is already associated with a target:

- a new target is created and the pointer becomes associated with this target
- any previous association with the pointer is broken
- any previous target that had been created by allocation and is not associated with any other pointers becomes inaccessible

Use the **ALLOCATED** intrinsic function to determine if an allocatable array is currently allocated. Use the **ASSOCIATED** intrinsic function to determine the association status of a pointer or whether a pointer is currently associated with a specified target.

Examples

```
CHARACTER, POINTER :: P(:,:)
CHARACTER, TARGET :: C(4,4)
INTEGER, ALLOCATABLE, DIMENSION(:) :: A
P => C
N = 2; M = N
ALLOCATE (P(N,M),STAT=I)        ! P is no longer associated with C
N = 3                           ! Target array for P maintains 2X2 shape
IF (.NOT.ALLOCATED(A)) ALLOCATE (A(N**2))
END
```

ALLOCATE

Related Information

- "ALLOCATABLE" on page 184
- "DEALLOCATE" on page 221
- "Allocation Status" on page 38
- "Pointer Association" on page 106
- "Deferred-shape Arrays" on page 47
- "ALLOCATED (ARRAY)" on page 367
- "ASSOCIATED (POINTER, TARGET)" on page 368

ASSIGN

Purpose

The **ASSIGN** statement assigns a statement label to an integer variable.

Format

```
►►──ASSIGN──stmt_label──TO──variable_name──────────────►◄
```

stmt_label   specifies the statement label of an executable statement or a **FORMAT** statement in the scoping unit containing the **ASSIGN** statement

variable_name
    is the name of a scalar default integer variable

Rules

A statement containing the designated statement label must appear in the same scoping unit as the **ASSIGN** statement. If the statement containing the statement label is an executable statement, you can use the label name in an assigned **GO TO** statement that is in the same scoping unit. If the statement containing the statement label is a **FORMAT** statement, you can use the label name as the format specifier in a **READ**, **WRITE**, or **PRINT** statement that is in the same scoping unit.

You can redefine an integer variable defined with a statement label value with the same or different statement label value or an integer value. However, you must define the variable with a statement label value before you reference it in an assigned **GO TO** statement or as a format identifier in an input/output statement.

The value of *variable_name* is not the integer constant represented by the label itself, and you cannot use it as such.

Examples

```
      ASSIGN 30 TO LABEL
      NUM = 40
      GO TO LABEL
      NUM = 50              ! This statement is not executed
30    ASSIGN 1000 TO IFMT
      PRINT IFMT, NUM       ! IFMT is the format specifier
1000  FORMAT(1X,I4)
      END
```

ASSIGN

Related Information

- "Statement Labels" on page 13
- "GO TO (Assigned)" on page 260

BACKSPACE

Purpose

The **BACKSPACE** statement positions an external file, connected for sequential access, before the preceding record.

Format

```
►►──BACKSPACE──┬──u────────────────┬──────────────►◄
               └──(──position_list──)──┘
```

u	is an external unit identifier. The value of *u* must not be an asterisk.
position_list	is a list that must contain one unit specifier ([**UNIT=**]*u*) and can also contain one of each of the other valid specifiers:
[UNIT=] *u*	is a unit specifier in which *u* must be an external unit identifier whose value is not an asterisk. An external unit identifier refers to an external file that is represented by a scalar integer expression. If the optional characters **UNIT=** are omitted, *u* must be the first item in *position_list*.
IOSTAT= *ios*	is an input/output status specifier that specifies the status of the input/output operation. *ios* is a scalar default integer variable. When the **BACKSPACE** statement finishes executing, *ios* is defined with:

- A zero value if no error condition occurs.
- A positive value if an error occurs.

ERR= *stmt_label*	is an error specifier that specifies the statement label of an executable statement in the same scoping unit to which control is to transfer in the case of an error. Coding the **ERR=** specifier suppresses error messages.

Rules

If there is no preceding record, the file position does not change. If the preceding record is the endfile record, the file is positioned before the endfile record. You cannot backspace over records that were written using list-directed or namelist formatting.

If the **ERR=** and **IOSTAT=** specifiers are set and an error is encountered, transfer is made to the statement specified by the **ERR=** specifier and a positive integer value is assigned to *ios*.

BACKSPACE

Examples

```
      BACKSPACE 15
      BACKSPACE (UNIT=15,ERR=99)
         ⋮
   99 PRINT *, "Unable to backspace file."
      END
```

Related Information

- "Input/Output Concepts" on page 141

BLOCK DATA

Purpose

A **BLOCK DATA** statement is the first statement in a block data program unit, which provides initial values for variables in named common blocks.

Format

```
►►──BLOCK DATA──────────────────────────────────────►◄
                └─block_data_name─┘
```

block_data_name
is the name of a block data program unit

Rules

You can have more than one block data program unit in an executable program, but only one can be unnamed.

The name of the block data program unit, if given, must not be the same as an external subprogram, entry, main program, module, or common block in the executable program. It also must not be the same as a local entity in this program unit.

Examples

```
BLOCK DATA ABC
   PARAMETER (I=10)
   DIMENSION Y(5)
   COMMON /L4/ Y
   DATA Y /5*I/
END BLOCK DATA ABC
```

Related Information

- "Block Data Program Unit" on page 125
- "END" on page 235, for details on the **END BLOCK DATA** statement

CALL

Purpose

The **CALL** statement invokes a subroutine to be executed.

Format

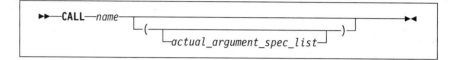

name   is the name of an internal, external, or module subroutine, an
              entry in an external or module subroutine, an intrinsic subroutine,
              or a generic name.

Rules

Executing a **CALL** statement results in the following order of events:

1. Actual arguments that are expressions are evaluated.
2. Actual arguments are associated with their corresponding dummy
   arguments.
3. Control transfers to the specified subroutine.
4. The subroutine is executed.
5. Control returns from the subroutine.

A subprogram can call itself recursively, directly or indirectly, if the subroutine
statement specifies the **RECURSIVE** keyword.

If a **CALL** statement includes one or more alternate return specifiers among its
arguments, control may be transferred to one of the statement labels indicated,
depending on the action specified by the subroutine in the **RETURN** statement.

Examples

```
INTERFACE
  SUBROUTINE SUB3(D1,D2)
    REAL D1,D2
  END SUBROUTINE
END INTERFACE
ARG1=7 ; ARG2=8
CALL SUB3(D2=ARG2,D1=ARG1)     ! subroutine call with argument keywords
END

SUBROUTINE SUB3(F1,F2)
  REAL F1,F2,F3,F4
```

```
      F3 = F1/F2
      F4 = F1-F2
      PRINT *, F3, F4
   END SUBROUTINE
```

Related Information

- "Recursion" on page 140
- "Actual Argument Specification" on page 130
- "Asterisks as Dummy Arguments" on page 137

CASE

Purpose

The **CASE** statement initiates a **CASE** statement block in a **CASE** construct, which has a concise syntax for selecting, at most, one of a number of statement blocks for execution.

Format

case_selector

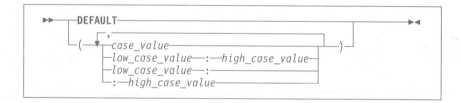

case_construct_name
    is a name given to the **CASE** construct for identification

case_value   is a scalar initialization expression of type integer, character, or logical

low_case_value, high_case_value
    are each scalar initialization expressions of type integer, character, or logical

Rules

The case index, determined by the **SELECT CASE** statement, is compared to each *case_selector* in a **CASE** statement. When a match occurs, the *stmt_block* associated with that **CASE** statement is executed. If no match occurs, no *stmt_block* is executed. No two case value ranges can overlap.

A match is determined as follows:

case_value

> DATA TYPE: integer, character or logical
>
> MATCH for integer and character: *case index= case_value*
>
> MATCH for logical: *case index* **.EQV.** *case_value* is true

low_case_value : high_case_value

> DATA TYPE: integer or character
>
> MATCH: *low_case_value* ≤ *case index* ≤ *high_case_value*

low_case_value :

> DATA TYPE: integer or character
>
> MATCH: *low_case_value* ≤ *case index*

: high_case_value

> DATA TYPE: integer or character
>
> MATCH: *case index* ≤ *high_case_value*

DEFAULT

> DATA TYPE: not applicable
>
> MATCH: if no other match occurs.

There must be only one match. If there is a match, the statement block associated with the matched *case_selector* is executed, completing execution of the case construct. If there is no match, execution of the case construct is complete.

If the *case_construct_name* is specified, it must match the name specified on the **SELECT CASE** and **END SELECT** statements.

DEFAULT is the default *case_selector*. Only one of the **CASE** statements may have **DEFAULT** as the *case_selector*.

Each case value must be of the same data type as the *case_expr*, as defined in the **SELECT CASE** statement.

When the *case_expr* and the case values are of type character, they can have different lengths.

CASE

Examples

```
ZERO: SELECT CASE(N)

    CASE DEFAULT ZERO           ! Default CASE statement for
                                ! CASE construct ZERO
            OTHER: SELECT CASE(N)
                CASE(:-1)       ! CASE statement for CASE
                                ! construct OTHER
                    SIGNUM = -1
                CASE(1:) OTHER
                    SIGNUM = 1
            END SELECT OTHER
    CASE (0)
        SIGNUM = 0

END SELECT ZERO
```

Related Information

- "CASE Construct" on page 90
- "SELECT CASE" on page 330
- "END (Construct)" on page 237, for details on the **END SELECT** statement

CHARACTER

Purpose

A **CHARACTER** type declaration statement specifies the kind, length, and attributes of objects and functions of type character. Initial values can be assigned to objects.

Format

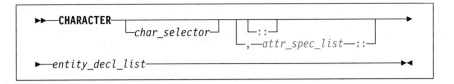

where:

attr_spec
ALLOCATABLE
DIMENSION (*array_spec*)
EXTERNAL
INTENT (*intent_spec*)
INTRINSIC
OPTIONAL
PARAMETER
POINTER
PRIVATE
PUBLIC
SAVE
TARGET

char_selector specifies the character length

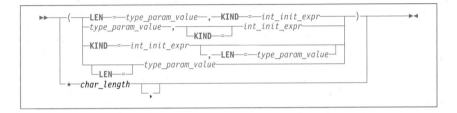

CHARACTER

type_param_value
 is a specification expression or an asterisk (*)

int_init_expr is a scalar integer initialization expression that must be nonnegative and must specify a representation method that exists on the processor

char_length is either a scalar integer literal constant (which cannot specify a kind type parameter) or a *type_param_value* enclosed in parentheses

attr_spec For detailed information on rules about a particular attribute, refer to the statement of the same name.

intent_spec is either **IN**, **OUT**, or **INOUT**

:: is the double colon separator. It is required if attributes are specified or if = *initialization_expr* is used.

array_spec is a list of dimension bounds

entity_decl

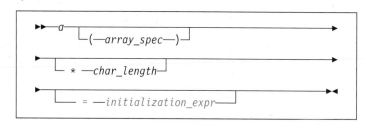

a is an object name or function name. *array_spec* cannot be specified for a function name.

initialization_expr
 provides an initial value, by means of an initialization expression, for the entity specified by the immediately preceding name

Rules

Entities in type declaration statements are constrained by the rules of any attributes specified for the entities, as detailed in the corresponding attribute statements.

The type declaration statement overrides the implicit type rules in effect. You can use a type declaration statement that confirms the type of an intrinsic function. The appearance of a generic or specific intrinsic function name in a type declaration statement does not cause the name to lose its intrinsic property.

An object cannot be initialized in a type declaration statement if it is a dummy argument, an allocatable array, a pointer, a function result, an object in blank common, an external name, an intrinsic name, or an automatic object. The object may be initialized if it appears in a named common block in a block data program unit.

The specification expression of a *type_param_value* or an *array_spec* can be a nonconstant expression if the specification expression appears in an interface body or in the specification part of a subprogram. Any object being declared that uses this nonconstant expression and is not a dummy argument is called an *automatic object*.

An attribute cannot be repeated in a given type declaration statement, nor can an entity be explicitly given the same attribute more than once in a scoping unit.

initialization_expr must be specified if the statement contains the **PARAMETER** attribute. If *initialization_expr* is specified and **PARAMETER** is not, the object is a variable that is initially defined. *a* becomes defined with the value determined by *initialization_expr*, in accordance with the rules for intrinsic assignment. If the variable is an array, its shape must be specified either in the type declaration statement or in a previous specification statement in the same scoping unit. A variable or variable subobject cannot be initialized more than once. The presence of *initialization_expr* implies that *a* is a saved object, except for an object with the **PARAMETER** attribute or in a named common block.

An *array_spec* specified in an *entity_decl* takes precedence over the *array_spec* in the **DIMENSION** attribute. A *char_length* specified in an *entity_decl* takes precedence over any length specified in *char_selector*.

An array function result that does not have the **POINTER** attribute must have an explicit-shape array specification.

If the entity declared is a function, it must not have an accessible explicit interface unless it is an intrinsic function.

The optional comma after *char_length* in a **CHARACTER** type declaration statement is permitted only if no double colon separator (::) appears in the statement.

If the **CHARACTER** type declaration statement is in the scope of a module, block data program unit, or main program, and you specify the length of the entity as inherited length, the entity must be the name of a named character constant. The character constant assumes the length of its corresponding expression defined by the **PARAMETER** attribute.

If the **CHARACTER** type declaration statement is in the scope of a procedure and the length of the entity is inherited, the entity name must be the name of a dummy argument or a named character constant. If the statement is in the scope of an external function, it can also be the function or entry name in a **FUNCTION** or **ENTRY** statement in the same program unit. If the entity name is the name of a dummy argument, the dummy argument assumes the length of the associated actual argument for each reference to the procedure. If the entity name is the name of a character constant, the character constant assumes the length of its corresponding expression defined by the **PARAMETER** attribute. If the entity name is a function or entry name, the entity assumes the length specified in the calling scoping unit.

The length of a character function is either a specification expression (which must be a constant expression if the function type is not declared in an interface block) or it is an asterisk, indicating the length of a dummy procedure name. The length cannot be an asterisk if the function is an internal or module function, recursive, or if the function returns array or pointer values.

Examples

```
I=7
CHARACTER(KIND=1,LEN=6) APPLES /'APPLES'/
CHARACTER(7), TARGET :: ORANGES = 'ORANGES'
CALL TEST(APPLES,I)
CONTAINS
  SUBROUTINE  TEST(VARBL,I)
    CHARACTER*(*), OPTIONAL :: VARBL    ! VARBL inherits a length of 6
    CHARACTER(I) :: RUNTIME             ! Automatic object with length of 7
  END SUBROUTINE
END
```

Related Information

- "Character" on page 26
- "Initialization Expressions" on page 66
- "How Type Is Determined" on page 33 for details on the implicit typing rules
- "Array Declarators" on page 43
- "Automatic Objects" on page 22
- "DATA" on page 216, for details on initial values

CLOSE

Purpose

The **CLOSE** statement disconnects an external file from a unit.

Format

```
►►──CLOSE──(──close_list──)────────────────────────────►◄
```

close_list   is a list that must contain one unit specifier (**UNIT=**u) and can also contain one of each of the other valid specifiers. The valid specifiers are:

[UNIT=] u is a unit specifier in which u must be an external unit identifier whose value is not an asterisk. An external unit identifier refers to an external file that is represented by a scalar integer expression. If the optional characters **UNIT=** are omitted, u must be the first item in close_list.

IOSTAT= ios   is an input/output status specifier that specifies the status of the input/output operation. ios is a scalar default integer variable. When the input/output statement containing this specifier finishes executing, ios is defined with:

- A zero value if no error condition occurs.
- A positive value if an error occurs.

ERR= stmt_label

is an error specifier that specifies the statement label of an executable statement in the same scoping unit to which control is to transfer in the case of an error. Coding the **ERR=** specifier suppresses error messages.

STATUS= char_expr

specifies the status of the file after it is closed. char_expr is a character expression whose value, when any trailing blanks are removed, is either **KEEP** or **DELETE**.

- If **KEEP** is specified for a file that exists, the file will continue to exist after the **CLOSE** statement. If **KEEP** is specified for a file that does not exist, the file will not exist after the **CLOSE** statement. **KEEP** must not be specified for a file whose status prior to executing the **CLOSE** statement is **SCRATCH**.
- If **DELETE** is specified, the file will not exist after the **CLOSE** statement.

CLOSE

The default is **DELETE** if the file status is **SCRATCH**; otherwise, the default is **KEEP**.

Rules

A **CLOSE** statement that refers to a unit can occur in any program unit of an executable program and need not occur in the same scoping unit as the **OPEN** statement referring to that unit. You can specify a unit that does not exist or has no file connected; the **CLOSE** statement has no effect in this case.

When an executable program stops for reasons other than an error condition, all units that are connected are closed. Each unit is closed with the status **KEEP** unless the file status prior to completion was **SCRATCH**, in which case the unit is closed with the status **DELETE**. The effect is as though a **CLOSE** statement without a **STATUS=** specifier were executed on each connected unit.

If a preconnected unit is disconnected by a **CLOSE** statement, the rules of implicit opening apply if the unit is later specified in a **WRITE** statement (without having been explicitly opened).

Examples

```
CLOSE(15)
CLOSE(UNIT=16,STATUS='DELETE')
```

Related Information

- "Connection of a Unit" on page 144
- "OPEN" on page 295

COMMON

Purpose

The **COMMON** statement specifies common blocks and their contents. A common block is a storage area that two or more scoping units can share, allowing them to define and reference the same data and to share storage units.

Format

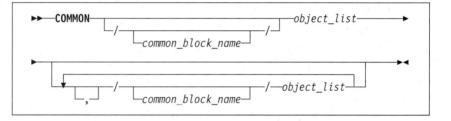

object

Rules

object cannot refer to a dummy argument, automatic object, allocatable array, function, function result, or entry to a procedure.

If an *explicit_shape_spec_list* is present, *variable_name* must not have the **POINTER** attribute. Each dimension bound must be a constant specification expression. This form specifies that *variable_name* has the **DIMENSION** attribute.

If *object* is of derived type, it must be a sequence derived type. Given a sequenced structure where all the components are nonpointers and are either all of default noncharacter type (or double precision real) or all of default character type, the structure is treated as if its components are enumerated directly in the common block.

A pointer object in a common block can only be storage associated with pointers of the same type, type parameters, and rank.

COMMON

If you specify *common_block_name*, all variables specified in the *object_list* that follows are declared to be in that named common block. If you omit *common_block_name*, all variables that you specify in the *object_list* that follows are in the blank common block.

Within a scoping unit, a common block name can appear more than once in the same or in different **COMMON** statements. Each successive appearance of the same common block name continues the common block specified by that name. Common block names are global entities.

The variables in a common block can have different data types. You can mix character and noncharacter data types within the same common block. Variable names in common blocks can appear in only one **COMMON** statement in a scoping unit, and you cannot duplicate them within the same **COMMON** statement.

Common Association

Within an executable program, all nonzero-sized named common blocks with the same name have the same first storage unit. There can be one blank common block, and all scoping units that refer to nonzero-sized blank common refer to the same first storage unit.

All zero-sized common blocks with the same name are storage associated with one another. All zero-sized blank common blocks are associated with one another and with the first storage unit of any nonzero-sized blank common blocks. Use association or host association can cause these associated objects to be accessible in the same scoping unit.

A nonpointer object that is of default noncharacter type (or a structure made up of only such objects) can only be associated with similar objects of these types.

Common Block Storage Sequence

Storage units for variables within a common block in a scoping unit are assigned in the order that their names appear within the **COMMON** statement.

You can extend a common block by using an **EQUIVALENCE** statement, but only by adding beyond the last entry, not before the first entry. For example, these statements specify X:

```
COMMON /X/ A,B      ! common block named X
REAL C(2)
EQUIVALENCE (B,C)
```

The contents of common block X are as follows:

```
            |   |   |   |   |   |   |   |   |   |   |   |   |
Variable A: |       A       |
Variable B:                 |       B       |
Array C:                    |      C(1)     |      C(2)      |
```

Only **COMMON** and **EQUIVALENCE** statements that appear in a scoping unit contribute to the common block storage sequences formed in that unit, not including variables in common made accessible by use association or host association.

An **EQUIVALENCE** statement cannot cause the storage sequences of two different common blocks to become associated. While a common block can be declared in the scoping unit of a module, it must not be declared in another scoping unit that accesses entities from the module through use association.

Size of a Common Block

The size of a common block is equal to the storage sequence needed to hold all the variables in the common block, including any extensions resulting from equivalence association.

Differences Between Named and Blank Common Blocks

- Within an executable program, there can be more than one named common block, but only one blank common block.
- In all scoping units of an executable program, named common blocks of the same name must have the same size, but blank common blocks can have different sizes. (If you specify blank common blocks with different sizes in different scoping units, the length of the longest block becomes the length of the blank common block in the executable program.)
- You can initially define objects in a named common block by using a **BLOCK DATA** program unit containing a **DATA** statement or a type declaration statement. You cannot initially define any elements of a common block in a blank common block.

  Each named common block can be initialized in only one block data program unit.

Examples

```
INTEGER MONTH,DAY,YEAR
COMMON /DATE/ MONTH,DAY,YEAR
REAL        R4
REAL        R8
CHARACTER(1) C1
COMMON /MIXED/ R8,C1,R4
```

COMMON

Related Information

- "Block Data Program Unit" on page 125
- "Explicit-shape Arrays" on page 44
- "The Scope of a Name" on page 102, for details on global entities

COMPLEX

Purpose

A **COMPLEX** type declaration statement specifies the length and attributes of objects and functions of type complex. Initial values can be assigned to objects.

Format

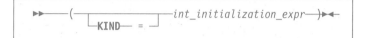

where:

attr_spec
ALLOCATABLE
DIMENSION (*array_spec*)
EXTERNAL
INTENT (*intent_spec*)
INTRINSIC
OPTIONAL
PARAMETER
POINTER
PRIVATE
PUBLIC
SAVE
TARGET

kind_selector

specifies the kind of complex entities, where *int_initialization_expr* represents the precision and range of each part of the complex entity

attr_spec   For detailed information on rules about a particular attribute, refer to the statement of the same name.

COMPLEX

intent_spec	is either **IN**, **OUT**, or **INOUT**
::	is the double colon separator. It is required if attributes are specified or if = *initialization_expr* is used.
array_spec	is a list of dimension bounds
entity_decl	

a	is an object name or function name. *array_spec* cannot be specified for a function name.
initialization_expr	provides an initial value, by means of an initialization expression, for the entity specified by the immediately preceding name

Rules

Entities in type declaration statements are constrained by the rules of any attributes specified for the entities, as detailed in the corresponding attribute statements.

The type declaration statement overrides the implicit type rules in effect. You can use a type declaration statement that confirms the type of an intrinsic function. The appearance of a generic or specific intrinsic function name in a type declaration statement does not cause the name to lose its intrinsic property.

An object cannot be initialized in a type declaration statement if it is a dummy argument, an allocatable array, a pointer, a function result, an object in blank common, an external name, an intrinsic name, or an automatic object. The object may be initialized if it appears in a named common block in a block data program unit.

The specification expression of an *array_spec* can be a nonconstant expression if the specification expression appears in an interface body or in the specification part of a subprogram. Any object being declared that uses this nonconstant expression and is not a dummy argument is called an *automatic object*.

An attribute cannot be repeated in a given type declaration statement, nor can an entity be explicitly given the same attribute more than once in a scoping unit.

initialization_expr must be specified if the statement contains the **PARAMETER** attribute. If *initialization_expr* is specified and **PARAMETER** is not, the object is a variable that is initially defined. *a* becomes defined with the value determined by *initialization_expr*, in accordance with the rules for intrinsic assignment. If the variable is an array, its shape must be specified either in the type declaration statement or in a previous specification statement in the same scoping unit. A variable or variable subobject cannot be initialized more than once. The presence of *initialization_expr* implies that *a* is a saved object, except for an object with the **PARAMETER** attribute or in a named common block.

An *array_spec* specified in the *entity_decl* takes precedence over the *array_spec* in the **DIMENSION** attribute.

An array function result that does not have the **POINTER** attribute must have an explicit-shape array specification.

If the entity declared is a function, it must not have an accessible explicit interface unless it is an intrinsic function.

Examples

```
COMPLEX, DIMENSION (2,3) :: ABC(3) ! ABC has 3 (not 6) array elements
```

Related Information

- "Complex" on page 25
- "Initialization Expressions" on page 66
- "How Type Is Determined" on page 33, for details on the implicit typing rules
- "Array Declarators" on page 43
- "Automatic Objects" on page 22
- "DATA" on page 216, for details on initial values

CONTAINS

Purpose

The **CONTAINS** statement separates the body of a main program, external subprogram, or module subprogram from any internal subprograms that it may contain. Similarly, it separates the specification part of a module from any module subprograms.

Format

```
▶▶──CONTAINS──────────────────────────────────────────────▶◀
```

Rules

When a **CONTAINS** statement exists, at least one subprogram must follow it.

The **CONTAINS** statement cannot appear in a block data program unit or in an internal subprogram.

Any label of a **CONTAINS** statement is considered part of the main program, subprogram, or module that contains the **CONTAINS** statement.

Examples

```
MODULE A
    ⋮
  CONTAINS                   ! Module subprogram must follow
  SUBROUTINE B(X)
      ⋮
    CONTAINS                 ! Internal subprogram must follow
    FUNCTION C(Y)
        ⋮
    END FUNCTION
  END SUBROUTINE
END MODULE
```

Related Information

- "Program Units, Procedures and Subprograms" on page 108

CONTINUE

Purpose

The **CONTINUE** statement is an executable control statement that takes no action; it has no effect. This statement is often used as the terminal statement of a loop.

Format

```
►►──CONTINUE─────────────────────────────────────────────────────►◄
```

Examples

```
      DO 100 I = 1,N
         X = X + N
100   CONTINUE
```

Related Information

- "Control" on page 87

CYCLE

Purpose

The **CYCLE** statement terminates the current execution cycle of a **DO** or **DO WHILE** construct.

Format

```
►►──CYCLE───────────────────────────────────────────────►◄
             └─DO_construct_name─┘
```

DO_construct_name
            is the name of a **DO** or **DO WHILE** construct

Rules

The **CYCLE** statement is placed within a **DO** or **DO WHILE** construct and belongs to the particular **DO** or **DO WHILE** construct specified by *DO_construct_name* or, if not specified, to the **DO** or **DO WHILE** construct that immediately surrounds it. The statement terminates only the current cycle of the construct that it belongs to.

When the **CYCLE** statement is executed, the current execution cycle of the **DO** or **DO WHILE** construct is terminated. Any executable statements after the **CYCLE** statement, including any terminating labeled action statement, will not be executed. For **DO** constructs, program execution continues with incrementation processing, if any. For **DO WHILE** constructs, program execution continues with loop control processing.

A **CYCLE** statement can have a statement label. However, it cannot be used as a labeled action statement that terminates a **DO** construct.

Examples

```fortran
LOOP1: DO I = 1, 20
   N = N + 1
   IF (N > NMAX) CYCLE LOOP1          ! cycle to LOOP1

   LOOP2: DO WHILE (K==1)
      IF (K > KMAX) CYCLE             ! cycle to LOOP2
      K = K + 1
   END DO LOOP2

   LOOP3:  DO J = 1, 10
      N = N + 1
      IF (N > NMAX) CYCLE LOOP1       ! cycle to LOOP1
```

```
        CYCLE LOOP3                      ! cycle to LOOP3
      END DO LOOP3

    END DO LOOP1
    END
```

Related Information

- "DO" on page 225
- "DO WHILE" on page 227

DATA

DATA

Purpose

The **DATA** statement provides initial values for variables.

Format

data_object is a variable or an implied-**DO** list. Any subscript or substring expression must be an initialization expression.

     *implied-**DO** list*

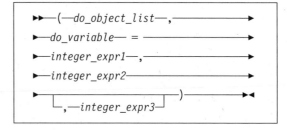

  do_object is an array element, scalar structure component, or implied-**DO** list

  do_variable is a named scalar integer variable called the implied-**DO** variable. This variable is a statement entity.

  integer_expr1, integer_expr2, and *integer_expr3*
       are each scalar integer expressions. The primaries of an expression can only contain constants or implied-**DO** variables of other implied-**DO** lists that have this implied-**DO** list within their ranges. Each operation must be intrinsic.

initial_value

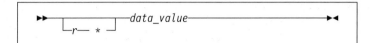

r	is a nonnegative scalar integer constant that cannot specify a kind type parameter. If *r* is a named constant, it must have been declared previously in the scoping unit or made accessible by use or host association. If *r* is omitted, the default value is 1. The form *r∗data_value* is equivalent to *r* successive appearances of the data value.
data_value	is a scalar constant, signed integer literal constant, signed real literal constant, structure constructor, or *boz_literal_constant*

boz_literal_constant

is an unsigned binary, octal, or hexadecimal literal constant that must correspond to a scalar integer variable. A *boz_literal_constant* can only appear in a **DATA** statement.

A binary constant has the form:

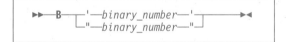

binary_number is a string formed from the digits 0 and 1.

An octal constant has the form:

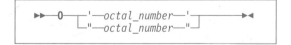

octal_number is a string composed of digits (0-7).

A hexadecimal constant has the form:

DATA

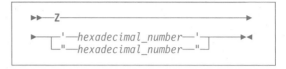

hexadecimal_number is a string composed of digits (0-9) and letters (A-F and, if representable, a-f).

Rules

Specifying an array object as a *data_object* is the same as specifying a list of all the elements in the array object in the order they are stored. Each *data_object_list* must specify the same number of items as its corresponding *initial_value_list*. There is a one-to-one correspondence between the items in these two lists. This correspondence establishes the initial value of each *data_object*.

The definition of each *data_object* by its corresponding *initial_value* must follow the rules for intrinsic assignment.

If *initial_value* is a structure constructor, each component must be an initialization expression. If *data_object* is a variable, any substring, subscript, or stride expressions must be initialization expressions.

If *data_value* is a named constant or structure constructor, the named constant or derived type must have been declared previously in the scoping unit or made accessible by use or host association.

Zero-sized arrays, implied-**DO** lists with iteration counts of zero, and values with a repeat factor of zero contribute no variables to the expanded *initial_value_list*, although a zero-length scalar character variable contributes one variable to the list.

You can use an implied-**DO** list in a **DATA** statement to initialize array elements, scalar structure components and substrings. The implied-**DO** list is expanded into a sequence of scalar structure components, array elements, or substrings, under the control of the implied-**DO** variable. Array elements and scalar structure components must not have constant parents. Each scalar structure component must contain at least one component reference that specifies a subscript list.

The range of an implied-**DO** list is the *do_object_list*. The iteration count and the values of the implied-**DO** variable are established from *integer_expr1*, *integer_expr2*, and *integer_expr3*, the same as for a **DO** statement. When the implied-**DO** list is executed, it specifies the items in the *do_object_list* once for each iteration of the implied-**DO** list, with the appropriate substitution of values for any occurrence of the implied-**DO** variables. If the implied-**DO** variable has an iteration count of 0, no variables are added to the expanded sequence.

Each subscript expression in a *do_object* can only contain constants or implied-**DO** variables of implied-**DO** lists that have the subscript expression within their ranges. Each operation must be intrinsic.

In a block data program unit, you can use a **DATA** statement or type declaration statement to provide an initial value for a variable in a named common block.

In an internal or module subprogram, if the *data_object* is the same name as an entity in the host, and the *data_object* is not declared in any other specification statement in the internal subprogram, the *data_object* must not be referenced or defined before the **DATA** statement.

A **DATA** statement cannot provide an initial value for:

- An automatic object
- A dummy argument
- A variable in a blank common block
- The result variable of a function
- A pointer or an object containing a pointer
- A variable that has the **ALLOCATABLE** attribute

You must not initialize a variable more than once in an executable program. If you associate two or more variables, you can only initialize one of the data objects.

Examples

```
        INTEGER Z(100),EVEN_ODD(0:9)
        LOGICAL FIRST_TIME
        CHARACTER*10 CHARARR(1)
        DATA    FIRST_TIME / .TRUE. /
        DATA    Z / 100* 0 /
! Implied-DO list
        DATA  (EVEN_ODD(J),J=0,8,2) / 5 * 0 /  &
    &       ,(EVEN_ODD(J),J=1,9,2) / 5 * 1 /
! Nested example
        DIMENSION TDARR(3,4)  ! Initializes a two-dimensional array
        DATA ((TDARR(I,J),J=1,4),I=1,3) /12 * 0/
```

DATA

Related Information

- "Data Types and Data Objects" on page 21
- "Executing a DO Statement" on page 94
- "Statement Entity" on page 104

DEALLOCATE

Purpose

The **DEALLOCATE** statement dynamically deallocates allocatable arrays and pointer targets. A specified pointer becomes disassociated while any other pointers associated with the target become undefined.

Format

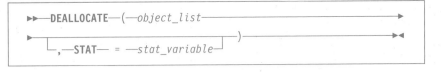

object   is a pointer or an allocatable array

stat_variable   is a scalar integer variable

Rules

An allocatable array that appears in a **DEALLOCATE** statement must be currently allocated. An allocatable array with the **TARGET** attribute cannot be deallocated through an associated pointer. Deallocation of such an array causes the association status of any associated pointer to become undefined. An allocatable array that has an undefined allocation status cannot be subsequently referenced, defined, allocated, or deallocated. Successful execution of a **DEALLOCATE** statement causes the allocation status of an allocatable array to become not allocated.

A pointer that appears in a **DEALLOCATE** statement must be associated with a whole target that was created with an **ALLOCATE** statement. Deallocation of a pointer target causes the association status of any other pointer associated with all or part of the target to become undefined.

> **Tips**
>
> Use the **DEALLOCATE** statement instead of the **NULLIFY** statement if no other pointer is associated with the allocated memory.
>
> Deallocate memory that a pointer function has allocated.

If the **STAT=** specifier is not present and an error condition occurs during execution of the statement, the program terminates. If the **STAT=** specifier is present, successful execution of the **DEALLOCATE** statement causes the stat_variable to be assigned the value zero, while an error condition during

DEALLOCATE

execution causes the *stat_variable* to be assigned a processor-dependent positive integer value.

The *stat_variable* must not be deallocated within the **DEALLOCATE** statement in which it appears.

Examples

```
INTEGER, ALLOCATABLE :: A(:,:)
INTEGER X,Y
   ⋮
ALLOCATE (A(X,Y))
   ⋮
DEALLOCATE (A,STAT=I)
END
```

Related Information

- "ALLOCATE" on page 186
- "ALLOCATABLE" on page 184
- "Allocation Status" on page 38
- "Pointer Association" on page 106
- "Deferred-shape Arrays" on page 47

Derived Type

Purpose

The **Derived Type** statement is the first statement of a derived-type definition.

Format

```
►►──TYPE─┬──────────────────────┬──::──type_name────────────►◄
         └─,─access_spec─┘
```

access_spec is either **PRIVATE** or **PUBLIC**

type_name   is the name of the derived type

Rules

access_spec can only be specified if the derived-type definition is within the specification part of a module.

type_name cannot be the same as the name of any intrinsic type or the name of any other accessible derived type.

If a label is specified on the **Derived Type** statement, the label belongs to the scoping unit of the derived-type definition.

If the corresponding **END TYPE** statement specifies a name, it must be the same as type_name.

Examples

```
MODULE ABC
   TYPE, PRIVATE :: SYSTEM        ! Derived type SYSTEM can only be accessed
     SEQUENCE                     !   within module ABC
     REAL :: PRIMARY
     REAL :: SECONDARY
     CHARACTER(20), DIMENSION(5) :: STAFF
   END TYPE
END MODULE
```

Related Information

- "Derived Types" on page 28
- "END TYPE" on page 240
- "SEQUENCE" on page 332
- "PRIVATE" on page 310

DIMENSION

Purpose

The **DIMENSION** attribute specifies the name and dimensions of an array.

Format

```
▶▶──DIMENSION──┬──────┬──array_declarator_list──────────────▶◀
               └─ :: ─┘
```

Rules

You can specify an array with up to seven dimensions.

Only one dimension specification for an array name can appear in a scoping unit.

```
┌──── Attributes Compatible with the DIMENSION Attribute ─────┐
│                                                             │
│   •  ALLOCATABLE        •  PARAMETER        •  PUBLIC        │
│   •  INTENT             •  POINTER          •  SAVE          │
│   •  OPTIONAL           •  PRIVATE          •  TARGET        │
│                                                             │
└─────────────────────────────────────────────────────────────┘
```

Examples

```
CALL SUB(5,6)
CONTAINS
SUBROUTINE SUB(I,M)
  DIMENSION LIST1(I,M)                    ! automatic array
  INTEGER, ALLOCATABLE, DIMENSION(:,:) :: A    ! deferred-shape array
     ⋮
END SUBROUTINE
END
```

Related Information

*   "Array Concepts" on page 41

DO

Purpose

The **DO** statement controls the execution of the statements that follow it, up to and including a specified terminal statement. Together, these statements form a **DO** construct.

Format

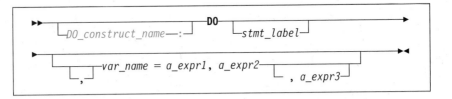

DO_construct_name
> is a name given to the **DO** construct for identification

stmt_label
> is the statement label of an executable statement appearing after the **DO** statement in the same scoping unit. This statement denotes the end of the **DO** construct.

var_name
> is a scalar variable name of type integer or real, called the **DO** variable

a_expr1, *a_expr2*, and *a_expr3*
> are each scalar expressions of type integer or real

Rules

If you specify a *DO_construct_name* on the **DO** statement, you must terminate the construct with an **END DO** and the same *DO_construct_name*. Conversely, if you do not specify a *DO_construct_name* on the **DO** statement, and you terminate the **DO** construct with an **END DO** statement, you must not have a *DO_construct_name* on the **END DO** statement.

If you specify a statement label in the **DO** statement, you must terminate the **DO** construct with a statement that is labeled with that statement label. You can terminate a labeled **DO** statement with an **END DO** statement that is labeled with that statement label, but you cannot terminate it with an unlabeled **END DO** statement. If you do not specify a label in the **DO** statement, you must terminate the **DO** construct with an **END DO** statement.

If the control clause (the clause beginning with *var_name*) is absent, the statement is an infinite **DO**. The loop will iterate indefinitely until interrupted (e.g., by the **EXIT** statement).

DO

Examples

```
INTEGER :: SUM=0
OUTER: DO
  INNER: DO M=1,10
    READ (5,*) J
    IF (J.LE.I) THEN
      PRINT *, 'VALUE MUST BE GREATER THAN ', I
      CYCLE INNER
    END IF
    SUM=SUM+J
    IF (SUM.GT.500) EXIT OUTER
    IF (SUM.GT.100) EXIT INNER
  END DO INNER
  SUM=SUM+I
  I=I+10
END DO OUTER
PRINT *, 'SUM =',SUM
END
```

Related Information

- "DO Construct" on page 93
- "END (Construct)" on page 237, for details on the **END DO** statement
- "EXIT" on page 248
- "CYCLE" on page 214

DO WHILE

Purpose

The **DO WHILE** statement is the first statement in the **DO WHILE** construct, which indicates that you want the following statement block, up to and including a specified terminal statement, to be repeatedly executed for as long as the logical expression specified in the statement continues to be true.

Format

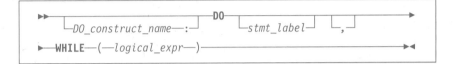

DO_construct_name
> is a name given to the **DO WHILE** construct for identification

stmt_label is the statement label of an executable statement appearing after the **DO WHILE** statement in the same scoping unit. It denotes the end of the **DO WHILE** construct.

logical_expr is a scalar logical expression

Rules

If you specify a *DO_construct_name* on the **DO WHILE** statement, you must terminate the construct with an **END DO** and the same *DO_construct_name*. Conversely, if you do not specify a *DO_construct_name* on the **DO WHILE** statement, and you terminate the **DO WHILE** construct with an **END DO** statement, you must not have a *DO_construct_name* on the **END DO** statement.

If you specify a statement label in the **DO WHILE** statement, you must terminate the **DO WHILE** construct with a statement that is labeled with that statement label. You can terminate a labeled **DO WHILE** statement with an **END DO** statement that is labeled with that statement label, but you cannot terminate it with an unlabeled **END DO** statement. If you do not specify a label in the **DO WHILE** statement, you must terminate the **DO WHILE** construct with an **END DO** statement.

DO WHILE

Examples

```
            MYDO: DO 10 WHILE (I .LE. 5)   ! MYDO is the construct name
                SUM = SUM + INC
                I = I + 1
10          END DO MYDO
            END

            SUBROUTINE EXAMPLE2
              REAL X(10)
              LOGICAL FLAG1
              DATA     FLAG1 /.TRUE./
              DO 20 WHILE (I .LE. 10)
                 X(I) = A
                 I = I + 1
20            IF (.NOT. FLAG1) STOP
            END SUBROUTINE EXAMPLE2
```

Related Information

- "DO WHILE Construct" on page 97
- "END (Construct)" on page 237, for details on the **END DO** statement
- "EXIT" on page 248
- "CYCLE" on page 214

DOUBLE PRECISION

Purpose

A **DOUBLE PRECISION** type declaration statement specifies the attributes of objects and functions of type double precision. Initial values can be assigned to objects.

Format

where:

attr_spec
ALLOCATABLE
DIMENSION (*array_spec*)
EXTERNAL
INTENT (*intent_spec*)
INTRINSIC
OPTIONAL
PARAMETER
POINTER
PRIVATE
PUBLIC
SAVE
TARGET

attr_spec   For detailed information on rules about a particular attribute, refer to the statement of the same name.

intent_spec   is either **IN**, **OUT**, or **INOUT**

::   is the double colon separator. It is required if attributes are specified or if = *initialization_expr* is used.

array_spec   is a list of dimension bounds

DOUBLE PRECISION

entity_decl

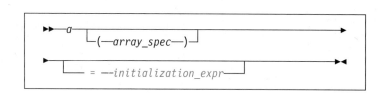

a
: is an object name or function name. *array_spec* cannot be specified for a function name.

initialization_expr
: provides an initial value, by means of an initialization expression, for the entity specified by the immediately preceding name

Rules

Entities in type declaration statements are constrained by the rules of any attributes specified for the entities, as detailed in the corresponding attribute statements.

The type declaration statement overrides the implicit type rules in effect. You can use a type declaration statement that confirms the type of an intrinsic function. The appearance of a generic or specific intrinsic function name in a type declaration statement does not cause the name to lose its intrinsic property.

An object cannot be initialized in a type declaration statement if it is a dummy argument, an allocatable array, a pointer, a function result, an object in blank common, an external name, an intrinsic name, or an automatic object. The object may be initialized if it appears in a named common block in a block data program unit.

The specification expression of an *array_spec* can be a nonconstant expression if the specification expression appears in an interface body or in the specification part of a subprogram. Any object being declared that uses this nonconstant expression and is not a dummy argument is called an *automatic object*.

An attribute cannot be repeated in a given type declaration statement, nor can an entity be explicitly given the same attribute more than once in a scoping unit.

initialization_expr must be specified if the statement contains the **PARAMETER** attribute. If *initialization_expr* is specified and **PARAMETER** is not, the object is a variable that is initially defined. *a* becomes defined with the value determined by *initialization_expr*, in accordance with the rules for intrinsic assignment. If the variable is an array, its shape must be specified either in the type declaration statement or in a previous specification statement in the same scoping unit. A variable or variable subobject cannot be initialized more than once. The presence of *initialization_expr* implies that *a* is a saved object, except for an object with the **PARAMETER** attribute or in a named common block.

An *array_spec* specified in the *entity_decl* takes precedence over the *array_spec* in the **DIMENSION** attribute.

An array function result that does not have the **POINTER** attribute must have an explicit-shape array specification.

If the entity declared is a function, it must not have an accessible explicit interface unless it is an intrinsic function.

Examples

```
DOUBLE PRECISION, POINTER :: PTR
DOUBLE PRECISION, TARGET  :: TAR
```

Related Information

- "Real" on page 23
- "Initialization Expressions" on page 66
- "How Type Is Determined" on page 33, for details on the implicit typing rules
- "Array Declarators" on page 43
- "Automatic Objects" on page 22
- "DATA" on page 216, for details on initial values

ELSE

ELSE

Purpose

The **ELSE** statement is the first statement of the optional **ELSE** block within an **IF** construct.

Format

```
►►──ELSE───────────────────────────────────────►◄
          └─IF_construct_name─┘
```

IF_construct_name
>   is a name given to the **IF** construct for identification

Format

Control branches to the **ELSE** block if every previous logical expression in the **IF** construct evaluates as false. The statement block of the **ELSE** block is executed and the **IF** construct is complete.

If the *IF_construct_name* is specified, it must be the same name as specified in the block **IF** statement.

Examples

```
IF (A.GT.0) THEN
  B = B-A
ELSE              ! the next statement is executed if a<=0
  B = B+A
END IF
```

Related Information

- "IF Construct" on page 88
- "END (Construct)" on page 237, for details on the **END IF** statement
- "ELSE IF" on page 233

ELSE IF

Purpose

The **ELSE IF** statement is the first statement of an optional **ELSE IF** block within an **IF** construct.

Format

```
▶▶──ELSE IF──(──scalar_logical_expr──)──THEN──────────────────▶
 ▶────────────────────────────────────────────────────────────▶◀
              └─IF_construct_name─┘
```

IF_construct_name is a name given to the **IF** construct for identification

Rules

scalar_logical_expr is evaluated if no previous logical expressions in the **IF** construct are evaluated as true. If *scalar_logical_expr* is true, the statement block that follows is executed and the **IF** construct is complete.

If the *IF_construct_name* is specified, it must be the same name as specified in the block **IF** statement.

Examples

```
IF (I.EQ.1) THEN
    J=J-1
ELSE IF (I.EQ.2) THEN
    J=J-2
ELSE IF (I.EQ.3) THEN
    J=J-3
ELSE
    J=J-4
END IF
```

Related Information

- "IF Construct" on page 88
- "END (Construct)" on page 237, for details on the **END IF** statement
- "ELSE" on page 232

ELSEWHERE

Purpose

The **ELSEWHERE** statement is the first statement of the optional **ELSEWHERE** block within a **WHERE** construct.

Format

```
►►──ELSEWHERE────────────────────────────────────────────────►◄
```

Rules

The mask expression that applies to all assignment statements in the **ELSEWHERE** block is (.NOT. *mask_expr*), where *mask_expr* is defined in the construct's **WHERE** statement.

Examples

```
INTEGER A(10),B(10)
WHERE (A>=0)
  B = SIN(A)
ELSEWHERE       ! Mask expression evaluates for A<0
  B = COS(A)
END WHERE
```

Related Information

- "WHERE Construct" on page 81
- "WHERE" on page 351
- "END (Construct)" on page 237, for details on the **END WHERE** statement

END

Purpose

An **END** statement indicates the end of a program unit or procedure.

Format

The **END** statement is the only required statement in a program unit.

For an internal subprogram or module subprogram, you must specify the **FUNCTION** or **SUBROUTINE** keyword on the **END** statement. For block data program units, external subprograms, the main program, modules and interface bodies, the corresponding keyword is optional.

The program name can be included in the **END PROGRAM** statement only if the optional **PROGRAM** statement is used and if the name is identical to the program name specified in the **PROGRAM** statement.

The block data name can be included in the **END BLOCK DATA** statement only if it is provided in the **BLOCK DATA** statement and if the name is identical to the block data name specified in the **BLOCK DATA** statement.

If a name is specified in an **END MODULE**, **END FUNCTION**, or **END SUBROUTINE** statement, it must be identical to the name specified in the corresponding **MODULE**, **FUNCTION**, or **SUBROUTINE** statement, respectively.

The **END**, **END FUNCTION**, **END PROGRAM**, and **END SUBROUTINE** statements are executable statements that can be branched to. In both fixed-form and free-form formats, no other statement may follow the **END** statement on the same line. In fixed-form format, you cannot continue a program unit **END** statement, nor can a statement whose initial line appears to be a program unit **END** statement be continued.

END

The **END** statement of a main program terminates execution of the program. The **END** statement of a function or subroutine has the same effect as a **RETURN** statement. An inline comment can appear on the same line as an **END** statement. Any comment line appearing after an **END** statement belongs to the next program unit.

Examples

```
PROGRAM TEST
  CALL SUB()
  CONTAINS
    SUBROUTINE SUB
      :
    END SUBROUTINE    ! Reference to subroutine name SUB is optional
END PROGRAM TEST
```

Related Information

- "Program Units and Procedures" on page 101

END (Construct)

Purpose

The **END DO**, **END IF**, **END SELECT**, and **END WHERE** statements terminate **DO** (or **DO WHILE**), **IF**, **CASE**, and **WHERE** constructs, respectively.

Format

DO_construct_name
>   is a name given to identify a **DO** or **DO WHILE** construct

IF_construct_name
>   is a name given to identify an **IF** construct

CASE_construct_name
>   is a name given to identify a **CASE** construct

Rules

If you label the **END DO** statement, you can use it as the terminal statement of a labeled or unlabeled **DO** or **DO WHILE** construct. An **END DO** statement terminates the innermost **DO** or **DO WHILE** construct only. If a **DO** or **DO WHILE** statement does not specify a statement label, the terminal statement of the **DO** or **DO WHILE** construct must be an **END DO** statement.

You can branch to an **END DO**, **END IF**, or **END SELECT** statement from within the **DO** (or **DO WHILE**), **IF**, or **CASE** construct, respectively. An **END IF** statement can also be branched to from outside of the **IF** construct.

If you specify a construct name on the statement that begins the construct, the **END** statement that terminates the construct must have the same construct name. Conversely, if you do not specify a construct name on the statement that begins the construct, you must not specify a construct name on the **END** statement.

END (Construct)

Examples

```
DECR: DO WHILE (I.GT.0)
    ⋮
  IF (J.LT.K) THEN
    ⋮
    END IF                  ! Cannot reference a construct name
    I=I-1
  END DO DECR               ! Reference to construct name DECR mandatory
```

Related Information

- "Control" on page 87
- "DO" on page 225
- "IF (Block)" on page 265
- "SELECT CASE" on page 330
- "WHERE" on page 351

END INTERFACE

Purpose

The **END INTERFACE** statement terminates a procedure interface block.

Format

```
►►──END INTERFACE──────────────────────────────────────►◄
```

Rules

Each **INTERFACE** statement must have a corresponding **END INTERFACE** statement.

Examples

```
INTERFACE OPERATOR (.DETERMINANT.)
  FUNCTION DETERMINANT (X)
    INTENT(IN) X
    REAL X(50,50), DETERMINANT
  END FUNCTION
END INTERFACE
```

Related Information

- "INTERFACE" on page 281
- "Interface Concepts" on page 110

END TYPE

Purpose

The **END TYPE** statement indicates the completion of a derived-type definition.

Format

```
►►──END TYPE─────────────────────────────►◄
              └─type_name─┘
```

Rules

If *type_name* is specified, it must match the *type_name* in the corresponding **Derived Type** statement.

If a label is specified on the **END TYPE** statement, the label belongs to the scoping unit of the derived-type definition.

Examples

```
TYPE A
  INTEGER :: B
  REAL :: C
END TYPE A
```

Related Information

- "Derived Types" on page 28
- "Derived Type" on page 223

ENDFILE

Purpose

The **ENDFILE** statement writes an endfile record as the next record of an external file connected for sequential access. This record becomes the last record in the file.

Format

```
►►──ENDFILE──┬─u─────────────────┬──────────────────►◄
             └─(─position_list─)─┘
```

u	is an external unit identifier. The value of *u* must not be an asterisk.
position_list	is a list that must contain one unit specifier ([**UNIT=**]*u*) and can also contain one of each of the other valid specifiers:
[UNIT=] *u*	is a unit specifier in which *u* must be an external unit identifier whose value is not an asterisk. An external unit identifier refers to an external file that is represented by a scalar integer expression. If the optional characters **UNIT=** are omitted, *u* must be the first item in *position_list*.
IOSTAT= *ios*	is an input/output status specifier that specifies the status of the input/output operation. *ios* is a scalar default integer variable. When the **ENDFILE** statement finishes executing, *ios* is defined with:

- A zero value if no error condition occurs.
- A positive value if an error occurs.

ERR= *stmt_label*
is an error specifier that specifies the statement label of an executable statement in the same scoping unit to which control is to transfer in the case of an error. Coding the **ERR=** specifier suppresses error messages.

Rules

If the **ERR=** and **IOSTAT=** specifiers are set and an error is encountered, transfer is made to the statement specified by the **ERR=** specifier and a positive integer value is assigned to *ios*.

ENDFILE

Examples

```
ENDFILE 12
ENDFILE (IOSTAT=IOSS,UNIT=11)
```

Related Information

- "Input/Output Concepts" on page 141

ENTRY

Purpose

A function subprogram or subroutine subprogram has a primary entry point that is established through the **SUBROUTINE** or **FUNCTION** statement. The **ENTRY** statement establishes an alternate entry point for an external subprogram or a module subprogram.

Format

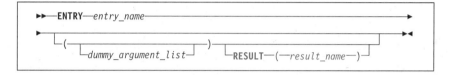

entry_name   is the name of an entry point in a function subprogram or subroutine subprogram

Rules

The **ENTRY** statement cannot appear in a main program, block data program unit, internal subprogram, **IF** construct, **DO** construct, **CASE** construct, derived-type definition, or interface block.

An **ENTRY** statement can appear anywhere after the **FUNCTION** or **SUBROUTINE** statement (and after any **USE** statements) of an external or module subprogram, except in a statement block within a control construct, in a derived-type definition, or in an interface block. **ENTRY** statements are nonexecutable and do not affect control sequencing during the execution of a subprogram.

The result variable is *result_name*, if specified; otherwise, it is *entry_name*. If the characteristics of the **ENTRY** statement's result variable are the same as those of the **FUNCTION** statement's result variable, the result variables identify the same variable, even though they can have different names. Otherwise, they are storage-associated and must be all nonpointer scalars of default intrinsic (noncharacter) type. *result_name* can be the same as the result variable name specified for the **FUNCTION** statement or another **ENTRY** statement.

The result variable cannot be specified in a **COMMON**, **DATA**, or **EQUIVALENCE** statement, nor can it have the **ALLOCATABLE**, **PARAMETER**, **INTENT**, **OPTIONAL**, or **SAVE** attributes.

ENTRY

If the **RESULT** keyword is specified, the **ENTRY** statement must be within a function subprogram, *entry_name* must not appear in any specification statement in the scope of the function subprogram, and *result_name* cannot be the same as *entry_name*.

A result variable cannot be initialized in a type declaration statement.

The entry name in an external subprogram is a global entity; an entry name in a module subprogram is not a global entity. An interface for an entry can appear in an interface block only when the entry name is used as the procedure name in an interface body.

In a function subprogram, *entry_name* identifies an external or module function that can be referenced as a function from the calling procedure. In a subroutine subprogram, *entry_name* identifies a subroutine and can be referenced as a subroutine from the calling procedure. When the reference is made, execution begins with the first executable statement following the **ENTRY** statement.

The result variable must be defined prior to exiting from the function, when the function is invoked through that entry.

A name in the *dummy_argument_list* must not appear:

- In an executable statement preceding the **ENTRY** statement unless it also appears in a **FUNCTION**, **SUBROUTINE**, or **ENTRY** statement that precedes the executable statement.
- In the expression of a statement function statement unless the name is also a dummy argument of the statement function, appears in a **FUNCTION** or **SUBROUTINE** statement, or appears in an **ENTRY** statement that precedes the statement function statement.

The order, number, type, and kind type parameters of the dummy arguments can differ from those of the **FUNCTION** or **SUBROUTINE** statement, or other **ENTRY** statements.

If a dummy argument is used in a specification expression to specify an array bound or character length of an object, you can only specify the object in a statement that is executed during a procedure reference if the dummy argument is present and appears in the dummy argument list of the procedure name referenced.

Recursion

An **ENTRY** statement can reference itself directly, only if the subprogram statement specifies **RECURSIVE** and the **ENTRY** statement specifies **RESULT**. The entry procedure then has an explicit interface within the subprogram. The **RESULT** clause is not required for an entry to reference itself indirectly.

If *entry_name* is of type character, its length cannot be an asterisk if the function is recursive.

Examples

```
RECURSIVE FUNCTION FNC() RESULT (RES)
    ⋮
  ENTRY ENT () RESULT (RES)          ! The result variable name can be
                                     ! the same as for the function
      ⋮
END FUNCTION
```

Related Information

- "FUNCTION" on page 257
- "SUBROUTINE" on page 336
- "Recursion" on page 140
- "Dummy Arguments" on page 131

EQUIVALENCE

Purpose

The **EQUIVALENCE** statement specifies that two or more objects in a scoping unit are to share the same storage.

Format

```
►►──EQUIVALENCE──▼─(──equiv_object──,──equiv_object_list──)──┘──►◄
```

equiv_object   is a variable name, array element, or substring. Any subscript or substring expression must be an integer initialization expression.

Rules

equiv_object must not be a target, pointer, dummy argument, function name, entry name, result name, structure component, named constant, automatic data object, allocatable array, object of nonsequence derived type, object of sequence derived type that contains a pointer in the structure, or subobject of any of these.

Because all items named within a pair of parentheses have the same first storage unit, they become associated. This is called *equivalence association*. It may cause the association of other items as well.

If you specify an array element in an **EQUIVALENCE** statement, the number of subscript quantities must equal the number of dimensions in the array. If you specify a multidimensional array using an array element with a single subscript *n*, the *n*th element in the array's storage sequence is specified. A nonzero-sized array without a subscript refers to the first element of the array.

If *equiv_object* is of derived type, it must be of a sequence derived type.

The lengths of associated items do not have to be equal.

Any zero-sized items are storage-associated with one another and with the first storage unit of any nonzero-sized sequences.

An **EQUIVALENCE** statement cannot associate the storage sequences of two different common blocks. It must not specify that the same storage unit is to occur more than once in a storage sequence. An **EQUIVALENCE** statement must not contradict itself or any previously established associations caused by an **EQUIVALENCE** statement.

You can cause names not in common blocks to share storage with a name in a common block using the **EQUIVALENCE** statement.

You can extend a common block by using an **EQUIVALENCE** statement, but only by adding beyond the last entry, not before the first entry. For example, if the variable that you associate to a variable in a common block, using the **EQUIVALENCE** statement, is an element of an array, the implicit association of the rest of the elements of the array can extend the size of the common block.

Examples

```
DOUBLE PRECISION A(3)
REAL B(5)
EQUIVALENCE (A,B(3))
```

Association of storage units:

```
              |     |     |     |     |     |     |     |
Array A:      |     |     |  A(1)  |  A(2)  |  A(3)  |
Array B: | B(1) | B(2) | B(3) | B(4) | B(5) |
```

Related Information

- "Definition Status of Variables" on page 34

EXIT

Purpose

The **EXIT** statement terminates execution of a **DO** construct or **DO WHILE** construct before the construct completes all of its iterations.

Format

```
▶▶──EXIT────────────────────────────────────────────▶◀
            └─DO_construct_name─┘
```

DO_construct_name
> is the name of the **DO** or **DO WHILE** construct

Rules

The **EXIT** statement is placed within a **DO** or **DO WHILE** construct and belongs to the **DO** or **DO WHILE** construct specified by *DO_construct_name* or, if not specified, by the **DO** or **DO WHILE** construct that immediately surrounds it. When a *DO_construct_name* is specified, the **EXIT** statement must be in the range of that construct.

When the **EXIT** statement is executed, the **DO** or **DO WHILE** construct that the **EXIT** statement belongs to becomes inactive. If the **EXIT** statement is nested in any other **DO** or **DO WHILE** constructs, they also become inactive. Any **DO** variable present retains its last defined value. If the **DO** construct has no construct control, it will iterate infinitely unless it becomes inactive. The **EXIT** statement can be used to make the construct inactive.

An **EXIT** statement can have a statement label; it cannot be used as the labeled action statement which terminates a **DO** or **DO WHILE** construct.

Examples

```
       LOOP1: DO I = 1, 20
          N = N + 1
10        IF (N > NMAX) EXIT LOOP1        ! EXIT from LOOP1


       LOOP2: DO WHILE (K==1)
          KMAX = KMAX - 1
20        IF (K > KMAX) EXIT             ! EXIT from LOOP2
       END DO LOOP2


       LOOP3:  DO J = 1, 10
          N = N + 1
30        IF (N > NMAX) EXIT LOOP1       ! EXIT from LOOP1
          EXIT LOOP3                     ! EXIT from LOOP3
       END DO LOOP3

       END DO LOOP1
```

Related Information

- "DO Construct" on page 93
- "DO WHILE Construct" on page 97

EXTERNAL

Purpose

The **EXTERNAL** attribute specifies that a name represents an external procedure, a dummy procedure, or a block data program unit. A procedure name with the **EXTERNAL** attribute can be used as an actual argument.

Format

```
►►──EXTERNAL──name_list──────────────────────────────────►◄
```

name   is the name of an external procedure, dummy procedure, or
            BLOCK DATA program unit

Rules

If an external procedure name or dummy argument name is used as an actual argument, it must be declared with the **EXTERNAL** attribute or by an interface block in the scoping unit, but may not appear in both.

If an intrinsic procedure name is specified with the **EXTERNAL** attribute in a scoping unit, the name becomes the name of a user-defined external procedure. Therefore, you cannot invoke that intrinsic procedure by that name from that scoping unit.

You can specify a name to have the **EXTERNAL** attribute only once in a scoping unit.

A name in an **EXTERNAL** statement must not also be specified as a specific procedure name in an interface block in the scoping unit.

```
┌─ Attributes Compatible with the EXTERNAL Attribute ──────
│
│   • OPTIONAL           • PRIVATE           • PUBLIC
│
└
```

Examples

```
PROGRAM MAIN
  EXTERNAL AAA
  CALL SUB(AAA)          ! Procedure AAA is passed to SUB
END

SUBROUTINE SUB(ARG)
  CALL ARG()             ! This results in a call to AAA
END SUBROUTINE
```

Related Information

- "Procedures as Dummy Arguments" on page 136
- Item 4 under "FORTRAN 77 Compatibility" on page 415

FORMAT

Purpose

The **FORMAT** statement provides format specifications for input/output statements.

Format

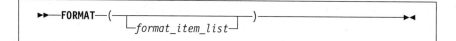

format_item

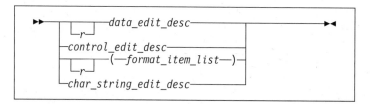

> *r*   is an unsigned, positive, integer literal constant that cannot specify a kind type parameter. It is called a repeat specification. It specifies the number of times to repeat the *format_item_list* or the *data_edit_desc*. The default is 1.
>
> *data_edit_desc*
> > is a data edit descriptor
>
> *control_edit_desc*
> > is a control edit descriptor
>
> *char_string_edit_desc*
> > is a character string edit descriptor

Data Edit Descriptors

Forms	Use	Page
A **A**w	Edits character values	152
Bw **B**w.m	Edits binary values	153

Forms	Use	Page
E*w.d* E*w.dEe* D*w.d* EN*w.d* EN*w.dEe* ES*w.d* ES*w.dEe*	Edits real and complex numbers with exponents	154
F*w.d*	Edits real and complex numbers without exponents	157
G*w.d* G*w.dEe*	Edits data fields of any intrinsic type, with the output format adapting to the type of the data and, if the data is of type real, the magnitude of the data	158
I*w* I*w.m*	Edits integer numbers	160
L*w*	Edits logical values	161
O*w* O*w.m*	Edits octal values	162
Z*w* Z*w.m*	Edits hexadecimal values	163

where:

w	specifies the width of a field, including all blanks
m	specifies the number of digits to be printed
d	specifies the number of digits to the right of the decimal point
e	specifies the number of digits in the exponent field

w, *m*, *d*, and *e* is an unsigned integer literal constant.

You cannot specify kind parameters for *w*, *m*, *d*, or *e*.

Control Edit Descriptors

Forms	Use	Page
/ *r/*	Specifies the end of data transfer on the current record	164
:	Specifies the end of format control if there are no more items in the input/output list	165
BN	Ignores nonleading blanks in numeric input fields	165
BZ	Interprets nonleading blanks in numeric input fields as zeros	165
*k***P**	Specifies a scale factor for real and complex items	167

FORMAT

Forms	Use	Page
S SS	Specifies plus signs are not to be written	168
SP	Specifies plus signs are to be written	168
T*c*	Specifies the absolute position in a record from which, or to which, the next character is transferred	168
TL*c*	Specifies the relative position (backward from the current position in a record) from which, or to which, the next character is transferred	168
TR*c*	Specifies the relative position (forward from the current position in a record) from which, or to which, the next character is transferred	168
*o*X	Specifies the relative position (forward from the current position in a record) from which, or to which, the next character is transferred	168

where:

r   is a repeat specifier. It is an unsigned, positive, integer literal constant.

k   specifies the scale factor to be used. It is an optionally signed, integer literal constant.

c   specifies the character position in a record. It is an unsigned, nonzero, integer literal constant.

o   is the relative character position in a record. It is an unsigned, nonzero, integer literal constant.

Kind type parameters cannot be specified for *r*, *k*, *c*, or *o*.

Character String Edit Descriptors

Forms	Use	Page
*n*H*str*	Outputs a character string (str)	166
'*str*' "*str*"	Outputs a character string (*str*)	165

n   is the number of characters in a literal field. It is an unsigned, positive, integer literal constant. Blanks are included in character count. A kind type parameter cannot be specified.

Rules

When a format identifier in a formatted **READ**, **WRITE**, or **PRINT** statement is a statement label or a variable that is assigned a statement label, the statement label identifies a **FORMAT** statement.

The **FORMAT** statement must have a statement label. **FORMAT** statements cannot appear in block data program units, interface blocks, the scope of a module, or derived-type definitions.

Commas separate edit descriptors. You can omit the comma between a **P** edit descriptor and an **F**, **E**, **EN**, **ES**, **D**, or **G** edit descriptor immediately following it, before a slash edit descriptor when the optional repeat specification is not present, after a slash edit descriptor, and before or after a colon edit descriptor.

FORMAT specifications can also be given as character expressions in input/output statements.

If a processor can represent both uppercase and lowercase letters, the use of characters in edit descriptors is not case-sensitive, except in character string edit descriptors.

Character Format Specification

When a format identifier (page 316) in a formatted **READ**, **WRITE**, or **PRINT** statement is a character array name or character expression, the value of the array or expression is a character format specification.

If the format identifier is a character array element name, the format specification must be completely contained within the array element. If the format identifier is a character array name, the format specification can continue beyond the first element into following consecutive elements.

Blanks can precede the format specification. Character data can follow the right parenthesis that ends the format specification without affecting the format specification.

FORMAT

Examples

```
          CHARACTER*32 CHARVAR
          CHARVAR="('integer: ',I2,'  binary: ',B8)"  ! Character format specification
          M = 56
          J = 1                                        !      OUTPUT:
          X = 2355.95843                               !
          WRITE (6,770) M,X                            !  56    2355.96
          WRITE (6,CHARVAR) M,M                        ! integer: 56  binary: 00111000
          WRITE (6,880) J,M                            !  1
                                                       ! 56
    770   FORMAT(I3, 2F10.2)
    880   FORMAT(I2)
          END
```

Related Information

- "Input/Output Formatting" on page 149
- "PRINT" on page 307
- "READ" on page 315
- "WRITE" on page 353

FUNCTION

Purpose

The **FUNCTION** statement is the first statement of a function subprogram.

Format

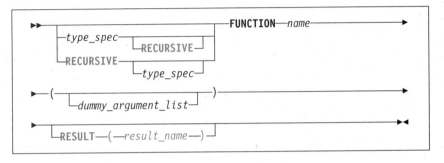

type_spec   specifies the type and type parameters of the function result. See "Type Declaration" on page 343 for details about *type_spec*.

name   is the name of the function subprogram

Rules

The type and type parameters of the function result can be specified by either *type_spec* or by declaring the result variable in the declaration part of the function subprogram, but not by both. If not specified at all, the implicit typing rules are in effect.

If **RESULT** is specified, *result_name* becomes the function result variable. *name* must not be declared in any specification statement in the subprogram, although it can be referenced. *result_name* must not be the same as *name*. If **RESULT** is not specified, *name* becomes the function result variable.

If the result variable is an array or pointer, the **DIMENSION** or **POINTER** attributes, respectively, must be specified within the function body.

If the function result is a pointer, the shape of the result variable determines the shape of the value returned by the function. If the result variable is a pointer, the function must either associate a target with the pointer or define the association status of the pointer as disassociated.

If the result variable is not a pointer, the function must define its value.

If the name of an external function is of derived type, the derived type must be a sequence derived type if the type is not use-associated or host-associated.

The function result variable must not be specified in a **COMMON**, **DATA**, or **EQUIVALENCE** statement, nor can it have the **ALLOCATABLE**, **PARAMETER**, **INTENT**, **OPTIONAL**, or **SAVE** attributes.

The function result variable is associated with any entry procedure result variables. This is called entry association. The definition of any of these result variables becomes the definition of all the associated variables having that same type, and is the value of the function regardless of the entry point.

If the function subprogram contains entry procedures, the result variables are not required to be of the same type unless the type is of character or derived type, if the variables have the **POINTER** attribute, or if they are not scalars. The variable whose name is used to reference the function must be in a defined state when a **RETURN** or **END** statement is executed in the subprogram. An associated variable of a different type must not become defined during the execution of the function reference, unless an associated variable of the same type redefines it later during execution of the subprogram.

Recursion

The **RECURSIVE** keyword must be specified if, directly or indirectly:

- the function invokes itself
- the function invokes a function defined by an **ENTRY** statement in the same subprogram
- an entry procedure in the same subprogram invokes itself
- an entry procedure in the same subprogram invokes another entry procedure in the same subprogram
- an entry procedure in the same subprogram invokes the subprogram defined by the **FUNCTION** statement

A function that directly invokes itself requires that both the **RECURSIVE** and **RESULT** keywords be specified. The presence of both keywords makes the procedure interface explicit within the subprogram.

If *name* is of type character, its length cannot be an asterisk if the function is recursive.

Examples

```
RECURSIVE FUNCTION FACTORIAL (N) RESULT (RES)
  INTEGER RES
  IF (N.EQ.0) THEN
    RES=1
  ELSE
    RES=N*FACTORIAL(N-1)
  END IF
END FUNCTION FACTORIAL
```

Related Information

- "Function and Subroutine Subprograms" on page 127
- "ENTRY" on page 243
- "Function Reference" on page 128
- "Dummy Arguments" on page 131
- "Statement Function" on page 333
- "Recursion" on page 140

GO TO (Assigned)

GO TO (Assigned)

Purpose

The assigned **GO TO** statement transfers program control to an executable statement, whose statement label is designated in an **ASSIGN** statement.

Format

```
►►──GO TO──variable_name───────────────────────────────────────►◄
                          └────────┬──(──stmt_label_list──)──┘
                                 └─,─┘
```

variable_name
> is a scalar variable name of type default integer that you have assigned a statement label to in an **ASSIGN** statement.

stmt_label
> is the statement label of an executable statement in the same scoping unit as the assigned **GO TO**. The same statement label can appear more than once in *stmt_label_list*.

Rules

When the assigned **GO TO** statement is executed, the variable you specify by *variable_name* with the value of a statement label must be defined. You must establish this definition with an **ASSIGN** statement in the same scoping unit as the assigned **GO TO** statement. If the integer variable is a dummy argument in a subprogram, you must assign it a statement label in the subprogram in order to use it in an assigned **GO TO** in that subprogram. Execution of the assigned **GO TO** statement transfers control to the statement identified by that statement label.

If *stmt_label_list* is present, the statement label assigned to the variable specified by *variable_name* must be one of the statement labels in the list.

The assigned **GO TO** cannot be the terminal statement of a **DO** or **DO WHILE** construct.

Examples

```
      INTEGER RETURN_LABEL
         ⋮
!  Simulate a call to a local procedure
      ASSIGN 100 TO RETURN_LABEL
      GOTO 9000
100   CONTINUE
         ⋮
9000  CONTINUE
!  A "local" procedure
         ⋮
      GOTO RETURN_LABEL
```

Related Information

- "GO TO (Assigned)" on page 260
- "Statement Labels" on page 13
- "Branching" on page 98

GO TO (Computed)

Purpose

The computed **GO TO** statement transfers program control to one of possibly several executable statements.

Format

```
►►──GO TO──(──stmt_label_list──)──┬────┬──int_expr──────────────►◄
                                  └─,──┘
```

stmt_label	is the statement label of an executable statement in the same scoping unit as the computed **GO TO**. The same statement label can appear more than once in *stmt_label_list*.
int_expr	is a scalar integer expression

Rules

When a computed **GO TO** statement is executed, the *int_expr* is evaluated. The resulting value is used as an index into *stmt_label_list*. Control then transfers to the statement whose statement label you identify by the index. For example, if the value of *int_expr* is 4, control transfers to the statement whose statement label is fourth in the *stmt_label_list*, provided there are at least four labels in the list.

If the value of *int_expr* is less than 1 or greater than the number of statement labels in the list, the **GO TO** statement has no effect (like a **CONTINUE** statement), and the next statement is executed.

Examples

```
      INTEGER NEXT
        ⋮
      GO TO (100,200) NEXT
 10   PRINT *,'Control transfers here if NEXT does not equal 1 or 2'
        ⋮
100   PRINT *,'Control transfers here if NEXT = 1'
        ⋮
200   PRINT *,'Control transfers here if NEXT = 2'
```

Related Information

- "Statement Labels" on page 13
- "Branching" on page 98

GO TO (Unconditional)

Purpose

The unconditional **GO TO** statement transfers program control to a specified executable statement.

Format

```
►►──GO TO──stmt_label──────────────────────────────►◄
```

    stmt_label   is the statement label of an executable statement in the same scoping unit as the unconditional **GO TO**

Rules

The unconditional **GO TO** statement transfers control to the statement identified by *stmt_label*.

The unconditional **GO TO** statement cannot be the terminal statement of a **DO** or **DO WHILE** construct.

Examples

```
    REAL(8) :: X,Y
    GO TO 10
      ⋮
10  PRINT *, X,Y
    END
```

Related Information

- "Statement Labels" on page 13
- "Branching" on page 98

IF (Arithmetic)

IF (Arithmetic)

Purpose

The arithmetic **IF** statement transfers program control to one of three executable statements, depending on the evaluation of an arithmetic expression.

Format

```
►►──IF──(──arith_expr──)──stmt_label1──,──stmt_label2──,─────────►
  ►──stmt_label3─────────────────────────────────────────────►◄
```

arith_expr   is a scalar arithmetic expression of type integer or real

stmt_label1, *stmt_label2*, and *stmt_label3*
are statement labels of executable statements within the same scoping unit as the **IF** statement. The same statement label can appear more than once among the three statement labels.

Rules

The arithmetic **IF** statement evaluates *arith_expr* and transfers control to the statement identified by *stmt_label1*, *stmt_label2*, *or stmt_label3*, depending on whether the value of *arith_expr* is less than zero, zero, or greater than zero, respectively.

Examples

```
      IF (K-100) 10,20,30
10    PRINT *,'K is less than 100.'
      GO TO 40
20    PRINT *,'K equals 100.'
      GO TO 40
30    PRINT *,'K is greater than 100.'
40    CONTINUE
```

Related Information

- "Branching" on page 98
- "Statement Labels" on page 13

IF (Block)

Purpose

The block **IF** statement is the first statement in an **IF** construct.

Format

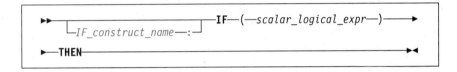

IF_construct_name
>   is a name given to the **IF** construct for identification

Rules

The block **IF** statement evaluates a logical expression and executes at most one of the blocks contained within the **IF** construct.

If the *IF_construct_name* is specified, it must appear on the **END IF** statement, and optionally on any **ELSE IF** or **ELSE** statements in the **IF** construct.

Examples

```
WHICHC: IF (CMD .EQ. 'RETRY') THEN
    IF (LIMIT .GT. FIVE) THEN          ! Nested IF constructs
        ⋮
        CALL STOP
    ELSE
        CALL RETRY
    END IF
ELSE IF (CMD .EQ. 'STOP') THEN WHICHC
    CALL STOP
ELSE IF (CMD .EQ. 'ABORT') THEN
    CALL ABORT
ELSE WHICHC
    GO TO 100
END IF WHICHC
```

IF (Block)

Related Information

- "IF Construct" on page 88
- "ELSE IF" on page 233
- "ELSE" on page 232
- "END (Construct)" on page 237, for details on the **END IF** statement

IF (Logical)

Purpose

The logical **IF** statement evaluates a logical expression and, if true, executes a specified statement.

Format

```
►►──IF──(──logical_expr──)──stmt────────────────────────►◄
```

logical_expr   is a scalar logical expression

stmt   is an unlabeled executable statement

Rules

When a logical **IF** statement is executed, the *logical_expr* is evaluated. If the value of *logical_expr* is true, *stmt* is executed. If the value of *logical_expr* is false, *stmt* does not execute and the **IF** statement has no effect (like a **CONTINUE** statement).

Execution of a function reference in *logical_expr* can change the values of variables that appear in *stmt*.

stmt cannot be a **SELECT CASE, CASE, END SELECT, DO, DO WHILE, END DO**, block **IF, ELSE IF, ELSE, END IF**, another logical **IF, WHERE** (for construct), **ELSEWHERE, END WHERE, END, END FUNCTION**, or **END SUBROUTINE** statement.

Examples

```
IF (ERR.NE.0) CALL ERROR(ERR)
```

Related Information

- "Control" on page 87

IMPLICIT

Purpose

The **IMPLICIT** statement changes or confirms the default implicit typing for local entities or, with the form **IMPLICIT NONE** specified, voids the implicit type rules altogether.

Format

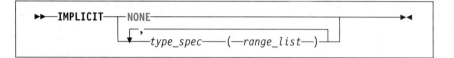

type_spec	specifies a data type. See "Type Declaration" on page 343.
range	is either a single letter or range of letters. A range of letters has the form $letter_1$-$letter_2$, where $letter_1$ is the first letter in the range and $letter_2$, which follows $letter_1$ alphabetically, is the last letter in the range.

Rules

Letter ranges cannot overlap; that is, no more than one type can be specified for a given letter.

In a given scoping unit, if a character has not been specified in an **IMPLICIT** statement, the implicit type for entities in a program unit or interface body is default integer for entities that begin with the characters I-N, and default real otherwise. The default for an internal or module procedure is the same as the implicit type used by the host scoping unit.

For any data entity name that begins with the character specified by *range_list*, and for which you do not explicitly specify a type, the type specified by the immediately preceding *type_spec* is provided. Note that implicit typing can be to a derived type that is inaccessible in the local scope if the derived type is accessible to the host scope.

If you specify the form **IMPLICIT NONE** in a scoping unit, you must use type declaration statements to specify data types for names local to that scoping unit. You cannot refer to a name that does not have an explicitly defined data type; this lets you control all names that are inadvertently referenced. When **IMPLICIT NONE** is specified, you cannot specify any other **IMPLICIT** statement in the same scoping unit.

An **IMPLICIT** statement does not change the data type of an intrinsic function.

Examples

```
      IMPLICIT INTEGER (B), COMPLEX (D, K-M), REAL (R-Z,A)
!  This IMPLICIT statement establishes the following
!  implicit typing:
!
!         A: real
!         B: integer
!         C: real
!         D: complex
!  E to H: real
!    I, J: integer
!  K, L, M: complex
!         N: integer
!  O to Z: real
```

Related Information

- "How Type Is Determined" on page 33 for a discussion of the implicit rules

INQUIRE

Purpose

The **INQUIRE** statement obtains information about the properties of a named file or the connection to a particular unit.

There are three forms of the **INQUIRE** statement:

- Inquire by file, which requires the **FILE=** specifier to be specified.
- Inquire by unit, which requires the **UNIT=** specifier to be specified.
- Inquire by output list, which requires only the **IOLENGTH=** specifier to be specified.

Format

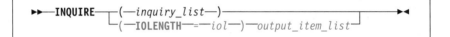

```
►►──INQUIRE──┬──(──inquiry_list──)──────────────────────────┬──►◄
             └──(──IOLENGTH──=──iol──)──output_item_list──┘
```

iol indicates the processor-dependent value that would result from the use of the output list in an unformatted output statement. *iol* is a scalar integer variable.

output_item See the **PRINT** or **WRITE** statement

inquiry_list is a list of inquiry specifiers for the inquire-by-file and inquire-by-unit forms of the **INQUIRE** statement. The inquire-by-file form cannot contain a unit specifier, and the inquire-by-unit form cannot contain a file specifier. No specifier can appear more than once in any **INQUIRE** statement. The inquiry specifiers are:

[UNIT=] *u* is a unit specifier. It specifies the unit about which the inquire-by-unit form of the statement is inquiring. *u* must be an external unit identifier whose value is not an asterisk. An external unit identifier refers to an external file that is represented by a scalar integer expression. If the optional characters **UNIT=** are omitted, *u* must be the first item in *inquiry_list*.

IOSTAT= *ios* is an input/output status specifier that specifies the status of the input/output operation. *ios* is a scalar variable of type default integer. When the input/output statement containing this specifier is finished executing, *ios* is defined with:

- A zero value if no error condition occurs.
- A positive value if an error occurs.

Coding the **IOSTAT=** specifier suppresses error messages.

ERR= *stmt_label*

    is an error specifier that specifies the statement label of an executable statement in the same scoping unit to which control is to transfer in the case of an error. Coding the **ERR=** specifier suppresses error messages.

FILE= *char_expr*

    is a file specifier. It specifies the name of the file about which the inquire-by-file form of the statement is inquiring. *char_expr* is a scalar character expression whose value, when any trailing blanks are removed, is a valid processor file name. The named file does not have to exist, nor does it have to be associated with a unit.

ACCESS= *char_var*

    indicates whether the file is connected for sequential access or direct access. *char_var* is a scalar default character variable that is assigned the value **SEQUENTIAL** if the file is connected for sequential access. The value assigned is **DIRECT** if the file is connected for direct access. If there is no connection, *char_var* is assigned the value **UNDEFINED**.

FORM= *char_var*

    indicates whether the file is connected for formatted or unformatted input/output. *char_var* is a scalar character variable that is assigned the value **FORMATTED** if the file is connected for formatted input/output. The value assigned is **UNFORMATTED** if the file is connected for unformatted input/output. If there is no connection, *char_var* is assigned the value **UNDEFINED**.

RECL= *rcl*   indicates the value of the record length of a file connected for direct access, or the value of the maximum record length of a file connected for sequential access. *rcl* is a scalar variable of type default integer that is assigned the value of the record length. If the file is connected for formatted input/output, the length is the number of characters for all records that contain character data. If the file is connected for unformatted input/output, the length is measured in processor-dependent units. If there is no connection, *rcl* becomes undefined.

BLANK= *char_var*

    indicates the default treatment of blanks for a file connected for formatted input/output. *char_var* is a scalar default character variable that is assigned the value **NULL** if all blanks in numeric input fields are ignored, or the value **ZERO** if all nonleading blanks are interpreted as zeros. If there is no connection, or if the connection is not for formatted input/output, *char_var* is assigned the value **UNDEFINED**.

EXIST= *ex*   indicates if a file or unit exists. *ex* is a scalar variable of type default logical that is assigned the value `true` or `false`. For the inquire-by-file form of the statement, the value `true` is assigned if the file specified by the **FILE=** specifier exists. The value `false` is assigned if the file does not exist. For the inquire-by-unit form of the statement, the value `true` is assigned if the unit specified by **UNIT=** exists. The value `false` is assigned if it is an invalid unit.

OPENED= *od*

indicates if a file or unit is connected. *od* is a scalar variable of type default logical that is assigned the value `true` or `false`. For the inquire-by-file form of the statement, the value `true` is assigned if the file specified by **FILE=** *char_var* is connected to a unit. The value `false` is assigned if the file is not connected to a unit. For the inquire-by-unit form of the statement, the value `true` is assigned if the unit specified by **UNIT=** is connected to a file. The value `false` is assigned if the unit is not connected to a file. For preconnected files that have not been closed, the value is `true` both before and after the first input/output operation.

NUMBER= *num*

indicates the external unit identifier currently associated with the file. *num* is a scalar variable of type default integer that is assigned the value of the external unit identifier of the unit that is currently connected to the file. If there is no unit connected to the file, *num* is assigned the value -1.

NAMED= *nmd*

indicates if the file has a name. *nmd* is a scalar variable of type default logical that is assigned the value `true` if the file has a name. The value assigned is `false` if the file does not have a name.

NAME= *fn*   indicates the name of the file. *fn* is a scalar default character variable that is assigned the name of the file to which the unit is connected.

SEQUENTIAL= *seq*

indicates if the file is connected for sequential access. *seq* is a scalar default character variable that is assigned the value **YES** if the file can be accessed sequentially. The value assigned is **NO** if the file cannot be accessed sequentially. The value assigned is **UNKNOWN** if access cannot be determined.

DIRECT= *dir*   indicates if the file is connected for direct access. *dir* is a scalar default character variable that is assigned the value **YES** if the file can be accessed directly. The value assigned is **NO** if the file cannot be accessed directly. The value assigned is **UNKNOWN** if it cannot be determined.

FORMATTED= *fmt*

indicates if the file can be connected for formatted input/output. *fmt* is a scalar default character variable that is assigned the value **YES** if the file can be connected for formatted input/output. The value assigned is **NO** if the file cannot be connected for formatted input/output. The value assigned is **UNKNOWN** if formatting cannot be determined.

UNFORMATTED= *unf*

indicates if the file can be connected for unformatted input/output. *fmt* is a scalar default character variable that is assigned the value **YES** if the file can be connected for unformatted input/output, the value **NO** if the file cannot be connected for unformatted input/output, or the value **UNKNOWN** if formatting cannot be determined.

NEXTREC= *nr*

indicates where the next record can be read or written on a file connected for direct access. *nr* is a scalar variable of type default integer that is assigned the value n + 1, where n is the record number of the last record read or written on the file connected for direct access. If the file is connected but no records were read or written since the connection, *nr* is assigned the value 1. If the file is not connected for direct access or if the position of the file cannot be determined because of a previous error, *nr* becomes undefined.

POSITION= *pos*

indicates the position of the file. *pos* is a scalar default character variable that is assigned the value **REWIND** if the file is connected by an **OPEN** statement for positioning at its initial point, **APPEND** if the file is connected for positioning before its endfile record or at its terminal point, **ASIS** if the file is connected without changing its position, or **UNDEFINED** if there is no connection or if the file is connected for direct access.

If the file has been repositioned to its initial point since it was opened, *pos* is assigned the value **REWIND**. If the file has been repositioned just before its endfile record since it was opened (or, if there is no endfile record, at its terminal point), *pos* is assigned the value **APPEND**. If both of the above are true and the file is empty, *pos* is assigned the value **APPEND**. If the file is positioned after the endfile record, *pos* is assigned the value **ASIS**.

ACTION= *act* indicates if the file is connected for read and/or write access. *act* is a scalar default character variable that is assigned the value **READ** if the file is connected for input only, **WRITE** if the file is connected for output only, **READWRITE** if the file is connected for both input and output, and **UNDEFINED** if there is no connection.

READ= *rd* indicates if the file can be read. *rd* is a scalar default character variable that is assigned the value **YES** if the file can be read, **NO** if the file cannot be read, and **UNKNOWN** if it cannot be determined if the file can be read.

WRITE= *wrt* indicates if the file can be written to. *wrt* is a scalar default character variable that is assigned the value **YES** if the file can be written to, **NO** if the file cannot be written to, and **UNKNOWN** if it cannot be determined if the file can be written to.

READWRITE= *rw*

indicates if the file can be both read from and written to. *rw* is a scalar default character variable that is assigned the value **YES** if the file can be both read from and written to, **NO** if the file cannot be both read from and written to, and **UNKNOWN** if it cannot be determined if the file can be both read from and written to.

DELIM= *del* indicates the form, if any, that is used to delimit character data that is written by list-directed or namelist formatting. *del* is a scalar default character variable that is assigned the value **APOSTROPHE** if apostrophes are used to delimit data, **QUOTE** if quotation marks are used to delimit data, **NONE** if neither apostrophes nor quotation marks are used to delimit data, and **UNDEFINED** if there is no file connection or no connection to formatted data.

PAD= *pd* indicates if the connection of the file had specified **PAD=NO**. *pd* is a scalar default character variable that is assigned the value **NO** if the connection of the file had specified **PAD=NO**, and **YES** for all other cases.

Rules

An **INQUIRE** statement can be executed before, while, or after a file is associated with a unit. Any values assigned as the result of an **INQUIRE** statement are values that are current at the time the statement is executed.

The same variable name must not be specified for more than one specifier in the same **INQUIRE** statement, and must not be associated with any other variable in the list of specifiers.

Examples

```
SUBROUTINE SUB(N)
  CHARACTER(N) A(5)
  INQUIRE (IOLENGTH=IOL) A(1)  ! Inquire by output list
  OPEN (7,RECL=IOL)
    ⋮
END SUBROUTINE
```

Related Information

- "Input/Output Concepts" on page 141

INTEGER

Purpose

An **INTEGER** type declaration statement specifies the length and attributes of objects and functions of type integer. Initial values can be assigned to objects.

Format

```
►►─INTEGER─────────────────────────────────────────────────►
            └kind_selector┘   ┌───┐
                              │└─::─┘
                              └─,─attr_spec_list─::─┘
►─entity_decl_list──────────────────────────────────────►◄
```

where:

```
attr_spec

    ALLOCATABLE
    DIMENSION (array_spec)
    EXTERNAL
    INTENT (intent_spec)
    INTRINSIC
    OPTIONAL
    PARAMETER
    POINTER
    PRIVATE
    PUBLIC
    SAVE
    TARGET
```

kind_selector

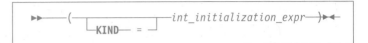

```
►►────(───────────────int_initialization_expr─)►◄
          └─KIND─ = ─┘
```

specifies the length of integer entities

attr_spec	For detailed information on rules about a particular attribute, refer to the statement of the same name.
intent_spec	is either **IN**, **OUT**, or **INOUT**
::	is the double colon separator. It is required if attributes are specified or if = *initialization_expr* is used.

array_spec   is a list of dimension bounds

entity_decl

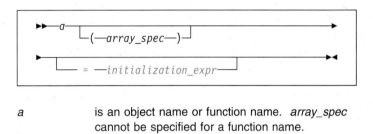

a is an object name or function name. *array_spec* cannot be specified for a function name.

initialization_expr

provides an initial value, by means of an initialization expression, for the entity specified by the immediately preceding name

Rules

Entities in type declaration statements are constrained by the rules of any attributes specified for the entities, as detailed in the corresponding attribute statements.

The type declaration statement overrides the implicit type rules in effect. You can use a type declaration statement that confirms the type of an intrinsic function. The appearance of a generic or specific intrinsic function name in a type declaration statement does not cause the name to lose its intrinsic property.

An object cannot be initialized in a type declaration statement if it is a dummy argument, an allocatable array, a pointer, a function result, an object in blank common, an external name, an intrinsic name, or an automatic object. The object may be initialized if it appears in a named common block in a block data program unit.

The specification expression of an *array_spec* can be a nonconstant expression if the specification expression appears in an interface body or in the specification part of a subprogram. Any object being declared that uses this nonconstant expression and is not a dummy argument is called an *automatic object*.

An attribute cannot be repeated in a given type declaration statement, nor can an entity be explicitly given the same attribute more than once in a scoping unit.

initialization_expr must be specified if the statement contains the **PARAMETER** attribute. If *initialization_expr* is specified and **PARAMETER** is not, the object is

INTEGER

a variable that is initially defined. *a* becomes defined with the value determined by *initialization_expr*, in accordance with the rules for intrinsic assignment. If the variable is an array, its shape must be specified either in the type declaration statement or in a previous specification statement in the same scoping unit. A variable or variable subobject cannot be initialized more than once. The presence of *initialization_expr* implies that *a* is a saved object, except for an object with the **PARAMETER** attribute or in a named common block.

An *array_spec* specified in the *entity_decl* takes precedence over the *array_spec* in the **DIMENSION** attribute.

An array function result that does not have the **POINTER** attribute must have an explicit-shape array specification.

If the entity declared is a function, it must not have an accessible explicit interface unless it is an intrinsic function.

Examples

```
MODULE INT
  INTEGER, DIMENSION(3) :: A,B,C
  INTEGER :: X=234,Y=678
END MODULE INT
```

Related Information

- "Integer" on page 23
- "Initialization Expressions" on page 66
- "How Type Is Determined" on page 33, for details on the implicit typing rules
- "Array Declarators" on page 43
- "Automatic Objects" on page 22
- "DATA" on page 216, for details on initial values

INTENT

Purpose

The **INTENT** attribute specifies the intended use of dummy arguments.

Format

```
►►──INTENT──(──┬──IN───┬──)──┬────┬──dummy_arg_name_list──────►◄
               ├──OUT──┤     └─::─┘
               └─INOUT─┘
```

dummy_arg_name
> is the name of a dummy argument, which cannot be a dummy procedure or a dummy pointer

Rules

The **INTENT** attribute can take three forms:

- **INTENT(IN)** specifies that the dummy argument must not be redefined or become undefined during the execution of the subprogram.

- **INTENT(OUT)** specifies that the dummy argument must be defined before it is referenced within the subprogram. Such a dummy argument becomes undefined on invocation of the subprogram.

- **INTENT(INOUT)** specifies that the dummy argument can both receive and return data to the invoking subprogram.

An actual argument that becomes associated with a dummy argument with an intent of **OUT** or **INOUT** must be definable. Hence, a dummy argument with an intent of **IN**, or an actual argument that is a constant, a subobject of a constant, or an expression, cannot be passed as an actual argument to a subprogram expecting an argument with an intent of **OUT** or **INOUT**.

An actual argument that is an array section with a vector subscript cannot be associated with a dummy array that is defined or redefined (i.e.,with an intent of **OUT** or **INOUT**).

```
┌─ Attributes Compatible with the INTENT Attribute ─────────┐
│                                                           │
│  • DIMENSION          • OPTIONAL          • TARGET         │
│                                                           │
└───────────────────────────────────────────────────────────┘
```

INTENT

Examples

```
PROGRAM MAIN
  DATA R,S /12.34,56.78/
  CALL SUB(R+S,R,S)
END PROGRAM

SUBROUTINE SUB (A,B,C)
  INTENT(IN) A
  INTENT(OUT) B
  INTENT(INOUT) C
  C=C+A+ABS(A)           ! Valid references to A and C
                         ! Valid redefinition of C
  B=C**2                 ! Valid redefinition of B
END SUBROUTINE
```

Related Information

- "Intent of Dummy Arguments" on page 133
- "Argument Association" on page 132
- "Dummy Arguments" on page 131

INTERFACE

Purpose

The **INTERFACE** statement is the first statement of an interface block, which can specify an explicit interface for an external or dummy procedure.

Format

```
►►──INTERFACE──────────────────────────────────────►◄
               └─generic_spec─┘
```

generic_spec

defined_operator
         is a defined unary operator, defined binary operator, or extended intrinsic operator

Rules

If *generic_spec* is present, the interface block is generic. If *generic_spec* is absent, the interface block is nongeneric. *generic_name* specifies a single name to reference all procedures in the interface block. At most, one specific procedure is invoked each time there is a procedure reference with a generic name.

A specific procedure must not have more than one explicit interface in a given scoping unit.

You can always reference a procedure through its specific interface, if accessible. If a generic interface exists for a procedure, the procedure can also be referenced through the generic interface.

If *generic_spec* is **OPERATOR***(defined_operator)*, the interface block can define a defined operator or extend an intrinsic operator.

If *generic_spec* is **ASSIGNMENT***(=)*, the interface block can extend intrinsic assignment.

INTERFACE

Examples

```
INTERFACE                              ! Nongeneric interface block
  FUNCTION VOL(RDS,HGT)
    REAL VOL, RDS, HGT
  END FUNCTION VOL
  FUNCTION AREA (RDS)
    REAL AREA, RDS
  END FUNCTION AREA
END INTERFACE

INTERFACE OPERATOR (.DETERMINANT.)     ! Defined operator interface
  FUNCTION DETERMINANT(X)
    INTENT(IN) X
    REAL X(50,50), DETERMINANT
  END FUNCTION
END INTERFACE

INTERFACE ASSIGNMENT(=)                ! Defined assignment interface
  SUBROUTINE BIT_TO_NUMERIC (N,B)
    INTEGER, INTENT(OUT) :: N
    LOGICAL, INTENT(IN)  :: B(:)
  END SUBROUTINE
END INTERFACE
```

Related Information

- "Explicit Interface" on page 112
- "Extended Intrinsic and Defined Operations" on page 75
- "Defined Operators" on page 118
- "Defined Assignment" on page 119
- "FUNCTION" on page 257
- "SUBROUTINE" on page 336
- "MODULE PROCEDURE" on page 290
- "Procedure References" on page 128
- "Generic Procedure References That Are Unambiguous" on page 116, for details about the rules on how any two procedures with the same generic name must differ

INTRINSIC

Purpose

The **INTRINSIC** attribute identifies a name as an intrinsic procedure and allows you to use specific names of intrinsic procedures as actual arguments.

Format

```
►►──INTRINSIC──name_list──────────────────────────────►◄
```

name   is the name of an intrinsic procedure

Rules

If you use a specific intrinsic procedure name as an actual argument in a scoping unit, it must have the **INTRINSIC** attribute. Generic names can have the **INTRINSIC** attribute, but you cannot pass them as arguments unless they are also specific names.

A generic or specific procedure that has the **INTRINSIC** attribute keeps its generic or specific properties.

A generic intrinsic procedure that has the **INTRINSIC** attribute can also be the name of a generic interface block. The generic interface block defines extensions to the generic intrinsic procedure.

```
┌─── Attributes Compatible with the INTRINSIC Attribute ───┐
│                                                          │
│  • PRIVATE                        • PUBLIC            ·   │
│                                                          │
└──────────────────────────────────────────────────────────┘
```

Examples

```
PROGRAM MAIN
  INTRINSIC SIN, ABS
  INTERFACE ABS
    LOGICAL FUNCTION MYABS(ARG)
      LOGICAL ARG
    END FUNCTION
  END INTERFACE

  LOGICAL LANS,LVAR
  REAL(KIND(0.0D0)) DANS,DVAR ! double precision entities
  DANS = ABS(DVAR)           ! Calls the DABS intrinsic procedure
  LANS = ABS(LVAR)           ! Calls the MYABS external procedure
```

INTRINSIC

```
! Pass intrinsic procedure name to subroutine
  CALL DOIT(0.5,SIN,X)        ! Passes the SIN specific intrinsic
END PROGRAM

SUBROUTINE DOIT(RIN,OPER,RESULT)
  RESULT = OPER(RIN)
END SUBROUTINE
```

Related Information

- Generic and specific intrinsic procedures are listed in "Intrinsic Procedures" on page 359. See this section to find out if a specific intrinsic name can be used as an actual argument.
- "Generic Interface Blocks" on page 116

LOGICAL

Purpose

A **LOGICAL** type declaration statement specifies the length and attributes of objects and functions of type logical. Initial values can be assigned to objects.

Format

```
►►──LOGICAL──────────────────────────────────────────────►
              └kind_selector┘   ┌──::──┐
                                └─,─attr_spec_list─::─┘
►──entity_decl_list─────────────────────────────────────►◄
```

where:

attr_spec
ALLOCATABLE
DIMENSION (*array_spec*)
EXTERNAL
INTENT (*intent_spec*)
INTRINSIC
OPTIONAL
PARAMETER
POINTER
PRIVATE
PUBLIC
SAVE
TARGET

kind_selector

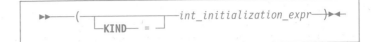

```
►►──────(──────────────int_initialization_expr──)►◄─
           └KIND─ = ─┘
```

specifies the length of logical entities

attr_spec   For detailed information on rules about a particular attribute, refer to the statement of the same name.

intent_spec   is either **IN**, **OUT**, or **INOUT**

::   is the double colon separator. It is required if attributes are specified or if = *initialization_expr* is used.

array_spec   is a list of dimension bounds

entity_decl

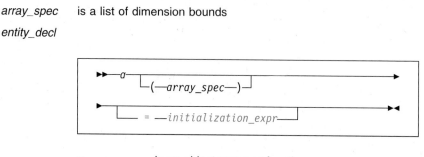

a   is an object name or function name. *array_spec*
                         cannot be specified for a function name.

initialization_expr

provides an initial value, by means of an
initialization expression, for the entity specified by
the immediately preceding name

Rules

Entities in type declaration statements are constrained by the rules of any
attributes specified for the entities, as detailed in the corresponding attribute
statements.

The type declaration statement overrides the implicit type rules in effect. You
can use a type declaration statement that confirms the type of an intrinsic
function. The appearance of a generic or specific intrinsic function name in a
type declaration statement does not cause the name to lose its intrinsic
property.

An object cannot be initialized in a type declaration statement if it is a dummy
argument, an allocatable array, a pointer, a function result, an object in blank
common, an external name, an intrinsic name, or an automatic object. The
object may be initialized if it appears in a named common block in a block data
program unit.

The specification expression of an *array_spec* can be a nonconstant expression
if the specification expression appears in an interface body or in the
specification part of a subprogram. Any object being declared that uses this
nonconstant expression and is not a dummy argument is called an *automatic
object*.

An attribute cannot be repeated in a given type declaration statement, nor can
an entity be explicitly given the same attribute more than once in a scoping unit.

initialization_expr must be specified if the statement contains the **PARAMETER**
attribute. If *initialization_expr* is specified and **PARAMETER** is not, the object is

a variable that is initially defined. *a* becomes defined with the value determined by *initialization_expr*, in accordance with the rules for intrinsic assignment. If the variable is an array, its shape must be specified either in the type declaration statement or in a previous specification statement in the same scoping unit. A variable or variable subobject cannot be initialized more than once. The presence of *initialization_expr* implies that *a* is a saved object, except for an object with the **PARAMETER** attribute or in a named common block.

An *array_spec* specified in the *entity_decl* takes precedence over the *array_spec* in the **DIMENSION** attribute.

An array function result that does not have the **POINTER** attribute must have an explicit-shape array specification.

If the entity declared is a function, it must not have an accessible explicit interface unless it is an intrinsic function.

Examples

```
LOGICAL, ALLOCATABLE :: L(:,:)
LOGICAL :: Z=.TRUE.
```

Related Information

- "Logical" on page 26
- "Initialization Expressions" on page 66
- "How Type Is Determined" on page 33, for details on the implicit typing rules
- "Array Declarators" on page 43
- "Automatic Objects" on page 22
- "DATA" on page 216, for details on initial values

MODULE

MODULE

Purpose

The **MODULE** statement is the first statement of a module program unit, which contains specifications and definitions that can be made accessible to other program units.

Format

```
►►──MODULE──module_name──────────────────────────────────────────►◄
```

Rules

The module name is a global entity that is referenced by the **USE** statement in other program units to access the public entities of the module. The module name must not have the same name as any other program unit, external procedure or common block in the program, nor can it be the same as any local name in the module.

If the **END** statement that completes the module specifies a module name, the name must be the same as that specified in the **MODULE** statement.

Examples

```
MODULE MM
   CONTAINS
     REAL FUNCTION SUM(CARG)
       COMPLEX CARG
       SUM_FNC(CARG) = IMAG(CARG) + REAL(CARG)
       SUM = SUM_FNC(CARG)
       RETURN
     ENTRY AVERAGE(CARG)
       AVERAGE = SUM_FNC(CARG) / 2.0
     END FUNCTION SUM
     SUBROUTINE SHOW_SUM(SARG)
       COMPLEX SARG
       REAL SUM_TMP
  10   FORMAT('SUM:',E10.3,' REAL:',E10.3,' IMAG',E10.3)
       SUM_TMP = SUM(CARG=SARG)
       WRITE(10,10) SUM_TMP, SARG
     END SUBROUTINE SHOW_SUM
END MODULE MM
```

Related Information

- "Modules" on page 122
- "USE" on page 348
- "Use Association" on page 106
- "END" on page 235, for details on the **END MODULE** statement
- "PRIVATE" on page 310
- "PUBLIC" on page 313

MODULE PROCEDURE

MODULE PROCEDURE

Purpose

The **MODULE PROCEDURE** statement lists those module procedures that have a generic interface.

Format

```
►►──MODULE PROCEDURE──procedure_name_list──────────────────►◄
```

Rules

The **MODULE PROCEDURE** statement must appear in an interface block that has a generic specification. **MODULE PROCEDURE** statements must be listed after any interface bodies in the interface block, which is contained in a scoping unit where *procedure_name* can be accessed as a module procedure.

procedure_name must be the name of a module procedure that is accessible in this scope. *procedure_name* must not have been previously associated with the generic specification of the interface block in which it appears, either by a previous appearance in an interface block or by use or host association.

The characteristics of module procedures are determined by module procedure definitions, not their interface bodies.

Examples

```
MODULE M
  CONTAINS
  SUBROUTINE S1(IARG)
    IARG=1
  END SUBROUTINE
  SUBROUTINE S2(RARG)
    RARG=1.1
  END SUBROUTINE
END MODULE

USE M
INTERFACE SS
  SUBROUTINE SS1(IARG,JARG)
  END SUBROUTINE
  MODULE PROCEDURE S1, S2
END INTERFACE
CALL SS(N)                  ! Calls subroutine S1 from M
CALL SS(I,J)                ! Calls subroutine SS1
END
```

Related Information

- "Interface Blocks" on page 112
- "INTERFACE" on page 281
- "Modules" on page 122

NAMELIST

Purpose

The **NAMELIST** statement specifies one or more lists of names for use in **READ**, **WRITE**, and **PRINT** statements.

Format

Nname   is a namelist group name

variable_name

must not be an array dummy argument with a nonconstant bound, a variable with nonconstant character length, an automatic object, a pointer, a variable of a type that has an ultimate component that is a pointer or an allocatable array.

Rules

The list of names belonging to a namelist group name ends with the appearance of another namelist group name or the end of the **NAMELIST** statement.

variable_name must either be accessed via use or host association, or have its type and type parameters specified by previous specification statements in the same scoping unit or by the implicit typing rules. If typed implicitly, any appearance of the object in a subsequent type declaration statement must confirm the implied type and type parameters. A derived-type object must not appear as a list item if any component ultimately contained within the object is not accessible within the scoping unit containing the namelist input/output statement on which its containing namelist group name is specified.

variable_name can belong to one or more namelist lists. If the namelist group name has the **PUBLIC** attribute, no item in the list can have the **PRIVATE** attribute or private components.

Nname can be specified in more than one **NAMELIST** statement in the scoping unit. The variable_name_list following each successive appearance of the same Nname in a scoping unit is treated as the continuation of the list for that Nname.

A namelist name can appear only in input/output statements. The rules for input/output conversion of namelist data are the same as the rules for data conversion.

Examples

```
DIMENSION X(5), Y(10)
NAMELIST /NAME1/ I,J,K
NAMELIST /NAME2/ A,B,C /NAME3/ X,Y
WRITE (10, NAME1)
PRINT NAME2
```

Related Information

- "Namelist Formatting" on page 173

NULLIFY

Purpose

The **NULLIFY** statement causes pointers to become disassociated.

Format

▶▶──NULLIFY──(──*pointer_object_list*──)────────────────▶◀

pointer_object

        is a pointer variable name or structure component

Rules

A *pointer_object* must have the **POINTER** attribute.

> ── Tip ───
>
> Always initialize a pointer with the **NULLIFY** statement or with pointer
> assignment.

Examples

```
TYPE T
  INTEGER CELL
  TYPE(T), POINTER :: NEXT
ENDTYPE T
TYPE(T) HEAD, TAIL
TARGET :: TAIL
HEAD%NEXT => TAIL
NULLIFY (TAIL%NEXT)
END
```

Related Information

- "Pointer Assignment" on page 84
- "Pointer Association" on page 106

OPEN

Purpose

The **OPEN** statement can be used to connect an existing external file to a unit, create an external file that is preconnected, create an external file and connect it to a unit, or change certain specifiers of a connection between an external file and a unit.

Format

```
►►──OPEN──(──open_list──)──────────────────────────────►◄
```

open_list   is a list that must contain one unit specifier (**UNIT=** *u*) and can also contain one of each of the other valid specifiers. The valid specifiers are:

[UNIT=] *u*   is a unit specifier in which *u* must be an external unit identifier whose value is not an asterisk. An external unit identifier refers to an external file that is represented by a scalar integer expression. If the optional characters **UNIT=** are omitted, *u* must be the first item in *open_list*.

IOSTAT= *ios*   is an input/output status specifier that specifies the status of the input/output operation. *ios* is a scalar variable of type default integer. When the input/output statement containing this specifier finishes execution, *ios* is defined with:

- A zero value if no error condition occurs.
- A positive value if an error occurs.

ERR= *stmt_label*

is an error specifier that specifies the statement label of an executable statement in the same scoping unit to which control is to transfer in the case of an error. Coding the **ERR=** specifier suppresses error messages.

FILE= *char_expr*

is a file specifier that specifies the name of the file to be connected to the specified unit. *char_expr* is a name that is allowed by the processor (after trailing blanks are removed). If **FILE=** is omitted and the unit is not implicitly connected, **STATUS=SCRATCH** must be specified; in this case, a processor-dependent file is connected.

STATUS= *char_expr*

specifies the status of the file when it is opened. *char_expr* is a scalar default character expression whose value, when any trailing blanks are removed, is one of the following:

- **OLD**, to connect an existing file to a unit. If **OLD** is specified, the file must exist. If the file does not exist, an error condition will occur.
- **NEW**, to create a new file, connect it to a unit, and change the status to **OLD**. If **NEW** is specified, the file must not exist. If the file already exists, an error condition will occur.
- **SCRATCH**, to create and connect a new file that will be deleted when it is disconnected. **SCRATCH** must not be specified with a named file (that is, **FILE=** *char_expr* must be omitted).
- **REPLACE**. If the file does not already exist, the file is created and the status is changed to **OLD**. If the file exists, the file is deleted, a new file is created with the same name, and the status is changed to **OLD**.
- **UNKNOWN**, to connect an existing file, or to create and connect a new file. If the file exists, it is connected as **OLD**. If the file does not exist, it is connected as **NEW**.

UNKNOWN is the default.

ACCESS= *char_expr*

specifies the access method for the connection of the file. *char_expr* is a scalar default character expression whose value, when any trailing blanks are removed, is either **SEQUENTIAL** or **DIRECT**. **SEQUENTIAL** is the default. If **ACCESS** is **DIRECT**, **RECL=** must be specified. If **ACCESS** is **SEQUENTIAL**, **RECL=** is optional.

FORM= *char_expr*

specifies whether the file is connected for formatted or unformatted input/output. *char_expr* is a scalar default character expression whose value, when any trailing blanks are removed, is either **FORMATTED** or **UNFORMATTED**. If the file is being connected for sequential access, **FORMATTED** is the default. If the file is being connected for direct access, **UNFORMATTED** is the default.

RECL= *integer_expr*

specifies the length of each record in a file being connected for direct access or the maximum length of a record in a file being connected for sequential access. *integer_expr* is a scalar integer expression whose value must be positive. This specifier must be present when a file is being connected for direct access. For formatted input/output, the length is the number of characters for all records that contain character data (of type default character). For unformatted input/output, the length is measured in processor-dependent units.

If **RECL=** is omitted when a file is being connected for sequential access (formatted or unformatted), the default value is processor-dependent.

BLANK= *char_expr*

controls the default interpretation of blanks when you are using a format specification. *char_expr* is a scalar default character expression whose value, when any trailing blanks are removed, is either **NULL** or **ZERO**. If **BLANK=** is specified, you must use **FORM= 'FORMATTED'**. If **BLANK=** is not specified and you specify **FORM='FORMATTED'**, **NULL** is the default.

POSITION= *char_expr*

specifies the file position for a file connected for sequential access. A file that did not exist previously is positioned at its initial point. *char_expr* is a scalar default character expression whose value, when any trailing blanks are removed, is either **ASIS**, **REWIND**, or **APPEND**. **REWIND** positions the file at its initial point. **APPEND** positions the file before the endfile record or, if there is no endfile record, at the terminal point. **ASIS** leaves the position unchanged. The default value is **ASIS**.

ACTION= *char_expr*

specifies the allowed input/output operations. *char_expr* is a scalar default character expression whose value evaluates to **READ**, **WRITE** or **READWRITE**. If **READ** is specified, **WRITE** and **ENDFILE** statements cannot refer to this connection. If **WRITE** is specified, **READ** statements cannot refer to this connection. The value **READWRITE** permits any input/output statement to refer to this connection. If the **ACTION=** specifier is omitted, the default value depends on the actual file permissions:

- If the **STATUS=** specifier has the value **OLD** or **UNKNOWN** and the file already exists:
  - The file is opened with **READWRITE**.
  - If the above is not possible, the file is opened with **READ**.
  - If neither of the above is possible, the file is opened with **WRITE**.
- If the **STATUS=** specifier has the value **NEW**, **REPLACE**, **SCRATCH** or **UNKNOWN** and the file does not exist:
  - The file is opened with **READWRITE**.

> — If the above is not possible, the file is opened with **WRITE**.

DELIM= *char_expr*

specifies what delimiter, if any, is used to delimit character constants written with list-directed or namelist formatting. *char_expr* is a scalar default character expression whose value must evaluate to **APOSTROPHE**, **QUOTE** or **NONE**. If the value is **APOSTROPHE**, apostrophes delimit character constants and all apostrophes within character constants are doubled. If the value is **QUOTE**, double quotation marks delimit character constants and all double quotation marks within character constants are doubled. If the value is **NONE**, character constants are not delimited and no characters are doubled. The default value is **NONE**. The **DELIM=** specifier is permitted only for files being connected for formatted input/output, although it is ignored during input of a formatted record.

PAD= *char_expr*

specifies if input records are padded with blanks. *char_expr* is a scalar default character expression that must evaluate to **YES** or **NO**. If the value is **YES**, a formatted input record is padded with blanks if an input list is specified and the format specification requires more data from a record than the record contains. If **NO** is specified, the input list and format specification must not require more characters from a record than the record contains. The default value is **YES**. The **PAD=** specifier is permitted only for files being connected for formatted input/output, although it is ignored during output of a formatted record.

Rules

If a unit is connected to a file that exists, an **OPEN** statement for that unit can be performed. If the **FILE=** specifier is not included in the **OPEN** statement, the file to be connected to the unit is the same as the file to which the unit is connected.

If the file to be connected to the unit is not the same as the file to which the unit is connected, the effect is as if a **CLOSE** statement without a **STATUS=** specifier had been executed for the unit immediately prior to the execution of the **OPEN** statement.

If the file to be connected to the unit is the same as the file to which the unit is connected, only the **BLANK=**, **DELIM=**, **PAD=**, **ERR=**, and **IOSTAT=** specifiers can have a value different from the one currently in effect. Execution of the **OPEN** statement causes any new value for the **BLANK=**, **DELIM=** or **PAD=** specifiers to be in effect, but does not cause any change in any of the unspecified specifiers or the position of the file. Any **ERR=** and **IOSTAT=** specifiers from **OPEN** statements previously executed have no effect on the current **OPEN** statement. To specify the same file as the one currently connected to the unit, you can specify the same file name, omit the **FILE=** specifier, or specify a file symbolically linked to the same file.

If a file is connected to a unit, an **OPEN** statement on that file and a different unit cannot be performed.

If the **ERR=** and **IOSTAT=** specifiers are set and an error is encountered, transfer is made to the statement specified by the **ERR=** specifier and a positive integer value is assigned to *ios*.

Examples

```
!   Open a new file with name fname

CHARACTER*20 FNAME
FNAME = 'INPUT.DAT'
OPEN(UNIT=8,FILE=FNAME,STATUS='NEW',FORM='FORMATTED')

OPEN (4,FILE="myfile")
OPEN (4,FILE="myfile", PAD="NO")   ! Changing PAD= value to NO
```

Related Information

- "Connection of a Unit" on page 144
- Item 3 under "FORTRAN 77 Compatibility" on page 415
- "CLOSE" on page 203

OPTIONAL

Purpose

The **OPTIONAL** attribute specifies that a dummy argument need not be associated with an actual argument in a reference to the procedure.

Format

```
►►─OPTIONAL─┬────┬─dummy_arg_name_list──────────────────►◄
            └─::─┘
```

Rules

A reference to a procedure that has an optional dummy argument specified must have an explicit interface.

Use the **PRESENT** intrinsic function to determine if an actual argument has been associated with an optional dummy argument. Avoid referencing an optional dummy argument without first verifying that the dummy argument is present.

A dummy argument is considered present in a subprogram if it is associated with an actual argument, which itself can also be a dummy argument that is present (an instance of propagation). A dummy argument that is not optional must be present; that is, it must be associated with an actual argument.

An optional dummy argument that is not present may be used as an actual argument corresponding to an optional dummy argument, which is then also considered not to be associated with an actual argument. An optional dummy argument that is not present is subject to the following restrictions:

- If it is a dummy data object or subobject, it cannot be defined or referenced.
- If it is a dummy procedure, it cannot be referenced.
- It cannot appear as an actual argument corresponding to a non-optional dummy argument, other than as the argument of the **PRESENT** intrinsic function.
- If it is an array, it must not be supplied as an actual argument to an elemental procedure unless an array of the same rank is supplied as an actual argument, which corresponds to a nonoptional argument of that elemental procedure.

The **OPTIONAL** attribute cannot be specified for dummy arguments in an interface body that specifies an explicit interface for a defined operator or defined assignment.

Attributes Compatible with the OPTIONAL Attribute

- DIMENSION   • INTENT   • TARGET
- EXTERNAL   • POINTER

Examples

```
SUBROUTINE SUB (X,Y)
  INTERFACE
    SUBROUTINE SUB2 (A,B)
      OPTIONAL :: B
    END SUBROUTINE
  END INTERFACE
  OPTIONAL :: Y
  IF (PRESENT(Y)) THEN            ! Reference to Y conditional
    X = X + Y                     ! on its presence
  ENDIF
  CALL SUB2(X,Y)
END SUBROUTINE

SUBROUTINE SUB2 (A,B)
  OPTIONAL :: B                   ! B and Y are argument associated,
  IF (PRESENT(B)) THEN            ! even if Y is not present, in
    B = B * A                     ! which case, B is also not present
  ENDIF
END SUBROUTINE
```

Related Information

- "Optional Dummy Arguments" on page 133
- "Interface Concepts" on page 110
- "PRESENT (A)" on page 397
- "Dummy Arguments" on page 131

PARAMETER

Purpose

The **PARAMETER** attribute specifies names for constants.

Format

```
>>--PARAMETER--(--,--constant_name-- = --init_expr--)--><
```

init_expr   is an initialization expression

Rules

A named constant must have its type, shape, and parameters specified in a previous specification statement in the same scoping unit or be declared implicitly. If a named constant is implicitly typed, its appearance in any subsequent type declaration statement or attribute specification statement must confirm the implied type and any parameter values.

You can define *constant_name* only once with a **PARAMETER** attribute in a scoping unit.

A named constant that is specified in the initialization expression must have been previously defined (possibly in the same **PARAMETER** or type declaration statement, if not in a previous statement) or made accessible through use or host association.

The initialization expression is assigned to the named constant using the rules for intrinsic assignment. If the named constant is of type character and it has inherited length, it takes on the length of the initialization expression.

┌─ **Attributes Compatible with the PARAMETER Attribute** ──────┐
│   │
│   • DIMENSION   • PRIVATE   • PUBLIC   │
│   │
└──┘

Examples

```
REAL, PARAMETER :: TWO=2.0

COMPLEX     XCONST
REAL        RPART,IPART
PARAMETER   (RPART=1.1,IPART=2.2)
PARAMETER   (XCONST = (1.1,2.2))

CHARACTER*2, PARAMETER :: BB='   '
   ⋮
END
```

Related Information

- "Initialization Expressions" on page 66
- "Data Objects" on page 22

PAUSE

Purpose

The **PAUSE** statement temporarily suspends the execution of a program and makes the character constant or digit string available in a processor-dependent manner.

Format

char_constant

  is a scalar character constant

digit_string is a string of one through five digits

Rules

Execution must be resumable. Resumption of execution is not under the program's control.

Examples

```
PAUSE 'Ensure backup tape is in tape drive'
PAUSE 10          ! Output:  PAUSE 10
```

POINTER

Purpose

The **POINTER** attribute designates objects as pointer variables.

Format

```
►►──POINTER───────────────────────────────────────────────►
              └─ :: ─┘

  ►─┬─object_name──────────────────────────────────┬─►◄
    │                                               │
    └─▲─                                            │
      '                                             │
          └─(──deferred_shape_spec_list──)─┘
```

deferred_shape_spec
      is a colon (:), where each colon represents a dimension

Rules

object_name refers to a data object or function result. If *object_name* is declared elsewhere in the scoping unit with the **DIMENSION** attribute, the array specification must be a *deferred_shape_spec_list*.

object_name may not appear in a **DATA**, **NAMELIST**, or **EQUIVALENCE** statement. If *object_name* is a component of a derived-type definition, any variables declared with that type cannot be specified in an **EQUIVALENCE**, **DATA**, or **NAMELIST** statement.

Pointer variables can appear in common blocks and block data program units.

An object having a component with the **POINTER** attribute can itself have the **TARGET**, **INTENT**, or **ALLOCATABLE** attributes, although it cannot appear in a data transfer statement.

┌─── **Attributes Compatible with the POINTER Attribute** ────────┐
│   │
│ • DIMENSION   • PRIVATE   • SAVE   │
│ • OPTIONAL   • PUBLIC   │
│   │
└──┘

These attributes apply only to the pointer itself, not to any associated targets, except for the **DIMENSION** attribute, which applies to associated targets.

POINTER

Examples

```
INTEGER, POINTER :: PTR(:)
INTEGER, TARGET :: TARG(5)
PTR => TARG                 ! PTR is associated with TARG and is
                            !   assigned an array specification of (5)


PTR(1) = 5                  ! TARG(1) has value of 5
PRINT *, FUNC()
CONTAINS
  REAL FUNCTION FUNC()
    POINTER :: FUNC         ! Function result is a pointer
       ⋮
  END FUNCTION
END
```

Related Information

- "Pointer Assignment" on page 84
- "TARGET" on page 338
- "ALLOCATED (ARRAY)" on page 367
- "DEALLOCATE" on page 221
- "Pointer Association" on page 106
- "Deferred-shape Arrays" on page 47

PRINT

Purpose

The **PRINT** statement is a data transfer output statement.

Format

```
►►──PRINT──format──────────────────────────────►◄
                  └─,──output_item_list─┘
```

output_item is an output list item. An output list specifies the data to be transferred. An output list item can be:

- A variable. An array is treated as if all of its elements were specified in the order they are arranged in storage.

  A pointer must be associated with a target and an allocatable array must be allocated. A derived-type object cannot have any ultimate component that is outside the scoping unit of this statement. The evaluation of output_item cannot result in a derived-type object that contains a pointer. The structure components of a structure in a formatted statement are treated as if they appear in the order of the derived-type definition; in an unformatted statement, the structure components are treated as a single value in their internal representation (including padding).

- An expression
- An implied-**DO** list, as described on page 308

format is a format specifier that specifies the format to be used in the output operation. *format* is a format identifier that can be:

- The statement label of a **FORMAT** statement. The **FORMAT** statement must be in the same scoping unit.

- The name of a scalar default integer variable that was assigned the statement label of a **FORMAT** statement. The **FORMAT** statement must be in the same scoping unit.

- A character constant. It must begin with a left parenthesis and end with a right parenthesis. Only the format codes described in the **FORMAT** statement can be used between the parentheses. Blank characters can precede the left parenthesis, or follow the right parenthesis.

- A character variable that contains character data whose left-most character positions constitute a valid format. A valid format begins with a left parenthesis and ends with a right parenthesis. Only the format codes listed under "FORMAT" on page 252 can be used between the parentheses. Blank characters can precede the left parenthesis, or follow the right parenthesis.

- An array of noncharacter intrinsic type.

- Any character expression, except one involving concatenation of an operand that specifies inherited length, unless the operand is the name of a constant.

- An asterisk, specifying list-directed formatting.

Implied-DO List

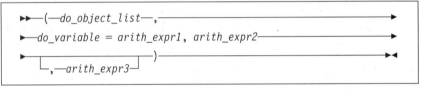

do_object   is an output list item

do_variable   is a named scalar variable of type integer, default real, or double precision

arith_expr1, *arith_expr2*, and *arith_expr3*
   are scalar expressions of type integer, default real, or double precision

The range of an implied-DO list is the list *do_object_list*. The iteration count and the values of the **DO** variable are established from *arith_expr1*, *arith_expr2*, and *arith_expr3*, the same as for a **DO** statement. When the implied-**DO** list is executed, the items in the *do_object_list* are specified once for each iteration of the implied-**DO** list, with the appropriate substitution of values for any occurrence of the **DO** variable.

Examples

```
      PRINT 10, A,B,C
10 FORMAT (E4.2,G3.2E1,B3)
```

Related Information

- "Input/Output Concepts" on page 141
- "Input/Output Formatting" on page 149

PRITATE

PRIVATE

Purpose

The **PRIVATE** attribute specifies that a module entity is not accessible outside the module through use association.

Format

```
>>──PRIVATE──────────────────────────────────────><
           └──┬────┬──access_id_list──┘
              └─::─┘
```

access_id   is a generic specification or the name of a variable, procedure, derived type, constant, or namelist group

Rules

The **PRIVATE** attribute can appear only in the scope of a module.

Although multiple **PRIVATE** statements may appear in a module, only one statement that omits an *access_id_list* is permitted. A **PRIVATE** statement without an *access_id_list* sets the default accessibility to private for all potentially accessible entities in the module. If the module contains such a statement, it cannot also include a **PUBLIC** statement without an *access_id_list*. If the module does not contain such a statement, the default accessibility is public. Entities whose accessibility is not explicitly specified have default accessibility.

A procedure that has a generic identifier that is public is accessible through that identifier, even if its specific identifier is private. If a module procedure contains a private dummy argument or function result whose type has private accessibility, the module procedure must be declared to have private accessibility and must not have a generic identifier that has public accessibility.

If a **PRIVATE** statement is specified within a derived-type definition, all the components of the derived type become private.

A structure must be private if its derived type is private. A namelist group must be private if it contains any object that is private or contains private components. A derived type that has a component of derived type that is private must itself be private or have private components. A subprogram must be private if any of its arguments are of a derived type that is private. A function must be private if its result variable is of a derived type that is private.

```
  ┌─ Attributes Compatible with the PRIVATE Attribute ──────────┐
  │                                                              │
  │   • ALLOCATABLE        • INTRINSIC         • SAVE            │
  │   • DIMENSION          • PARAMETER         • TARGET          │
  │   • EXTERNAL           • POINTER                             │
  │                                                              │
  └──────────────────────────────────────────────────────────────┘
```

Examples

```
MODULE MC
   PUBLIC                       ! Default accessibility declared as public
   INTERFACE GEN
      MODULE PROCEDURE SUB1, SUB2
   END INTERFACE
   PRIVATE SUB1                 ! SUB1 declared as private
   CONTAINS
      SUBROUTINE SUB1(I)
         INTEGER I
         I = I + 1
      END SUBROUTINE SUB1
      SUBROUTINE SUB2(I,J)
         I = I + J
      END SUBROUTINE
END MODULE MC

PROGRAM ABC
   USE MC
   K = 5
   CALL GEN(K)                  ! SUB1 referenced because GEN has public
                                ! accessibility and appropriate argument
                                ! is passed

   CALL SUB2(K,4)
   PRINT *, K                   ! Value printed is 10
END PROGRAM
```

Related Information

- "Derived Types" on page 28
- "Modules" on page 122
- "PUBLIC" on page 313

PROGRAM

Purpose

The **PROGRAM** statement specifies that a program unit is a main program, the program unit that receives control from the system when the executable program is invoked at run time.

Format

```
►►──PROGRAM──name──────────────────────────────────────────────►◄
```

name   is the name of the main program in which this statement appears

Rules

The **PROGRAM** statement is optional.

If specified, the **PROGRAM** statement must be the first statement of the main program.

If a program name is specified in the corresponding **END** statement, it must match *name*.

The program name is global to the executable program. The program must not have a name that is the same as the name of any common block, external procedure, or any other program unit in that executable program. The program name cannot be the same as any name local to the main program.

The name has no type and must not appear in any type declaration or specification statements. You cannot refer to a main program from a subprogram or from itself.

Examples

```
PROGRAM DISPLAY_NUMBER_2
   INTEGER A
   A = 2
   PRINT *, A
END PROGRAM DISPLAY_NUMBER_2
```

Related Information

* "Main Program" on page 121

PUBLIC

Purpose

The **PUBLIC** attribute specifies that a module entity can be accessed by other program units through use association.

Format

```
►►──PUBLIC──────────────────────────────────────────────►◄
             │   ┌─access_id_list─┐
             └─::─┘
```

access_id   is a generic specification or the name of a variable, procedure, derived type, constant, or namelist group

Rules

The **PUBLIC** attribute can appear only in the scope of a module.

Although multiple **PUBLIC** statements can appear in a module, only one statement that omits an *access_id_list* is permitted. A **PUBLIC** statement without an *access_id_list* sets the default accessibility to public for all potentially accessible entities in the module. If the module contains such a statement, it cannot also include a **PRIVATE** statement without an *access_id_list*. If the module does not contain such a statement, the default accessibility is public. Entities whose accessibility is not explicitly specified have default accessibility.

A procedure that has a generic identifier that is public is accessible through that identifier, even if its specific identifier is private. If a module procedure contains a private dummy argument or function result whose type has private accessibility, the module procedure must be declared to have private accessibility and must not have a generic identifier that has public accessibility.

Attributes Compatible with the PUBLIC Attribute

- ALLOCATABLE
- DIMENSION
- EXTERNAL
- INTRINSIC
- PARAMETER
- POINTER
- SAVE
- TARGET

PUBLIC

Examples

```
MODULE MC
   PRIVATE                          ! Default accessibility declared as private
   PUBLIC GEN                       ! GEN declared as public
   INTERFACE GEN
      MODULE PROCEDURE SUB1
   END INTERFACE
   CONTAINS
      SUBROUTINE SUB1(I)
         INTEGER I
         I = I + 1
      END SUBROUTINE SUB1
END MODULE MC
PROGRAM ABC
   USE MC
   K = 5
   CALL GEN(K)                      ! SUB1 referenced because GEN has public
                                    !   accessibility and appropriate argument
                                    !   is passed
   PRINT *, K                       ! Value printed is 6
END PROGRAM
```

Related Information

- "PRIVATE" on page 310
- "Modules" on page 122

READ

Purpose

The **READ** statement is the data transfer input statement.

Format

```
►►──READ──┬─format───────────────────────────┬──►◄
          │        └─,─input_item_list─┘      │
          └─(─io_control_list─)───────────────┘
                              └─input_item_list─┘
```

format	is a format identifier, described below under **FMT=**_format_.
input_item	is an input list item. An input list specifies the data to be transferred. An input list item can be:

- A variable name, but not for an assumed-size array. An array is treated as if all of its elements were specified in the order they are arranged in storage.

  A pointer must be associated with a definable target and an allocatable array must be allocated. A derived-type object cannot have any ultimate component that is outside the scoping unit of this statement. The evaluation of *input_item* cannot result in a derived-type object that contains a pointer. The structure components of a structure in a formatted statement are treated as if they appear in the order of the derived-type definition; in an unformatted statement, the structure components are treated as a single value in their internal representation (including padding).

- An implied-**DO** list, as described on page 318.

io_control	is a list that must contain one unit specifier (**UNIT=**), and can also contain one of each of the other valid specifiers:
[UNIT=] *u*	is a unit specifier that specifies the unit to be used in the input operation. *u* is an external unit identifier or internal file identifier.

An external unit identifier refers to an external file. It is one of the following:

- A scalar integer expression
- An asterisk

An internal file identifier refers to an internal file. It is the name of a default character variable that cannot be an array section with a vector subscript.

READ

If the optional characters **UNIT=** are omitted, *u* must be the first item in *io_control_list*. If the optional characters **UNIT=** are specified, either the optional characters **FMT=** or the optional characters **NML=** must also be present.

[FMT=] *format*

is a format specifier that specifies the format to be used in the input operation. *format* is a format identifier that can be:

- The statement label of a **FORMAT** statement. The **FORMAT** statement must be in the same scoping unit.

- The name of a scalar default integer variable that was assigned the statement label of a **FORMAT** statement. The **FORMAT** statement must be in the same scoping unit.

- A character constant. It must begin with a left parenthesis and end with a right parenthesis. Only the format codes described in the **FORMAT** statement can be used between the parentheses. Blank characters can precede the left parenthesis, or follow the right parenthesis.

- A character variable that contains character data whose left-most character positions constitute a valid format. A valid format begins with a left parenthesis and ends with a right parenthesis. Only the format codes listed under "FORMAT" on page 252 can be used between the parentheses. Blank characters can precede the left parenthesis, or follow the right parenthesis. If *format* is an array element, the format identifier must not exceed the length of the array element.

- An array of noncharacter intrinsic type. The data must be a valid format identifier as described under character array.

- Any character expression, except one involving concatenation of an operand that specifies inherited length, unless the operand is the name of a constant.

- An asterisk, specifying list-directed formatting.

If the optional characters **FMT=** are omitted, *format* must be the second item in *io_control_list* and the first item must be the unit specifier with the optional characters **UNIT=** omitted. Both **NML=** and **FMT=** cannot be specified in the same input statement.

REC= *integer_expr*

is a record specifier that specifies the number of the record to be read in a file connected for direct access. The **REC=** specifier is only permitted for direct input. *integer_expr* is an integer expression whose value is positive. A record specifier is not valid if list-directed or namelist formatting is used and if the unit specifier specifies an internal file. The record specifier represents the relative position of a record within a file. The relative position number of the first record is 1.

IOSTAT= *ios* is an input/output status specifier that specifies the status of the input/output operation. *ios* is a variable of type default integer. Coding the **IOSTAT=** specifier suppresses error messages. When the statement finishes execution, *ios* is defined with:

- A zero value if an error condition, end-of-file condition, or end-of-record condition does not occur.
- A positive value if an error occurs.
- A negative value if an end-of-file condition is encountered and no error occurs.
- A negative value different from the end-of-file value if an end-of-record condition occurs and no error condition or end-of-file condition occurs.

ERR= *stmt_label*

is an error specifier that specifies the statement label of an executable statement to which control is to transfer in the case of an error. Coding the **ERR=** specifier suppresses error messages.

END= *stmt_label*

is an end-of-file specifier that specifies a statement label at which the program is to continue if an endfile record is encountered and no error occurs. An external file is positioned after the endfile record, the **IOSTAT=** specifier, if present, is assigned a negative value, and the **NUM=** specifier, if present, is assigned an integer value. If an error occurs and the statement contains the **SIZE=** specifier, the specified variable becomes defined with an integer value. Coding the **END=** specifier suppresses the error message for end-of-file. This specifier can be specified for a unit connected for either sequential or direct access.

[NML=] *name*

is a namelist specifier that specifies the name of a namelist list that you have previously defined. If the optional characters **NML=** are not specified, the namelist name must appear as the second parameter in the list and the first item must be the unit specifier with **UNIT=** omitted. If both **NML=** and **UNIT=** are specified, all the parameters can appear in any order.

ADVANCE= *char_expr*
> is an advance specifier that determines whether nonadvancing input occurs for this statement. *char_expr* is a scalar default character expression that must evaluate to **YES** or **NO**. If **NO** is specified, nonadvancing input occurs. If **YES** is specified, advancing, formatted sequential input occurs. The default value is **YES**. **ADVANCE=** can be specified only in a formatted sequential **READ** statement with an explicit format specification that does not specify an internal file unit specifier.

SIZE= *count* is a character count specifier that determines how many characters are transferred by data edit descriptors during execution of the current input statement. *count* is a scalar default integer variable. Blanks that are inserted as padding are not included in the count.

EOR= *stmt_label*
> is an end-of-record specifier. If the specifier is present, an end-of-record condition occurs, and no error condition occurs during execution of the statement:
>
> 1. If the **PAD=** specifier has the value **YES**, the record is padded with blanks to satisfy the input list item and the corresponding data edit descriptor that requires more characters than the record contains.
> 2. Execution of the **READ** statement terminates.
> 3. The file specified in the **READ** statement is positioned after the current record.
> 4. If the **IOSTAT=** specifier is present, the specified variable becomes defined with a negative value different from an end-of-file value.
> 5. If the **SIZE=** specifier is present, the specified variable becomes defined with an integer value.
> 6. Execution continues with the statement containing the statement label specified by the **EOR=** specifier.
> 7. End-of-record messages are suppressed.

Implied-DO List

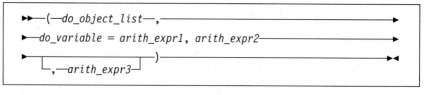

do_object   is an input list item

do_variable   is a named scalar variable of type integer, default real, or double precision

arith_expr1, *arith_expr2*, and *arith_expr3*
are scalar expressions of type integer, default real, or double precision

The range of an implied-**DO** list is the list *do_object_list*. The iteration count and the values of the **DO** variable are established from *arith_expr1*, *arith_expr2*, and *arith_expr3*, the same as for a **DO** statement. When the implied-**DO** list is executed, the items in the *do_object_list* are specified once for each iteration of the implied-**DO** list, with the appropriate substitution of values for any occurrence of the **DO** variable.

The **DO** variable or an associated data item must not appear as an input list item in the *do_object_list*, but can be read in the same **READ** statement outside of the implied-**DO** list.

Rules

Any statement label specified by the **ERR=**, **EOR=** and **END=** specifiers must refer to a branch target statement that appears in the same scoping unit as the **READ** statement.

If either the **EOR=** specifier or the **SIZE=** specifier is present, the **ADVANCE=** specifier must also be present and must have the value **NO**.

Variables specified for the **IOSTAT=**, **SIZE=** and **NUM=** specifiers must not be associated with any input list item, namelist list item, or the **DO** variable of an implied-**DO** list. If such a specifier variable is an array element, its subscript values must not be affected by the data transfer, any implied-**DO** processing, or the definition or evaluation of any other specifier.

A **READ** statement without *io_control_list* specified specifies the same unit as a **READ** statement with *io_control_list* specified in which the external unit identifier is an asterisk.

If the **ERR=** and **IOSTAT=** specifiers are set and an error is encountered, transfer is made to the statement specified by the **ERR=** specifier and a positive integer value is assigned to *ios*.

READ

Examples

```
INTEGER A(100)
CHARACTER*4 B
READ *, A(LBOUND(A,1):UBOUND(A,1))
READ (7,FMT='(A3)',ADVANCE='NO',EOR=100) B
    :
100 PRINT *, 'end of record reached'
END
```

Related Information

- "Input/Output Concepts" on page 141

REAL

Purpose

A **REAL** type declaration statement specifies the length and attributes of objects and functions of type real. Initial values can be assigned to objects.

Format

```
▶▶──REAL─────────────────────────────────────────────────────▶
          └kind_selector┘    ┌──::──┐
                             └─,─attr_spec_list─::─┘

   ▶──entity_decl_list──────────────────────────────────────▶◀
```

where:

attr_spec
ALLOCATABLE
DIMENSION (*array_spec*)
EXTERNAL
INTENT (*intent_spec*)
INTRINSIC
OPTIONAL
PARAMETER
POINTER
PRIVATE
PUBLIC
SAVE
TARGET

kind_selector

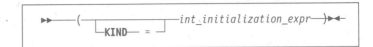

```
▶▶──(──────────────int_initialization_expr─)▶◀
        └KIND─ = ─┘
```

specifies the length of real entities

attr_spec   For detailed information on rules about a particular attribute, refer to the statement of the same name.

intent_spec   is either **IN**, **OUT**, or **INOUT**

::   is the double colon separator. It is required if attributes are specified or if = *initialization_expr* is used.

array_spec   is a list of dimension bounds

entity_decl

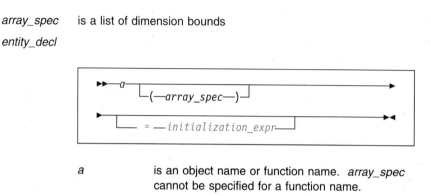

  a   is an object name or function name. *array_spec* cannot be specified for a function name.

initialization_expr

        provides an initial value, by means of an initialization expression, for the entity specified by the immediately preceding name

Rules

Entities in type declaration statements are constrained by the rules of any attributes specified for the entities, as detailed in the corresponding attribute statements.

The type declaration statement overrides the implicit type rules in effect. You can use a type declaration statement that confirms the type of an intrinsic function. The appearance of a generic or specific intrinsic function name in a type declaration statement does not cause the name to lose its intrinsic property.

An object cannot be initialized in a type declaration statement if it is a dummy argument, an allocatable array, a pointer, a function result, an object in blank common, an external name, an intrinsic name, or an automatic object. The object may be initialized if it appears in a named common block in a block data program unit.

The specification expression of an *array_spec* can be a nonconstant expression if the specification expression appears in an interface body or in the specification part of a subprogram. Any object being declared that uses this nonconstant expression and is not a dummy argument is called an *automatic object*.

An attribute cannot be repeated in a given type declaration statement, nor can an entity be explicitly given the same attribute more than once in a scoping unit.

initialization_expr must be specified if the statement contains the **PARAMETER** attribute. If *initialization_expr* is specified and **PARAMETER** is not, the object is a variable that is initially defined. *a* becomes defined with the value determined by *initialization_expr*, in accordance with the rules for intrinsic assignment. If the variable is an array, its shape must be specified either in the type declaration statement or in a previous specification statement in the same scoping unit. A variable or variable subobject cannot be initialized more than once. The presence of *initialization_expr* implies that *a* is a saved object, except for an object with the **PARAMETER** attribute or in a named common block.

An *array_spec* specified in the *entity_decl* takes precedence over the *array_spec* in the **DIMENSION** attribute.

An array function result that does not have the **POINTER** attribute must have an explicit-shape array specification.

If the entity declared is a function, it must not have an accessible explicit interface unless it is an intrinsic function.

Examples

```
REAL, POINTER :: RPTR
REAL, TARGET  :: RTAR
```

Related Information

- "Real" on page 23
- "Initialization Expressions" on page 66
- "How Type Is Determined" on page 33, for details on the implicit typing rules
- "Array Declarators" on page 43
- "Automatic Objects" on page 22
- "DATA" on page 216, for details on initial values

RETURN

Purpose

The **RETURN** statement:

- In a function subprogram, ends the execution of the subprogram and returns control to the referencing statement. The value of the function is available to the referencing procedure.
- In a subroutine subprogram, ends the subprogram and transfers control to the first executable statement after the procedure reference or to an alternate return point, if one is specified.

Format

```
►►──RETURN──────────────────────────────────────────►◄
           └─int_expr─┘
```

    int_expr   is a scalar integer expression

Rules

int_expr can be specified in a subroutine subprogram only, and it specifies an alternate return point. Letting *m* be the value of *int_expr*, if $1 \le m \le$ the number of asterisks in the **SUBROUTINE** or **ENTRY** statement, the *m*th asterisk in the dummy argument list is selected. Control then returns to the invoking procedure at the statement whose statement label is specified as the *m*th alternate return specifier in the **CALL** statement. For example, if the value of *m* is 5, control returns to the statement whose statement label is specified as the fifth alternate return specifier in the **CALL** statement.

If *int_expr* is omitted or if its value (*m*) is not in the range 1 through the number of asterisks in the **SUBROUTINE** or **ENTRY** statement, a normal return is executed. Control returns to the invoking procedure at the statement following the **CALL** statement.

Executing a **RETURN** statement terminates the association between the dummy arguments of the subprogram and the actual arguments supplied to that instance of the subprogram. All entities local to the subprogram become undefined, except as noted under "Events Causing Undefinition" on page 36.

A subprogram can contain more than one **RETURN** statement, but it does not require one. An **END** statement in a function or subroutine subprogram has the same effect as a **RETURN** statement.

Examples

```
CALL SUB(A,B)
CONTAINS
  SUBROUTINE SUB(A,B)
    INTEGER :: A,B
    IF (A.LT.B)
      RETURN              ! Control returns to the calling procedure
    ELSE
     ⋮
    END IF
  END SUBROUTINE
END
```

Related Information

- "Asterisks as Dummy Arguments" on page 137
- "Actual Argument Specification" on page 130 for a description of alternate return points
- "Events Causing Undefinition" on page 36

REWIND

Purpose

The **REWIND** statement positions an external file connected for sequential access at the beginning of the first record of the file.

Format

```
►►──REWIND──┬─u────────────────┬──────────────────────►◄
            └─(─position_list─)─┘
```

u	is an external unit identifier. The value of *u* must not be an asterisk.
position_list	is a list that must contain one unit specifier ([**UNIT=**]*u*) and can also contain one of each of the other valid specifiers. The valid specifiers are:
[UNIT=] *u*	is a unit specifier in which *u* must be an external unit identifier whose value is not an asterisk. An external unit identifier refers to an external file that is represented by a scalar integer expression. If the optional characters **UNIT=** are omitted, *u* must be the first item in *position_list*.
IOSTAT= *ios*	is an input/output status specifier that specifies the status of the input/output operation. *ios* is a scalar variable of type default integer. When the **REWIND** statement finishes executing, *ios* is defined with:

- A zero value if no error condition occurs.
- A positive value if an error occurs.

ERR= *stmt_label*

is an error specifier that specifies the statement label of an executable statement in the same scoping unit to which control is to transfer in the case of an error. Coding the **ERR=** specifier suppresses error messages.

Rules

If the external file connected to the specified unit does not exist, the **REWIND** statement has no effect. If it exists, an end-of-file marker is created, if necessary, and the file is positioned at the beginning of the first record. If the file is already positioned at its initial point, the **REWIND** statement has no effect. The **REWIND** statement causes a subsequent **READ** or **WRITE** statement referring to *u* to read data from or write data to the first record of the external file associated with *u*.

If the **ERR=** and **IOSTAT=** specifiers are set and an error is encountered, transfer is made to the statement specified by the **ERR=** specifier and a positive integer value is assigned to *ios*.

Examples

```
REWIND (9, IOSTAT=IOSS)
```

Related Information

- "Input/Output Concepts" on page 141

SAVE

Purpose

The **SAVE** attribute specifies the names of objects and named common blocks whose definition status you want to retain after control returns from the subprogram where you define the variables and named common blocks.

Format

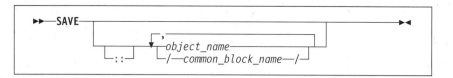

Rules

A **SAVE** statement without a list is treated as though it contains the names of all common items and local variables in the scoping unit. A common block name having the **SAVE** attribute has the effect of specifying all the entities in that named common block.

Within a function or subroutine subprogram, a variable whose name you specify with the **SAVE** attribute does not become undefined as a result of a **RETURN** or **END** statement in the subprogram.

object_name cannot be the name of a dummy argument, function result variable, procedure, automatic object, or common block entity.

If a local entity specified with the **SAVE** attribute (and not in a common block) is in a defined state at the time a **RETURN** or **END** statement is encountered in a subprogram, that entity is defined with the same value at the next reference of that subprogram. Saved objects are shared by all instances of the subprogram.

┌─ **Attributes Compatible with the SAVE Attribute** ─────────────┐

- ALLOCATABLE
- DIMENSION

- POINTER
- PRIVATE

- PUBLIC
- TARGET

└──┘

Examples

```
LOGICAL :: CALLED=.FALSE.
CALL SUB(CALLED)
CALLED=.TRUE.
CALL SUB(CALLED)
CONTAINS
  SUBROUTINE SUB(CALLED)
    INTEGER, SAVE :: J
    LOGICAL :: CALLED
    IF (CALLED.EQV..FALSE.) THEN
      J=2
    ELSE
      J=J+1
    ENDIF
    PRINT *, J                      ! Output on first call is 2
                                    ! Output on second call is 3

  END SUBROUTINE
END
```

Related Information

- "Definition Status of Variables" on page 34
- Item 2 under "FORTRAN 77 Compatibility" on page 415

SELECT CASE

Purpose

The **SELECT CASE** statement is the first statement of a **CASE** construct, which provides a concise syntax for selecting, at most, one of a number of statement blocks for execution.

Format

case_construct_name
> is a name given to the **CASE** construct for identification

case_expr   is a scalar expression of type integer, character or logical

Rules

When a **SELECT CASE** statement is executed, the *case_expr* is evaluated. The resulting value is called the case index, which is used for evaluating control flow within the case construct.

If the *case_construct_name* is specified, it must appear on the **END CASE** statement and optionally on any **CASE** statements within the construct.

Examples

```
ZERO: SELECT CASE(N)          ! start of CASE construct ZERO

    CASE DEFAULT ZERO
        OTHER: SELECT CASE(N) ! start of CASE construct OTHER
            CASE(:-1)
                SIGNUM = -1
            CASE(1:) OTHER
                SIGNUM = 1
        END SELECT OTHER
    CASE (0)
        SIGNUM = 0

END SELECT ZERO
```

Related Information

- "CASE Construct" on page 90
- "CASE" on page 196
- "END (Construct)" on page 237, for details on the **END SELECT** statement

---

SEQUENCE

Purpose

The **SEQUENCE** statement specifies that the order of the components in a derived-type definition establishes the storage sequence for objects of that type. Such a type becomes a *sequence derived type*.

Format

```
►►──SEQUENCE───────────────────────────────────────────────────►◄
```

Rules

The **SEQUENCE** statement can be specified only once in a derived-type definition.

If a component of a sequence derived type is of derived type, that derived type must also be a sequence derived type.

Use of sequence derived types can lead to misaligned data, which can adversely affect the performance of a program.

Examples

```
TYPE PERSON
  SEQUENCE
  CHARACTER*1 GENDER    ! Offset 0
  INTEGER(4) AGE        ! Offset 1
  CHARACTER(30) NAME    ! Offset 5
END TYPE PERSON
```

Related Information

- "Derived Types" on page 28
- "Derived Type" on page 223
- "END TYPE" on page 240

Statement Function

Purpose

A statement function defines a function in a single statement.

Format

►►—*name*—(—┬─────────────────────┬—)— = ───────────►
                    └─*dummy_argument_list*─┘

►—*scalar_expression*────────────────────────────►◄

name　　　　is the name of the statement function. It must not be supplied
　　　　　　　as a procedure argument.

dummy_argument
　　　　　　　can only appear once in the dummy argument list of any
　　　　　　　statement function. The dummy arguments have the scope of
　　　　　　　the statement function statement, and the same types and type
　　　　　　　parameters as the entities of the same names in the scoping unit
　　　　　　　containing the statement function.

Rules

A statement function is local to the scoping unit in which it is defined. It must
not be defined in the scope of a module.

name determines the data type of the value returned from the statement
function. If the data type of *name* does not match that of the scalar expression,
the value of the scalar expression is converted to the type of *name* in
accordance with the rules for assignment statements.

The names of the function and all the dummy arguments must be specified,
explicitly or implicitly, to be scalar data objects.

The scalar expression can be composed of constants, references to variables,
references to functions and function dummy procedures, and intrinsic
operations. If the expression contains a reference to a function or function
dummy procedure, the reference must not require an explicit interface, the
function must not require an explicit interface or be a transformational intrinsic,
and the result must be scalar. If an argument to a function or function dummy
procedure is array-valued, it must be an array name.

The scalar expression can reference another statement function that is either:

- declared previously in the same scoping unit, or

Statement Function

- declared in the host scoping unit.

Named constants and arrays whose elements are referenced in the expression must be declared earlier in the scoping unit or be made accessible by use or host association.

Variables that are referenced in the expression must be either:

- dummy arguments of the statement function, or
- accessible in the scoping unit

If an entity in the expression is typed by the implicit typing rules, its type must agree with the type and type parameters given in any subsequent type declaration statement.

An external function reference in the scalar expression must not cause any dummy arguments of the statement function to become undefined or redefined.

If the statement function is defined in an internal subprogram and if it has the same name as an accessible entity from the host, precede the statement function definition with an explicit declaration of the statement function name. For example, use a type declaration statement.

The length specification for a statement function of type character or a statement function dummy argument of type character must be a constant specification expression.

Examples

```
PARAMETER (PI = 3.14159)
REAL AREA,CIRCUM,R,RADIUS
AREA(R) = PI * (R**2)              ! Define statement functions
CIRCUM(R) = 2 * PI * R             !   AREA and CIRCUM

! Reference the statement functions
PRINT *,'The area is: ',AREA(RADIUS)
PRINT *,'The circumference is: ',CIRCUM(RADIUS)
```

Related Information

- "Dummy Arguments" on page 131
- "Function Reference" on page 128
- "How Type Is Determined" on page 33, for information on how the type of the statement function is determined

STOP

Purpose

When the **STOP** statement is executed, the program stops executing and the character constant or digit string, if specified, is available in a processor-dependent manner.

Format

```
►►─STOP──────────────────────────────────────────────►◄
         ┬─char_constant─┬
         └─digit_string──┘
```

char_constant
    is a scalar default character constant

digit_string   is a string of one through five digits

Rules

A **STOP** statement cannot terminate the range of a **DO** or **DO WHILE** construct.

Examples

```
STOP 'Abnormal Termination'    ! Output:  STOP Abnormal Termination
END

STOP                           ! No output
END
```

SUBROUTINE

Purpose

The **SUBROUTINE** statement is the first statement of a subroutine subprogram.

Format

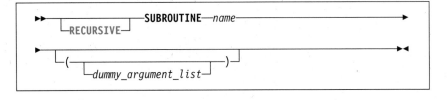

name   is the name of the subroutine subprogram

Rules

The subroutine name cannot appear in any other statement in the scope of the subroutine, unless recursion has been specified.

The **RECURSIVE** keyword must be specified if, directly or indirectly,

- the subroutine invokes itself.
- the subroutine invokes a procedure defined by an **ENTRY** statement in the same subprogram.
- an entry procedure in the same subprogram invokes itself.
- an entry procedure in the same subprogram invokes another entry procedure in the same subprogram.
- an entry procedure in the same subprogram invokes the subprogram defined by the **SUBROUTINE** statement.

If the **RECURSIVE** keyword is specified, the procedure interface is explicit within the subprogram.

Examples

```
RECURSIVE SUBROUTINE SUB(X,Y)
  INTEGER X,Y
  IF (X.LT.Y) THEN
    RETURN
  ELSE
    CALL SUB(X,Y+1)
  END IF
END SUBROUTINE SUB
```

Related Information

- "Function and Subroutine Subprograms" on page 127
- "Dummy Arguments" on page 131
- "Recursion" on page 140
- "CALL" on page 194
- "ENTRY" on page 243
- "RETURN" on page 324
- "Definition Status of Variables" on page 34

TARGET

Purpose

Variables with the **TARGET** attribute can become pointer targets.

Format

Rules

Although the target of a pointer can also be a pointer, this target cannot have the **TARGET** attribute.

A target cannot appear in an **EQUIVALENCE** statement.

```
┌─── Attributes Compatible with the TARGET Attribute ───┐
│                                                        │
│   •  ALLOCATABLE      •  OPTIONAL        •  PUBLIC      │
│   •  DIMENSION        •  PRIVATE         •  SAVE        │
│   •  INTENT                                             │
│                                                        │
└────────────────────────────────────────────────────────┘
```

Examples

```
REAL, POINTER :: A,B
REAL, TARGET  :: C = 3.14
B => C
A => B        ! A points to C
```

Related Information

- "POINTER" on page 305
- "ALLOCATED (ARRAY)" on page 367
- "DEALLOCATE" on page 221
- "Pointer Assignment" on page 84
- "Pointer Association" on page 106

TYPE

Purpose

A **TYPE** type declaration statement specifies the type and attributes of objects and functions of derived type. Initial values can be assigned to objects.

Format

```
►►──TYPE──(──type_name──)──────────────────────────────────►

                          └──:─:──┘
                          └──,──attr_spec_list──:─:──┘

►──entity_decl_list────────────────────────────────────────►◄
```

where:

attr_spec
ALLOCATABLE
DIMENSION (*array_spec*)
EXTERNAL
INTENT (*intent_spec*)
OPTIONAL
PARAMETER
POINTER
PRIVATE
PUBLIC
SAVE
TARGET

type_name   is the name of a derived type

attr_spec   For detailed information on rules about a particular attribute, refer to the statement of the same name.

intent_spec is either **IN**, **OUT**, or **INOUT**

::   is the double colon separator. It is required if attributes are specified or if = *initialization_expr* is used.

array_spec   is a list of dimension bounds

TYPE

entity_decl

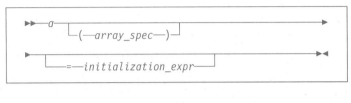

a	is an object name or function name. *array_spec* cannot be specified for a function name.

initialization_expr
provides an initial value, by means of an initialization expression, for the entity specified by the immediately preceding name

Rules

Entities in type declaration statements are constrained by the rules of any attributes specified for the entities, as detailed in the corresponding attribute statements.

Once a derived type has been defined, you can use it to define your data items using the **TYPE** type declaration statement. When an entity is explicitly declared to be of a derived type, that derived type must have been previously defined in the scoping unit or is accessible by use or host association.

The data object becomes an *object of derived type* or a *structure*. Each *structure component* is a subobject of the object of derived type.

If you specify the **DIMENSION** attribute, you are creating an array whose elements have a data type of that derived type.

Other than in specification statements, you can use objects of derived type as actual and dummy arguments, and they can also appear as items in input/output lists (unless the object has a component with the **POINTER** attribute), assignment statements, structure constructors, and the right side of a statement function definition. If a structure component is not accessible, a derived-type object cannot be used in an input/output list or as a structure constructor.

Objects of nonsequence derived type cannot be used as data items in **EQUIVALENCE** and **COMMON** statements.

A nonsequence derived-type dummy argument must specify a derived type that is accessible through use or host association to ensure that the same derived-type definition defines both the actual and dummy arguments.

The type declaration statement overrides the implicit type rules in effect.

An object cannot be initialized in a type declaration statement if it is a dummy argument, allocatable array, pointer, function result, object in blank common, external name, intrinsic name, or automatic object. The object may be initialized if it appears in a named common block in a block data program unit.

The specification expression of an *array_spec* can be a nonconstant expression if the specification expression appears in an interface body or in the specification part of a subprogram. Any object being declared that uses this nonconstant expression and is not a dummy argument is called an *automatic object*.

An attribute cannot be repeated in a given type declaration statement, nor can an entity be explicitly given the same attribute more than once in a scoping unit.

initialization_expr must be specified if the statement contains the **PARAMETER** attribute. If *initialization_expr* is specified and **PARAMETER** is not, the object is a variable that is initially defined. *a* becomes defined with the value determined by *initialization_expr*, in accordance with the rules for intrinsic assignment. If the variable is an array, its shape must be specified either in the type declaration statement or in a previous specification statement in the same scoping unit. A variable or variable subobject cannot be initialized more than once. The presence of *initialization_expr* implies that *a* is a saved object, except for an object with the **PARAMETER** attribute or in a named common block.

An *array_spec* specified in the *entity_decl* takes precedence over the *array_spec* in the **DIMENSION** attribute.

An array function result that does not have the **POINTER** attribute must have an explicit-shape array specification.

If the entity declared is a function, it must not have an accessible explicit interface unless it is an intrinsic function. The derived type can be specified on the **FUNCTION** statement, provided the derived type is defined within the body of the function or is accessible via host or use association.

TYPE

Examples

```
TYPE PEOPLE                              ! Defining derived type PEOPLE
  INTEGER AGE
  CHARACTER*20 NAME
END TYPE PEOPLE
TYPE(PEOPLE) :: SMITH = PEOPLE(25,'John Smith')
END
```

Related Information

- "Derived Types" on page 28
- "Derived Type" on page 223
- "Initialization Expressions" on page 66
- "How Type Is Determined" on page 33, for details on the implicit typing rules
- "Array Declarators" on page 43
- "Automatic Objects" on page 22
- "DATA" on page 216, for details on initial values

Type Declaration

Purpose

A type declaration statement specifies the type, length, and attributes of objects and functions. Initial values can be assigned to objects.

Format

```
►►─type_spec─┬──────────────────────┬─entity_decl_list─────►◄
             │       ┌─::─┐          │
             └─,─attr_spec_list─::─┘
```

where:

type_spec	attr_spec
CHARACTER [*char_selector*]	**ALLOCATABLE**
COMPLEX [*kind_selector*]	**DIMENSION** (*array_spec*)
DOUBLE PRECISION	**EXTERNAL**
INTEGER [*kind_selector*]	**INTENT** (*intent_spec*)
LOGICAL [*kind_selector*]	**INTRINSIC**
REAL [*kind_selector*]	**OPTIONAL**
TYPE (*type_name*)	**PARAMETER**
	POINTER
	PRIVATE
	PUBLIC
	SAVE
	TARGET

type_name   is the name of a derived type

kind_selector

```
►►────(──────────────────int_initialization_expr─)►◄
        └─KIND─ = ─┘
```

represents one of the permissible length specifications for its associated type. *int_literal_constant* cannot specify a kind type parameter.

char_selector specifies the character length

Type Declaration

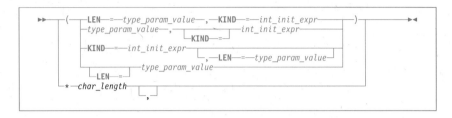

type_param_value
: is a specification expression or an asterisk (*)

int_init_expr
: is a scalar integer initialization expression that must be nonnegative and must specify a representation method that exists on the processor

char_length
: is either a scalar integer literal constant (which cannot specify a kind type parameter) or a type_param_value enclosed in parentheses

attr_spec
: For detailed information on rules about a particular attribute, refer to the statement of the same name.

intent_spec
: is either **IN**, **OUT**, or **INOUT**

::
: is the double colon separator. It is required if attributes are specified or if = initialization_expr is used.

array_spec
: is a list of dimension bounds

entity_decl

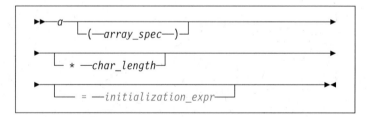

a
: is an object name or function name. array_spec cannot be specified for a function name.

initialization_expr
: provides an initial value, by mean of an initialization expression, for the entity specified by the immediately preceding name

Rules

Entities in type declaration statements are constrained by the rules of any attributes specified for the entities, as detailed in the corresponding attribute statements.

The type declaration statement overrides the implicit type rules in effect. You can use a type declaration statement that confirms the type of an intrinsic function. The appearance of a generic or specific intrinsic function name in a type declaration statement does not cause the name to lose its intrinsic property.

An object cannot be initialized in a type declaration statement if it is a dummy argument, allocatable array, pointer, function result, object in blank common, external name, intrinsic name, or automatic object. The object may be initialized if it appears in a named common block in a block data program unit.

The specification expression of a *type_param_value* or an *array_spec* can be a nonconstant expression if the specification expression appears in an interface body or in the specification part of a subprogram. Any object being declared that uses this nonconstant expression and is not a dummy argument is called an *automatic object*.

An attribute cannot be repeated in a given type declaration statement, nor can an entity be explicitly given the same attribute more than once in a scoping unit.

initialization_expr must be specified if the statement contains the **PARAMETER** attribute. If *initialization_expr* is specified and **PARAMETER** is not, the object is a variable that is initially defined. *a* becomes defined with the value determined by *initialization_expr*, in accordance with the rules for intrinsic assignment. If the variable is an array, its shape must be specified either in the type declaration statement or in a previous specification statement in the same scoping unit. A variable or variable subobject cannot be initialized more than once. The presence of *initialization_expr* implies that *a* is a saved object, except for an object with the **PARAMETER** attribute or in a named common block.

An *array_spec* specified in an *entity_decl* takes precedence over the *array_spec* in the **DIMENSION** attribute. A *char_length* specified in an *entity_decl* takes precedence over a *char_length* specified in *char_selector*.

An array function result that does not have the **POINTER** attribute must have an explicit-shape array specification.

If the entity declared is a function, it must not have an accessible explicit interface unless it is an intrinsic function.

Type Declaration

The optional comma after *char_length* in a **CHARACTER** type declaration statement is permitted only if no double colon separator (::) appears in the statement.

If the **CHARACTER** type declaration statement is in the scope of a module, block data program unit, or main program, and you specify the length of the entity as inherited length, the entity must be the name of a named character constant. The character constant assumes the length of its corresponding expression defined by the **PARAMETER** attribute.

If the **CHARACTER** type declaration statement is in the scope of a procedure and the length of the entity is inherited, the entity name must be the name of a dummy argument or a named character constant. If the statement is in the scope of an external function, it can also be the function or entry name in a **FUNCTION** or **ENTRY** statement in the same program unit. If the entity name is the name of a dummy argument, the dummy argument assumes the length of the associated actual argument for each reference to the procedure. If the entity name is the name of a character constant, the character constant assumes the length of its corresponding expression defined by the **PARAMETER** attribute. If the entity name is a function or entry name, the entity assumes the length specified in the calling scoping unit.

The length of a character function is either a specification expression (which must be a constant expression if the function type is not declared in an interface block) or it is an asterisk, indicating the length of a dummy procedure name. The length cannot be an asterisk if the function is an internal or module function, recursive, or if the function returns array or pointer values.

Examples

```
CHARACTER(KIND=1,LEN=6) APPLES /'APPLES'/
CHARACTER*7, TARGET :: ORANGES = 'ORANGES'
CALL TEST(APPLES)
END

SUBROUTINE  TEST(VARBL)
  CHARACTER*(*), OPTIONAL :: VARBL    ! VARBL inherits a length of 6

  COMPLEX, DIMENSION (2,3) :: ABC(3) ! ABC has 3 (not 6) array elements
  REAL, POINTER :: XCONST

  TYPE PEOPLE                         ! Defining derived type PEOPLE
    INTEGER AGE
    CHARACTER*20 NAME
  END TYPE PEOPLE
  TYPE(PEOPLE) :: SMITH = PEOPLE(25,'John Smith')
END
```

Related Information

- "Data Types and Data Objects" on page 21
- "Initialization Expressions" on page 66
- "How Type Is Determined" on page 33, for details on the implicit typing rules
- "Array Declarators" on page 43
- "Automatic Objects" on page 22
- "DATA" on page 216, for details on initial values

USE

Purpose

The **USE** statement is a module reference that provides local access to the public entities of a module.

Format

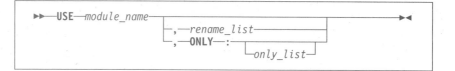

rename	is the assignment of a local name to an accessible data entity:
	local_name => use_name
only	is a *rename*, a generic specification, or the name of a variable, procedure, derived type, named constant, or namelist group

Rules

The **USE** statement can only appear prior to all other statements in *specification_part*. Multiple **USE** statements may appear within a scoping unit.

Entities in the scoping unit become *use-associated* with the module entities, and the local entities have the attributes of the corresponding module entities.

In addition to the **PRIVATE** attribute, the **ONLY** clause of the **USE** statement provides further constraint on which module entities can be accessed. If the **ONLY** clause is specified, only entities named in the *only_list* are accessible. If no list follows the keyword, no module entities are accessible. If the **ONLY** clause is absent, all public entities are accessible.

If a scoping unit contains multiple **USE** statements, all specifying the same module, and one of the statements does not include the **ONLY** clause, all public entities are accessible. If each **USE** statement includes the **ONLY** clause, only those entities named in one or more of the *only_lists* are accessible.

You can rename an accessible entity for local use. A module entity can be accessed by more than one local name. If no renaming is specified, the name of the use-associated entity becomes the local name. The local name of a use-associated entity cannot be redeclared. However, if the **USE** statement appears in the scoping unit of a module, the local name can appear in a **PUBLIC** or **PRIVATE** statement.

If multiple generic interfaces that are accessible to a scoping unit have the same local name, operator, or assignment, they are treated as a single generic interface. In such a case, one of the generic interfaces can contain an interface body to an accessible procedure with the same name. Otherwise, any two different use-associated entities can only have the same name if the name is not used to refer to an entity in the scoping unit. If a use-associated entity and host entity share the same name, the host entity becomes inaccessible through host association by that name.

A module must not reference itself, either directly or indirectly. For example, module X cannot reference module Y if module Y references module X.

Consider the situation where a module (e.g., module B) has access through use association to the public entities of another module (e.g., module A). The accessibility of module B's local entities (which includes those entities that are use-associated with entities from module A) to other program units is determined by the **PRIVATE** and **PUBLIC** attributes, or, if absent, through the default accessibility of module B. Of course, other program units can access the public entities of module A directly.

Examples

```
MODULE A
   REAL :: X=5.0
END MODULE A
MODULE B
   USE A
   PRIVATE :: X                    !  X cannot be accessed through module B
   REAL :: C=80, D=50
END MODULE B
PROGRAM TEST
   INTEGER :: TX=7
   CALL SUB
   CONTAINS

   SUBROUTINE SUB
   USE B, ONLY : C
   USE B, T1 => C
   USE B, TX => C                  !  C is given another local name
   USE A
   PRINT *, TX                     !  Value written is 80 because use-associated
                                   !  entity overrides host entity

   END SUBROUTINE
END
```

USE

Related Information

- "Modules" on page 122
- "PRIVATE" on page 310
- "PUBLIC" on page 313
- "Order of Statements and Execution Sequence" on page 18

WHERE

Purpose

The **WHERE** statement masks the evaluation of array expressions and array assignment. The **WHERE** statement can be the initial statement of the **WHERE** construct.

Format

```
►►──WHERE──(──mask_expr──)──────────────────────►◄
                          └─assignment_stmt─┘
```

mask_expr   is a logical array expression

Rules

If *assignment_stmt* is present, the **WHERE** statement is not part of a **WHERE** construct. If *assignment_stmt* is absent, the **WHERE** statement is the first statement of the **WHERE** construct and an **END WHERE** statement must follow.

The logical array expression determines the mask.

In each *assignment_stmt*, the *mask_expr* and the variable being defined must be arrays of the same shape. *assignment_stmt* must not be a defined assignment.

When an assignment statement in a **WHERE** statement is executed, the expression of the assignment statement is evaluated for all the elements where *mask_expr* is true and the result is assigned to the corresponding elements of the variable according to the rules of intrinsic assignment.

If a nonelemental function reference occurs in the expression or variable of an assignment statement, the function is evaluated without any masked control by *mask_expr*, that is, all of its argument expressions are fully evaluated and the function is fully evaluated. If the result is an array and the reference is not within the argument list of a nonelemental function, elements corresponding to true values in *mask_expr* are selected for use in evaluating each expression.

If an elemental intrinsic operation or function reference occurs in the expression or variable of an assignment statement and is not within the argument list of a nonelemental function reference, the operation is performed or the function is evaluated only for the elements corresponding to true values in *mask_expr*.

WHERE

If an array constructor appears in an assignment statement, the array constructor is evaluated without any masked control by *mask_expr* and then the assignment statement is evaluated.

If the **WHERE** statement is not the first statement of a **WHERE** construct, it can be used as the terminal statement of a **DO** or **DO WHILE** construct.

Examples

```
REAL, DIMENSION(10) :: A,B,C

!   In the following WHERE statement, the LOG of an element of A
!   is assigned to the corresponding element of B only if that
!   element of A is a positive value.

WHERE (A>0.0) B = LOG(A)
    ⋮
END
```

Related Information

- "WHERE Construct" on page 81
- "ELSEWHERE" on page 234
- "END (Construct)" on page 237, for details on the **END WHERE** statement

WRITE

Purpose

The **WRITE** statement is a data transfer output statement.

Format

```
►►──WRITE──(──io_control_list──)──┬─────────────────────┬──►◄
                                  └──output_item_list──┘
```

output_item   is an output list item. An output list specifies the data to be transferred. An output list item can be:

- A variable name. An array is treated as if all of its elements were specified in the order they are arranged in storage.

  A pointer must be associated with a target and an allocatable array must be allocated. A derived-type object cannot have any ultimate component that is outside the scoping unit of this statement. The evaluation of output_item cannot result in a derived-type object that contains a pointer. The structure components of a structure in a formatted statement are treated as if they appear in the order of the derived-type definition; in an unformatted statement, the structure components are treated as a single value in their internal representation (including padding).

- An expression
- An implied-**DO** list, as described on page 355

io_control   is a list that must contain one unit specifier (**UNIT=**), and can also contain one of each of the other valid specifiers:

[UNIT=] u   is a unit specifier that specifies the unit to be used in the output operation. u is an external unit identifier or internal file identifier.

An external unit identifier refers to an external file. It is one of the following:

- A scalar integer expression
- An asterisk

An internal file identifier refers to an internal file. It is the name of a default character variable, which cannot be an array section with a vector subscript.

If the optional characters **UNIT=** are omitted, u must be the first item in io_control_list. If **UNIT=** is specified, **FMT=** must also be specified.

WRITE

[FMT=] *format*

is a format specifier that specifies the format to be used in the output operation. *format* is a format identifier that can be:

- The statement label of a **FORMAT** statement. The **FORMAT** statement must be in the same scoping unit.

- The name of a scalar default integer variable that was assigned the statement label of a **FORMAT** statement. The **FORMAT** statement must be in the same scoping unit.

- A character constant that must begin with a left parenthesis and end with a right parenthesis. Only the format codes listed under "FORMAT" on page 252 can be used between the parentheses. Blank characters can precede the left parenthesis, or follow the right parenthesis.

- A character variable that contains character data whose left-most character positions constitute a valid format. A valid format begins with a left parenthesis and ends with a right parenthesis. Only the format codes described in the **FORMAT** statement can be used between the parentheses. Blank characters can precede the left parenthesis, or follow the right parenthesis. If *format* is an array element, the format identifier must not exceed the length of the array element.

- An array of noncharacter intrinsic type. The data must be a valid format identifier as described under character array.

- Any character expression, except one involving concatenation of an operand that specifies inherited length, unless the operand is the name of a constant.

- An asterisk, specifying list-directed formatting.

If the optional characters **FMT=** are omitted, *format* must be the second item in *io_control_list*, and the first item must be the unit specifier with **UNIT=** omitted. Both **NML=** and **FMT=** cannot be specified in the same output statement.

REC= *integer_expr*

is a record specifier that specifies the number of the record to be written in a file connected for direct access. The **REC=** specifier is only permitted for direct output. *integer_expr* is an integer expression whose value is positive. A record specifier is not valid if formatting is list-directed or if the unit specifier specifies an internal file. The record specifier represents the relative position of a record within a file. The relative position number of the first record is 1.

IOSTAT= *ios* is an input/output status specifier that specifies the status of the input/output operation. *ios* is a scalar variable of type default integer. Coding the **IOSTAT=** specifier suppresses error messages. When the statement finishes execution, *ios* is defined with:

- A zero value if no error condition occurs.
- A positive value if an error occurs.

ERR= *stmt_label*

is an error specifier that specifies the statement label of an executable statement in the same scoping unit to which control is to transfer in the case of an error. Coding the **ERR=** specifier suppresses error messages.

[NML=] *name*

is a namelist specifier that specifies the name of a namelist list that you have previously defined. If the optional characters **NML=** are not specified, the namelist name must appear as the second parameter in the list, and the first item must be the unit specifier with **UNIT=** omitted. If both **NML=** and **UNIT=** are specified, all the parameters can appear in any order.

ADVANCE= *char_expr*

is an advance specifier that determines whether nonadvancing output occurs for this statement. *char_expr* is a character expression that must evaluate to **YES** or **NO**. If **NO** is specified, nonadvancing output occurs. If **YES** is specified, advancing, formatted sequential output occurs. The default value is **YES**. **ADVANCE=** can be specified only in a formatted sequential **WRITE** statement with an explicit format specification that does not specify an internal file unit specifier.

Implied-DO List

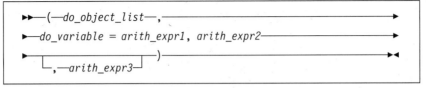

do_object   is an output list item

do_variable   is a named scalar variable of type integer, default real, or double precision

WRITE

arith_expr1, *arith_expr2*, and *arith_expr3*
> are scalar expressions of type integer, default real, or double precision

The range of an implied-**DO** list is the list *do_object_list*. The iteration count and values of the **DO** variable are established from *arith_expr1*, *arith_expr2*, and *arith_expr3*, the same as for a **DO** statement. When the implied-**DO** list is executed, the items in the *do_object_list* are specified once for each iteration of the implied-**DO** list, with the appropriate substitution of values for any occurrence of the **DO** variable.

Rules

Variables specified for the **IOSTAT=** and **NUM=** specifiers must not be associated with any output list item, namelist list item, or **DO** variable of an implied-**DO** list. If such a specifier variable is an array element, its subscript values must not be affected by the data transfer, any implied-**DO** processing, or the definition or evaluation of any other specifier.

If the **ERR=** and **IOSTAT=** specifiers are set and an error is encountered, transfer is made to the statement specified by the **ERR=** specifier and a positive integer value is assigned to *ios*.

PRINT format has the same effect as WRITE(*,format).

Examples

    WRITE (6,FMT='(10F8.2)') (LOG(A(I)),I=1,N+9,K),G

Related Information

- "Input/Output Concepts" on page 141

Part 3. Intrinsic Procedures

Chapter 10. Intrinsic Procedures

Fortran defines a number of procedures, called intrinsic procedures, that are available to any program. This chapter is an alphabetical reference to these procedures.

Related Information: "Intrinsic Procedures" on page 129 provides background information that you may need to be familiar with before proceeding with this chapter.

"INTRINSIC" on page 283 is a related statement.

Classes of Intrinsic Procedures

There are four classes of intrinsic procedures: inquiry functions, elemental procedures, transformational functions and subroutines.

Inquiry Intrinsic Functions

The result of an *inquiry function* depends on the properties of its principal argument, not the value of the argument. The value of the argument does not have to be defined.

ALLOCATED	LBOUND	RADIX
ASSOCIATED	**LEN**	RANGE
BIT_SIZE	MAXEXPONENT	SHAPE
DIGITS	MINEXPONENT	SIZE
EPSILON	PRECISION	TINY
HUGE	PRESENT	UBOUND
KIND		

Elemental Intrinsic Procedures

Some intrinsic functions and one intrinsic subroutine (**MVBITS**) are *elemental*. That is, they can be specified for scalar arguments, but also accept arguments that are arrays.

If all arguments are scalar, the result is a scalar.

If any argument is an array, all INTENT(OUT) and INTENT(INOUT) arguments must be arrays of the same shape and the remaining arguments must be conformable with them.

The shape of the result is the shape of the argument with the greatest rank. The elements of the result are the same as if the function was applied individually to the corresponding elements of each argument.

ABS	EXPONENT	MAX
ACHAR	FLOOR	MERGE
ACOS	FRACTION	MIN
ADJUSTL	IACHAR	MOD
ADJUSTR	IBCLR	MODULO
AIMAG	IBITS	MVBITS
AINT	IBSET	NEAREST
ANINT	ICHAR	NINT
ASIN	IEOR	NOT
ATAN	INDEX	REAL
ATAN2	INT	RRSPACING
BTEST	IOR	SCALE
CEILING	ISHFT	SCAN
CHAR	ISHFTC	SET_EXPONENT
CMPLX	LEN_TRIM	SIGN
CONJG	LGE	SIN
COS	LGT	SINH
COSH	LLE	SPACING
DBLE	LLT	SQRT
DIM	LOG	TAN
DPROD	LOG10	TANH
EXP	LOGICAL	VERIFY

Transformational Intrinsic Functions

All other intrinsic functions are classified as *transformational functions*. They generally accept array arguments and return array results that depend on the values of elements in the argument arrays.

ALL	MAXVAL	SELECTED_REAL_KIND
ANY	MINLOC	SPREAD
COUNT	MINVAL	SUM
CSHIFT	PACK	TRANSFER
DOT_PRODUCT	PRODUCT	TRANSPOSE
EOSHIFT	REPEAT	TRIM
MATMUL	RESHAPE	UNPACK
MAXLOC	SELECTED_INT_KIND	

For background information on arrays, see "Array Concepts" on page 41.

Intrinsic Subroutines

Some intrinsic procedures are subroutines. They perform a variety of tasks.

DATE_AND_TIME   RANDOM_NUMBER   SYSTEM_CLOCK
MVBITS   RANDOM_SEED

Data Representation Models

Integer Bit Model

The following model shows how the processor represents each bit of a nonnegative scalar integer object:

$$j = \sum_{k=0}^{s-1} w_k \times 2^k$$

j is the integer value

s is the number of bits

w_k is binary digit w located at position k

The examples of intrinsic functions in this section that require this model use the following integer kind type parameters and s parameters:

Integer Kind Parameter	s Parameter
1	8
2	16
4	32
8	64

The following intrinsic functions use this model:

BTEST   IBSET   ISHFTC
IAND   IEOR   MVBITS
IBCLR   IOR   NOT
IBITS   ISHFT

Integer Data Model

$$i = s \times \sum_{k=1}^{q} w_k \times r^{k-1}$$

i	is the integer value
s	is the sign (± 1)
q	is the number of digits (positive integer)
w_k	is a nonnegative digit $< r$
r	is the radix

The examples of intrinsic functions in this section that require this model use the following r and q parameters:

Integer Kind Parameter	r Parameter	q Parameter
1	2	7
2	2	15
4	2	31
8	2	63

The following intrinsic functions use this model:

DIGITS RADIX RANGE
HUGE

Real Data Model

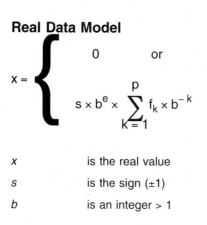

$$x = \begin{cases} 0 & \text{or} \\ s \times b^e \times \sum_{k=1}^{p} f_k \times b^{-k} \end{cases}$$

x	is the real value
s	is the sign (± 1)
b	is an integer > 1

e is an integer, where $e_{min} \leq e \leq e_{max}$

p is an integer > 1

f_k is a nonnegative integer $< b$ ($f_1 \neq 0$)

The examples of intrinsic functions in this section that require this model use the following parameters:

Real Kind parameter	b Parameter	p Parameter	e_{min} Parameter	e_{max} Parameter
4	2	24	-125	128
8	2	53	-1021	1024
16	2	106	-1021	1024

The following intrinsic functions use this model:

DIGITS	MINEXPONENT	RRSPACING
EPSILON	NEAREST	SCALE
EXPONENT	PRECISION	SET_EXPONENT
FRACTION	RADIX	SPACING
HUGE	RANGE	TINY
MAXEXPONENT		

Detailed Descriptions of Intrinsic Procedures

The following is an alphabetical list of all generic names for intrinsic procedures.

For each procedure, several items of information are listed.

Notes:

1. The argument names listed in the title can be used as the names for keyword arguments when calling the procedure.
2. For those procedures with specific names, a table lists each specific name along with information about the specific function.

   The column labelled "Pass as Arg?" indicates whether or not you can pass that specific name as an actual argument to a procedure. Only the specific name of an intrinsic procedure may be passed as an actual argument, and then only for some specific names. A specific name passed this way may only be referenced with scalar arguments.
3. The index contains entries for each specific name, if you know the specific name but not the generic one.

ABS (A)

Absolute value.

A   must be of type integer, real, or complex.

Class: Elemental function

Result Type and Attributes: The same as A except that if A is complex, the result is real.

Result Value

- If A is of type integer or real, the result is |A|.
- If A is of type complex with value (x,y), the result approximates

$$\sqrt{x^2 + y^2}$$

Examples: ABS ((3.0, 4.0)) has the value 5.0.

Specific Name	Argument Type	Result Type	Pass As Arg?
IABS	default integer	same as argument	yes
ABS	default real	default real	yes
DABS	double precision real	double precision real	yes
CABS	default complex	default real	yes

ACHAR (I)

Returns the character in a specified position of the ASCII collating sequence. It is the inverse of the IACHAR function.

I   must be of type integer.

Class: Elemental function

Result Type and Attributes: Character of length one with the same kind type parameter as KIND ('A').

Result Value

- If I has a value in the range $0 \le I \le 127$, the result is the character in position I of the ASCII collating sequence, provided that the character corresponding to I is representable.
- If I is outside the allowed value range, the result is processor-dependent.

Examples: ACHAR (88) has the value 'X'.

ACOS (X)

Arccosine (inverse cosine) function.

X   must be of type real with a value that satisfies the inequality |X| ≤ 1.

Class: Elemental function

Result Type and Attributes: Same as X.

Result Value

- It is expressed in radians and approximates arccos(X).
- It is in the range $0 \le ACOS(X) \le \pi$.

Examples: ACOS (1.0) has the value 0.0.

Specific Name	Argument Type	Result Type	Pass As Arg?
ACOS	default real	default real	yes
DACOS	double precision real	double precision real	yes

ADJUSTL (STRING)

Adjust to the left, removing leading blanks and inserting trailing blanks.

STRING must be of type character.

Class: Elemental function

Result Type and Attributes: Character of the same length and kind type parameter as STRING.

Result Value: The value of the result is the same as STRING except that any leading blanks have been deleted and the same number of trailing blanks have been inserted.

Examples: ADJUSTL ('ƀWORD') has the value 'WORDƀ'.

ADJUSTR (STRING)

Adjust to the right, removing trailing blanks and inserting leading blanks.

STRING must be of type character.

Class: Elemental function

Result Type and Attributes: Character of the same length and kind type parameter as STRING.

Result Value: The value of the result is the same as STRING except that any trailing blanks have been deleted and the same number of leading blanks have been inserted.

Examples: ADJUSTR ('WORDƀ') has the value 'ƀWORD'.

AIMAG (Z)

Imaginary part of a complex number.

Z   must be of type complex.

Class: Elemental function

Result Type and Attributes: Real with the same kind type parameter as Z.

Result Value: If Z has the value (x,y), the result has the value y.

Examples: AIMAG ((2.0, 3.0)) has the value 3.0.

Specific Name	Argument Type	Result Type	Pass As Arg?
AIMAG	default complex	default real	yes

AINT (A, KIND)

Truncates to a whole number.

A must be of type real.

KIND (optional) must be a scalar integer initialization expression.

Class: Elemental function

Result Type and Attributes

- The result type is real.
- If KIND is present, the kind type parameter is that specified by KIND; otherwise, the kind type parameter is that of A.

Result Value

- If $|A| < 1$, the result is zero.
- If $|A| \geq 1$, the result has a value equal to the integer whose magnitude is the largest integer that does not exceed the magnitude of A and whose sign is the same as the sign of A.

Examples

```
AINT(3.555) = 3.0
AINT(-3.555) = -3.0
```

Specific Name	Argument Type	Result Type	Pass As Arg?
AINT	default real	default real	yes
DINT	double precision real	double precision real	yes

ALL (MASK, DIM)

Determines if all values in an entire array, or in each vector along a single dimension, are true.

MASK is a logical array.

DIM (optional) is an integer scalar in the range $1 \leq DIM \leq rank(MASK)$. The corresponding actual argument must not be an optional dummy argument.

Class: Transformational function

Result Value: The result is a logical array with the same type and type parameters as MASK, and rank rank(MASK)-1. If the DIM is missing, or MASK has a rank of one, the result is a scalar of type logical.

The shape of the result is $(s_1, s_2, ..., s_{(DIM-1)}, s_{(DIM+1)}, ..., s_n)$, where n is the rank of MASK.

Each element in the result array is .TRUE. only if all the elements given by $MASK(m_1, m_2, ..., m_{(DIM-1)}, :, m_{(DIM+1)}, ..., m_n)$, are true. When the result is a scalar, either because DIM is not specified or because MASK is of rank one, it is .TRUE. only if all elements of MASK are true, or MASK has size zero.

Examples

```
! A is the array | 4 3 6 |, and B is the array | 3 5 2 |
!                | 2 4 1 |                      | 7 8 4 |

! Is every element in A less than the
! corresponding one in B?
      RES = ALL(A .LT. B)          ! result RES is false

! Are all elements in each column of A less than the
! corresponding column of B?
      RES = ALL(A .LT. B, DIM = 1) ! result RES is (f,t,f)

! Same question, but for each row of A and B.
      RES = ALL(A .LT. B, DIM = 2) ! result RES is (f,t)
```

ALLOCATED (ARRAY)

Indicate whether or not an allocatable array is currently allocated.

ARRAY is an allocatable array whose allocation status you want to know.

Class: Inquiry function

Result Type and Attributes: Default logical scalar.

Result Value: The result corresponds to the allocation status of ARRAY: .TRUE. if it is currently allocated, .FALSE. if it is not currently allocated, or undefined if its allocation status is undefined.

Examples

```
INTEGER, ALLOCATABLE, DIMENSION(:) :: A
PRINT *, ALLOCATED(A)      ! A is not allocated yet.
ALLOCATE (A(1000))
PRINT *, ALLOCATED(A)      ! A is now allocated.
END
```

Related Information: "Allocatable Arrays" on page 47, "ALLOCATE" on page 186, "Allocation Status" on page 38.

ANINT (A, KIND)

Nearest whole number.

A   must be of type real.

KIND (optional) must be a scalar integer initialization expression.

Class: Elemental function

Result Type and Attributes

• The result type is real.
• If KIND is present, the kind type parameter is that specified by KIND;

otherwise, the kind type parameter is that of A.

Result Value

• If A > 0, ANINT(A) = AINT(A + 0.5)
• If A ≤ 0, ANINT(A) = AINT(A - 0.5)

Note: The addition and subtraction of 0.5 are done in round-to-zero mode.

Examples

```
ANINT(3.555) = 4.0
ANINT(-3.555) = -4.0
```

Specific Name	Argument Type	Result Type	Pass As Arg?
ANINT	default real	default real	yes
DNINT	double precision real	double precision real	yes

ANY (MASK, DIM)

Determines if any of the values in an entire array, or in each vector along a single dimension, are true.

MASK is a logical array.

DIM (optional) is an integer scalar in the range 1 ≤ DIM ≤ rank(MASK). The corresponding actual argument must not be an optional dummy argument.

Class: Transformational function

Result Value: The result is a logical array of the same type and type parameters as MASK, and rank of rank(MASK)-1. If the DIM is missing, or MASK has a rank of one, the result is a scalar of type logical.

The shape of the result is $(s_1, s_2, ..., s_{(DIM-1)}, s_{(DIM+1)}, ..., s_n)$, where n is the rank of MASK.

Each element in the result array is .TRUE. if any of the elements given by $MASK(m_1, m_2, ..., m_{(DIM-1)}, :, m_{(DIM+1)}, ..., m_n)$ are true. When the result is a scalar, either because DIM is not specified or because MASK is of rank one, it is .TRUE. if any of the elements of MASK are true.

Examples

```
! A is the array | 9 -6 7 |, and B is the array | 2 7 8 |
!                | 3 -1 5 |                      | 5 6 9 |

! Is any element in A greater than or equal to the
! corresponding element in B?
      RES = ANY(A .GE. B)          ! result RES is true

! For each column in A, is there any element in the column
! greater than or equal to the corresponding element in B?
      RES = ANY(A .GE. B, DIM = 1) ! result RES is (t,f,f)

! Same question, but for each row of A and B.
      RES = ANY(A .GE. B, DIM = 2) ! result RES is (t,f)
```

ASIN (X)

Arcsine (inverse sine) function.

X   must be of type real. Its value must satisfy the inequality $|X| \leq 1$.

Class: Elemental function

Result Type and Attributes: Same as X.

Result Value

- It is expressed in radians and approximates arcsin(X).
- It is in the range $-\pi/2 \leq ASIN(X) \leq \pi/2$.

Examples: ASIN (1.0) approximates $\pi/2$.

Specific Name	Argument Type	Result Type	Pass As Arg?
ASIN	default real	default real	yes
DASIN	double precision real	double precision real	yes

ASSOCIATED (POINTER, TARGET)

Returns the association status of its pointer argument, or indicates whether the pointer is associated with the target.

POINTER
   A pointer whose association status you want to test. It can be of any type. Its association status must not be undefined.

TARGET (optional)
   A pointer or target that might or might not be associated with POINTER. Its association status must not be undefined.

Class: Inquiry function

Result Type and Attributes: Default logical scalar.

Result Value: If only the POINTER argument is specified, the result is .TRUE. if it is associated with any target and .FALSE. otherwise. If TARGET is also specified, the procedure tests whether POINTER is associated with TARGET, or with the same object that TARGET is associated with (if TARGET is also pointer).

The result is undefined if either POINTER or TARGET is associated with a zero-sized array, or if TARGET is a zero-sized array.

Objects with different types or shapes cannot be associated with each other.

Arrays with the same type and shape but different bounds can be associated with each other.

Examples

```
REAL, POINTER, DIMENSION(:,:) :: A
REAL, TARGET, DIMENSION(5,10) :: B, C

NULLIFY (A)
PRINT *, ASSOCIATED (A)   ! False, not associated yet

A => B
PRINT *, ASSOCIATED (A)   ! True, because A is
                          ! associated with B

PRINT *, ASSOCIATED (A,C) ! False, A is not
                          ! associated with C
END
```

ATAN (X)

Arctangent (inverse tangent) function.

X   must be of type real.

Class: Elemental function

Result Type and Attributes: Same as X.

Result Value

- It is expressed in radians and approximates arctan(X).
- It is in the range $-\pi/2 \le \text{ATAN}(X) \le \pi/2$.

Examples: ATAN (1.0) approximates $\pi/4$.

Specific Name	Argument Type	Result Type	Pass As Arg?
ATAN	default real	default real	yes
DATAN	double precision real	double precision real	yes

ATAN2 (Y, X)

Arctangent (inverse tangent) function. The result is the principal value of the nonzero complex number (X, Y) formed by the real arguments Y and X.

Y   must be of type real.

X   must be of the same type and kind type parameter as Y. If Y has the value zero, X must not have the value zero.

Class: Elemental function

Result Type and Attributes: Same as X.

Result Value

- It is expressed in radians and has a value equal to the principal value of the argument of the complex number (X, Y).
- It is in the range $-\pi < \text{ATAN2}(Y, X) \le \pi$.
- If $X \ne 0$, the result approximates arctan(Y/X).
- If $Y > 0$, the result is positive.
- If $Y < 0$, the result is negative.
- If $Y = 0$ and $X > 0$, the result is zero.
- If $Y = 0$ and $X < 0$, the result is π.
- If $X = 0$, the absolute value of the result is $\pi/2$.

Examples: ATAN2 (1.5574077, 1.0) has the value 1.0.

Given that

$$Y = \begin{vmatrix} 1 & 1 \\ -1 & -1 \end{vmatrix} \qquad X = \begin{vmatrix} -1 & 1 \\ -1 & 1 \end{vmatrix}$$

the value of ATAN2(Y,X) is approximately:

$$\text{ATAN2 (Y, X)} = \begin{vmatrix} 3\pi/4 & \pi/4 \\ -3\pi/4 & -\pi/4 \end{vmatrix}$$

BIT_SIZE •CEILING

Specific Name	Argument Type	Result Type	Pass As Arg?
ATAN2	default real	default real	yes
DATAN2	double precision real	double precision real	yes

BIT_SIZE (I)

Returns the number of bits in an integer type. Because only the type of the argument is examined, the argument need not be defined.

I   must be of type integer.

Class: Inquiry function

Result Type and Attributes: Scalar integer with the same kind type parameter as I.

Result Value: The result is the number of bits in the integer data type of the argument.

BTEST (I, POS)

Tests a bit of an integer value.

I   must be of type integer.

POS must be of type integer. It must be nonnegative and be less than BIT_SIZE (I).

Class: Elemental function

Result Type and Attributes: The result is of type default logical.

Result Value: The result has the value .TRUE. if bit POS of I has the value 1 and the value .FALSE. if bit POS of I has the value 0.

The bits are numbered 0 to BIT_SIZE(I)-1, from right to left.

Examples: BTEST (8, 3) has the value .TRUE..

```
If A has the value
  | 1 2 |
  | 3 4 |
the value of BTEST (A, 2) is
  | false false |
  | false true  |
and the value of BTEST (2, A) is
  | true  false |
  | false false |
```

See "Integer Bit Model" on page 361.

CEILING (A)

Returns the least integer greater than or equal to its argument.

A   must be of type real.

Class: Elemental function

Result Type and Attributes: Default integer.

Result Value: The result has a value equal to the least integer greater than or equal to A. The result is undefined if this value cannot be represented in the default integer type.

Examples: CEILING (3.7) has the value 4. CEILING (-3.7) has the value -3.

CHAR (I, KIND)

Returns the character in the given position of the collating sequence associated with the specified kind type parameter. It is the inverse of the function ICHAR.

I must be of type integer with a value in the range $0 \le I \le n-1$, where n is the number of characters in the collating sequence associated with the specified kind type parameter.

KIND (optional) must be a scalar integer initialization expression.

Class: Elemental function

Result Type and Attributes

- Character of length one.
- If KIND is present, the kind type parameter is that specified by KIND; otherwise, the kind type parameter is that of the default character type.

Result Value

- The result is the character in position I of the collating sequence associated with the specified kind type parameter.
- ICHAR (CHAR (I, KIND (C))) must have the value I for $0 \le I \le n-1$ and CHAR (ICHAR (C), KIND (C)) must have the value C for any representable character.

Examples: CHAR (88) has the value 'X' on a processor using the ASCII collating sequence.

Specific Name	Argument Type	Result Type	Pass As Arg?
CHAR	any integer	default character	no

CMPLX (X, Y, KIND)

Convert to complex type.

X must be of type integer, real, or complex.

Y (optional) must be of type integer or real. It must not be present if X is of type complex.

KIND (optional) must be a scalar integer initialization expression.

Class: Elemental function

Result Type and Attributes

- It is of type complex.
- If KIND is present, the kind type parameter is that specified by KIND; otherwise, the kind type parameter is that of the default real type.

Result Value

- If Y is absent and X is not complex, it is as if Y were present with the value zero.
- If Y is absent and X is complex, it is as if Y were present with the value AIMAG(X).
- CMPLX(X, Y, KIND) has the complex value whose real part is REAL(X, KIND) and whose imaginary part is REAL(Y, KIND).

Examples: CMPLX (-3) has the value (-3.0, 0.0).

CONJG (Z)

Conjugate of a complex number.

Z   must be of type complex.

Class: Elemental function

Result Type and Attributes: Same as Z.

Result Value: Given Z has the value (x, y), the result has the value (x, -y).

Examples: CONJG ((2.0, 3.0)) has the value (2.0, -3.0).

Specific Name	Argument Type	Result Type	Pass As Arg?
CONJG	default complex	default complex	yes

COS (X)

Cosine function.

X   must be of type real or complex.

Class: Elemental function

Result Type and Attributes: Same as X.

Result Value

- It has a value that approximates cos(X).
- If X is of type real, X is regarded as a value in radians.
- If X is of type complex, the real part of X is regarded as a value in radians.

Examples: COS (1.0) has the value 0.54030231 (approximately).

Specific Name	Argument Type	Result Type	Pass As Arg?
COS	default real	default real	yes
DCOS	double precision real	double precision real	yes
CCOS	default complex	default complex	yes

COSH (X)

Hyperbolic cosine function.

X   must be of type real.

Class: Elemental function

Result Type and Attributes: Same as X.

Result Value: The result value approximates cosh(X).

Examples: COSH (1.0) has the value 1.5430806 (approximately).

Specific Name	Argument Type	Result Type	Pass As Arg?
COSH	default real	default real	yes
DCOSH	double precision real	double precision real	yes

COUNT (MASK, DIM)

Counts the number of true array elements in an entire logical array, or in each vector along a single dimension. Typically, the logical array is one that is used as a mask in another intrinsic.

MASK is a logical array.

DIM (optional) is an integer scalar in the range $1 \leq \text{DIM} \leq \text{rank}(\text{MASK})$. The corresponding actual argument must not be an optional dummy argument.

Class: Transformational function

Result Value: If DIM is present, the result is an integer array of rank rank(MASK)-1. If DIM is missing, or MASK has a rank of one, the result is a scalar of type integer.

Each element of the resulting array ($R(s_1, s_2, ..., s_{(DIM-1)}, s_{(DIM+1)}, ..., s_n)$) equals the number of elements that are true in MASK along the corresponding dimension ($s_1, s_2, ..., s_{(DIM-1)}, :, s_{(DIM+1)}, ..., s_n$).

If MASK is a zero-sized array, the result equals zero.

Examples

```
! A is the array │ T F F │, and B is the array │ F F T │
!                │ F T T │                      │ T T T │

! How many corresponding elements in A and B
! are equivalent?
    RES = COUNT(A .EQV. B)        ! result RES is 3

! How many corresponding elements are equivalent
! in each column?
    RES = COUNT(A .EQV. B, DIM=1) ! result RES is (0,2,1)

! Same question, but for each row.
    RES = COUNT(A .EQV. B, DIM=2) ! result RES is (1,2)
```

CSHIFT (ARRAY, SHIFT, DIM)

Shifts the elements of all vectors along a given dimension of an array. The shift is circular; that is, elements shifted off one end are inserted again at the other end.

ARRAY is an array of any type.

SHIFT is an integer expression of rank rank(ARRAY)-1.

DIM (optional) is an integer scalar in the range $1 \leq \text{DIM} \leq \text{rank}(\text{ARRAY})$. If absent, it defaults to 1.

Class: Transformational function

Result Value: The result is an array with the same shape and the same data type as ARRAY.

If SHIFT is a scalar, the same shift is applied to each vector. Otherwise, each vector ARRAY($s_1, s_2, ..., s_{(DIM-1)}, :, s_{(DIM+1)}, ..., s_n$) is shifted according to the corresponding value in SHIFT($s_1, s_2, ..., s_{(DIM-1)}, s_{(DIM+1)}, ..., s_n$).

The absolute value of SHIFT determines the amount of shift. The sign of SHIFT determines the direction of the shift:

Positive SHIFT
moves each element of the vector toward the beginning of the vector.

Negative SHIFT
moves each element of the vector toward the end of the vector.

Zero SHIFT
does no shifting. The value of the vector remains unchanged.

DATE_AND_TIME

Examples

```
! A is the array | A D G |
!                | B E H |
!                | C F I |

! Shift the first column down one, the second column
! up one, and leave the third column unchanged.
       RES = CSHIFT (A, SHIFT = (/-1,1,0/), DIM = 1)
! The result is | C E G |
!               | A F H |
!               | B D I |

! Do the same shifts as before, but on the rows
! instead of the columns.
       RES = CSHIFT (A, SHIFT = (/-1,1,0/), DIM = 2)
! The result is | G A D |
!               | E H B |
!               | C F I |
```

DATE_AND_TIME (DATE, TIME, ZONE, VALUES)

Returns data from the real-time clock and the date in a form compatible with the representations defined in ISO 8601:1988.

DATE (optional) must be scalar and of type default character, and must have a length of at least eight to contain the complete value. It is an INTENT(OUT) argument. Its left-most eight characters are set to a value of the form CCYYMMDD, where CC is the century, YY the year within the century, MM the month within the year, and DD the day within the month. If no date is available, they are set to blank.

TIME (optional) must be scalar and of type default character, and must have a length of at least ten in order to contain the complete value. It is an INTENT(OUT) argument. Its left-most ten characters are set to a value of the form hhmmss.sss, where hh is the hour of the day, mm is the minutes of the hour, and ss.sss is the seconds and milliseconds of the minute. If no is clock available, they are set to blank.

ZONE (optional) must be scalar and of type default character, and must have a length at least five in order to contain the complete value. It is an INTENT(OUT) argument. Its left-most five characters are set to a value of the form ±hhmm, where hh and mm are the time difference with respect to Coordinated Universal Time (UTC) in hours and parts of an hour expressed in minutes, respectively. If no clock is available, they are set to blank.

VALUES (optional) must be of type default integer and of rank one. It is an INTENT(OUT) argument. Its size must be at least eight. The values returned in VALUES are as follows:

VALUES(1) is the year (for example, 1995), or -HUGE (0) if no date is available.

VALUES(2) is the month of the year, or -HUGE (0) if no date is available.

VALUES(3) is the day of the month, or -HUGE (0) if no date is available.

VALUES(4) is the time difference with respect to Coordinated Universal Time (UTC) in minutes, or -HUGE (0) if this information is not available.

VALUES(5) is the hour of the day, in the range 0 to 23, or -HUGE (0) if there is no clock.

VALUES(6) is the minutes of the hour, in the range 0 to 59, or -HUGE (0) if there is no clock.

VALUES(7) is the seconds of the minute, in the range 0 to 60, or -HUGE (0) if there is no clock.

VALUES (8) is the milliseconds of the second, in the range 0 to 999, or -HUGE (0) if there is no clock.

Class: Subroutine

Examples: The following program:

```
INTEGER DATE_TIME (8)
CHARACTER (LEN = 10) BIG_BEN (3)
CALL DATE_AND_TIME (BIG_BEN (1), BIG_BEN (2), &
                    BIG_BEN (3), DATE_TIME)
```

if executed in Geneva, Switzerland on 1985 April 12 at 15:27:35.5, would have assigned the value 19850412 to BIG_BEN(1), the value 152735.500 to BIG_BEN(2), the value +0100 to BIG_BEN(3), and the following values to DATE_TIME: 1985, 4, 12, 60, 15, 27, 35, 500.

Note that UTC is defined by CCIR Recommendation 460-2 (also known as Greenwich Mean Time).

DBLE (A)

Convert to double precision real type.

A must be of type integer, real, or complex.

Class: Elemental function

Result Type and Attributes: Double precision real.

Result Value

- If A is of type double precision real, DBLE(A) = A.
- If A is of type integer or real, the result has as much precision of the significant part of A as a double precision real datum can contain.
- If A is of type complex, the result has as much precision of the significant part of the real part of A as a double precision real datum can contain.

Examples: DBLE (-3) has the value -3.0D0.

DIGITS (X)

Returns the number of significant digits for numbers whose type and kind type parameter are the same as the argument.

X must be of type integer or real. It may be scalar or array valued.

Class: Inquiry function

Result Type and Attributes: Default integer scalar.

Result Value: The result is the number of significant digits for the model representing numbers of the same kind and type as X.

Examples: DIGITS (X) = 63, where X is of type integer(8) (see "Data Representation Models" on page 361).

DIM (X, Y)

The difference X-Y if it is positive; otherwise zero.

X must be of type integer or real.

Y must be of the same type and kind type parameter as X.

Class: Elemental function

Result Type and Attributes: Same as X.

Result Value

- If $X > Y$, the value of the result is X - Y.
- If $X \leq Y$, the value of the result is zero.

DOT_PRODUCT •DPROD

Examples: DIM (-3.0, 2.0) has the value 0.0. DIM (-3.0, -4.0) has the value 1.0.

Specific Name	Argument Type	Result Type	Pass As Arg?
IDIM	default integer	same as argument	yes
DIM	default real	default real	yes
DDIM	double precision real	double precision real	yes

DOT_PRODUCT (VECTOR_A, VECTOR_B)

Computes the dot product on two vectors.

VECTOR_A is a vector with a numeric or logical data type.

VECTOR_B must be of numeric type if VECTOR_A is of numeric type and of logical type if VECTOR_A is of logical type.

Class: Transformational function

Result Value: The result is a scalar whose data type depends on the data type of the two vectors.

If either vector is a zero-sized array, the result equals zero when it has a numeric data type, and false when it is of type logical.

If VCTR_A is of type integer or real, the result value equals SUM(VCTR_A * VCTR_B).

If VCTR_A is of type complex, the result equals SUM(CONJG(VCTR_A) * VCTR_B).

If VCTR_A is of type logical, the result equals ANY(VCTR_A .AND. VCTR_B).

Examples

```
! A is (/ 3, 1, -5 /), and B is (/ 6, 2, 7 /).
    RES = DOT_PRODUCT (A, B)
! calculated as
!   ( (3*6) + (1*2) + (-5*7) )
! = (   18  +   2   + (-35) )
! = -15
```

DPROD (X, Y)

Double precision real product.

X   must be of type default real.

Y   must be of type default real.

Class: Elemental function

Result Type and Attributes: Double precision real.

Result Value: The result has a value equal to the product of X and Y.

Examples: DPROD (-3.0, 2.0) has the value -6.0D0.

Specific Name	Argument Type	Result Type	Pass As Arg?
DPROD	default real	double precision real	yes

EOSHIFT (ARRAY, SHIFT, BOUNDARY, DIM)

Shifts the elements of all vectors along a given dimension of an array. The shift is end-off; that is, elements shifted off one end are lost, and copies of boundary elements are shifted in at the other end.

ARRAY is an array of any type.

SHIFT is an integer expression of rank rank(ARRAY)-1.

BOUNDARY (optional) is an expression of rank rank(ARRAY)-1, with the same data type and type parameters as ARRAY.

DIM (optional) is an integer scalar in the range $1 \leq$ DIM $\leq$ rank(ARRAY).

Class: Transformational function

Result Value: The result is an array with the same shape and data type as ARRAY.

The absolute value of SHIFT determines the amount of shift. The sign of SHIFT determines the direction of the shift:

Positive SHIFT moves each element of the vector toward the beginning of the vector. If an element is taken off the beginning of a vector, its value is replaced by the corresponding value from BOUNDARY at the end of the vector.

Negative SHIFT moves each element of the vector toward the end of the vector. If an element is taken off the end of a vector, its value is replaced by the corresponding value from BOUNDARY at the beginning of the vector.

Zero SHIFT does no shifting. The value of the vector remains unchanged.

Result Value: If BOUNDARY is a scalar value, this value is used in all shifts.

If BOUNDARY is an array of values, the values of the array elements of BOUNDARY with subscripts (s_1, s_2, ..., $s_{(DIM-1)}$, $s_{(DIM+1)}$, ..., s_n) are used for that dimension.

If BOUNDARY is not specified, the following default values are used, depending on the data type of ARRAY:

character	'ƀ' (one blank)
logical	false
integer	0
real	0.0
complex	(0.0, 0.0)

Examples

```
! A is | 1.1 4.4 7.7 |, SHIFT is S=(/0, -1, 1/),
!      | 2.2 5.5 8.8 |
!      | 3.3 6.6 9.9 |
! and BOUNDARY is the array B=(/-0.1, -0.2, -0.3/).

! Leave the first column alone, shift the second
! column down one, and shift the third column up one.
RES = EOSHIFT (A, SHIFT = S, BOUNDARY = B, DIM = 1)
! The result is | 1.1 -0.2  7.7 |
!               | 2.2  4.4  8.8 |
!               | 3.3  5.5 -0.3 |

! Do the same shifts as before, but on the
! rows instead of the columns.
RES = EOSHIFT (A, SHIFT = S, BOUNDARY = B, DIM = 2)
! The result is |  1.1 4.4  7.7 |
!               | -0.2 2.2  5.5 |
!               |  6.6 9.9 -0.3 |
```

EPSILON (X)

Returns a positive model number that is almost negligible compared to unity in the model representing numbers of the same type and kind type parameter as the argument.

X   must be of type real. It may be scalar or array valued.

Class: Inquiry function

Result Type and Attributes: Scalar of the same type and kind type parameter as X.

Result Value: The result is

$\text{RADIX}(X)ei0(1 - \text{DIGITS}(X))$

where *ei* is the exponent indicator (E, D) depending on the type of X.

Examples: EPSILON (X) = 1.1920929E-07 for X of type real(4). See "Real Data Model" on page 362.

EXP (X)

Exponential.

X   must be of type real or complex.

Class: Elemental function

Result Type and Attributes: Same as X.

Result Value

- The result has a value equal to e^x.
- If X is of type complex, its imaginary part is regarded as a value in radians.

Examples: EXP (1.0) has the value 2.7182818 (approximately).

Specific Name	Argument Type	Result Type	Pass As Arg?
EXP	default real	default real	yes
DEXP	double precision real	double precision real	yes
CEXP	default complex	default complex	yes

EXPONENT (X)

Returns the exponent part of the argument when represented as a model number.

X   must be of type real.

Class: Elemental function

Result Type and Attributes: Default integer.

Result Value

- If X ≠ 0, the result is the exponent of X (which is always within the range of a default integer).
- If X = 0, the exponent of X is zero.

Examples: EXPONENT (10.2) = 4. See "Real Data Model" on page 362

FLOOR (A)

Returns the greatest integer less than or equal to its argument.

A   must be of type real.

Class: Elemental function

Result Type and Attributes: Default integer.

Result Value: The result has the value equal to the greatest integer less than or equal to A. The result is undefined if this value cannot be represented in the default integer type.

Examples: FLOOR (3.7) has the value 3. FLOOR (-3.7) has the value -4.

FRACTION (X)

Returns the fractional part of the model representation of the argument value.

X   must be of type real.

Class: Elemental function

Result Type and Attributes: Same as X.

Result Value: The result is:
X $*$ (RADIX(X)$^{-\text{EXPONENT}(X)}$)

Examples

FRACTION(10.2) = $2^{-4} * 10.2 \approx 0.6375$

HUGE (X)

Returns the largest number in the model representing numbers of the same type and kind type parameter as the argument.

X   must be of type integer or real. It may be scalar or array valued.

Class: Inquiry function

Result Type and Attributes: Scalar of the same type and kind type parameter as X.

Result Value

- If X is of any integer type, the result is:
  $2^{\text{DIGITS}(X)} - 1$

- If X is of any real type, the result is:
  $(1.0 - 2.0^{-\text{DIGITS}(X)}) * (2.0^{\text{MAXEXPONENT}(X)})$

Examples: HUGE (X) = (1D0 - 2D0**-53) * (2D0**1024) for X of type real(8).

HUGE (X) = (2**63) - 1 for X of type integer(8).

See "Data Representation Models" on page 361.

IACHAR (C)

Returns the position of a character in the ASCII collating sequence.

C   must be of type default character and of length one.

Class: Elemental function

Result Type and Attributes: Default integer.

Result Value

- If C is in the collating sequence defined by the codes specified in ISO 646:1983 (International Reference Version), the result is the position of C in that sequence and satisfies the inequality (0 ≤ IACHAR (C) ≤ 127). An undefined value is returned if C is not in the ASCII collating sequence.
- The results are consistent with the LGE, LGT, LLE, and LLT lexical comparison functions. For example, LLE (C, D) is true, so IACHAR (C) .LE. IACHAR (D) is true too.

Examples: IACHAR ('X') has the value 88.

IAND (I, J)

Performs a logical AND.

I   must be of type integer.

J   must be of type integer with the same kind type parameter as I.

Class: Elemental function

Result Type and Attributes: Same as I.

Result Value: The result has the value obtained by combining I and J bit-by-bit according to the following table:

```
I   J   IAND (I,J)
------------------
1   1      1
1   0      0
0   1      0
0   0      0
```

The bits are numbered 0 to BIT_SIZE(I)-1, from right to left.

Examples: IAND (1, 3) has the value 1. See "Integer Bit Model" on page 361.

IBCLR (I, POS)

Clears one bit to zero.

I   must be of type integer.

POS must be of type integer. It must be nonnegative and less than BIT_SIZE (I).

Class: Elemental function

Result Type and Attributes: Same as I.

Result Value: The result has the value of the sequence of bits of I, except that bit POS of I is set to zero.

The bits are numbered 0 to BIT_SIZE(I)-1, from right to left.

Examples: IBCLR (14, 1) has the result 12.

If V has the value (/1, 2, 3, 4/), the value of IBCLR (POS = V, I = 31) is (/29, 27, 23, 15/).

See "Integer Bit Model" on page 361.

IBITS (I, POS, LEN)

Extracts a sequence of bits.

I   must be of type integer.

POS must be of type integer. It must be nonnegative and POS + LEN must be less than or equal to BIT_SIZE (I).

LEN must be of type integer and nonnegative.

Class: Elemental function

Result Type and Attributes: Same as I.

Result Value: The result has the value of the sequence of LEN bits in I beginning at bit POS, right-adjusted and with all other bits zero.

The bits are numbered 0 to BIT_SIZE(I)-1, from right to left.

Examples: IBITS (14, 1, 3) has the value 7. See "Integer Bit Model" on page 361.

IBSET (I, POS)

Sets one bit to one.

I   must be of type integer.

POS must be of type integer. It must be nonnegative and less than BIT_SIZE (I).

Class: Elemental function

Result Type and Attributes: Same as I.

Result Value: The result has the value of the sequence of bits of I, except that bit POS of I is set to one.

The bits are numbered 0 to BIT_SIZE(I)-1, from right to left.

Examples: IBSET (12, 1) has the value 14.

If V has the value (/1, 2, 3, 4/), the value of IBSET (POS = V, I = 0) is (/2, 4, 8, 16/).

See "Integer Bit Model" on page 361.

ICHAR (C)

Returns the position of a character in the collating sequence associated with the kind type parameter of the character.

C   must be of type character and of length one. Its value must be that of a representable character.

Class: Elemental function

Result Type and Attributes: Default integer.

Result Value

- The result is the position of C in the collating sequence associated with the kind type parameter of C and is in the range $0 \le$ ICHAR (C) $\le n$-1, where n is the number of characters in the collating sequence.
- For any representable characters C and D, C .LE. D is true if and only if ICHAR (C) .LE. ICHAR (D) is true and C .EQ. D is true if and only if ICHAR (C) .EQ. ICHAR (D) is true.

Examples: ICHAR ('X') has the value 88 in the ASCII collating sequence.

Specific Name	Argument Type	Result Type	Pass As Arg?
ICHAR	default character	default integer	no

IEOR (I, J)

Performs an exclusive OR.

I   must be of type integer.

J   must be of type integer with the same kind type parameter as I.

Class: Elemental function

Result Type and Attributes: Same as I.

Result Value: The result has the value obtained by combining I and J bit-by-bit according to the following truth table:

```
I  J  IEOR (I,J)
----------------
1  1      0
1  0      1
0  1      1
0  0      0
```

The bits are numbered 0 to BIT_SIZE(I)-1, from right to left.

Examples: IEOR (1, 3) has the value 2. See "Integer Bit Model" on page 361.

INDEX (STRING, SUBSTRING, BACK)

Returns the starting position of a substring within a string.

STRING must be of type character.

SUBSTRING must be of type character with the same kind type parameter as STRING.

BACK (optional) must be of type logical.

Class: Elemental function

Result Type and Attributes: Default integer.

Result Value

- Case (i): If BACK is absent or present with the value .FALSE., the result is the minimum positive value of I such that STRING (I : I + LEN (SUBSTRING) - 1) = SUBSTRING or zero if there is no such value. Zero is returned if LEN (STRING) < LEN (SUBSTRING). One is returned if LEN (SUBSTRING) = 0.
- Case (ii): If BACK is present with the value .TRUE., the result is the maximum value of I less than or equal to LEN (STRING) - LEN (SUBSTRING) + 1, such that STRING (I : I + LEN (SUBSTRING) - 1) = SUBSTRING or zero if there is no such value. Zero is returned if LEN (STRING) < LEN (SUBSTRING) and LEN (STRING) + 1 is returned if LEN (SUBSTRING) = 0.

Examples: INDEX ('FORTRAN', 'R') has the value 3.

INDEX ('FORTRAN', 'R', BACK = .TRUE.) has the value 5.

Specific Name	Argument Type	Result Type	Pass As Arg?
INDEX	default character	default integer	yes **1**

Note: When this specific name is passed as an argument, the procedure can only be referenced without the **BACK** optional argument.

INT (A, KIND)

Convert to integer type.

A   must be of type integer, real, or complex.

KIND (optional) must be a scalar integer initialization expression.

Class: Elemental function

Result Type and Attributes

- Integer.
- If KIND is present, the kind type parameter is that specified by KIND; otherwise, the kind type parameter is that of the default integer type.

Result Value

- Case (i): If A is of type integer, INT (A) = A.
- Case (ii): If A is of type real, there are two cases: if |A| < 1, INT (A) has the value 0; if |A| ≥ 1, INT (A) is the integer whose magnitude is the largest integer that does not exceed the magnitude of A and whose sign is the same as the sign of A.
- Case (iii): If A is of type complex, INT (A) is the value obtained by applying the case (ii) rule to the real part of A.
- The result is undefined if it cannot be represented in the specified integer type.

Examples: INT (-3.7) has the value -3.

Specific Name	Argument Type	Result Type	Pass As Arg?
INT	default real	default integer	no
IDINT	double precision real	default integer	no
IFIX	default real	default integer	no

IOR (I, J)

Performs an inclusive OR.

I   must be of type integer.

J   must be of type integer with the same kind type parameter as I.

Class: Elemental function

Result Type and Attributes: Same as I.

Result Value: The result has the value obtained by combining I and J bit-by-bit according to the following truth table:

```
I  J   IOR (I,J)
-----------------
1  1     1
1  0     1
0  1     1
0  0     0
```

The bits are numbered 0 to BIT_SIZE(I)-1, from right to left.

Examples: IOR (1, 3) has the value 3. See "Integer Bit Model" on page 361.

ISHFT (I, SHIFT)

Performs a logical shift.

I   must be of type integer.

SHIFT must be of type integer. The absolute value of SHIFT must be less than or equal to BIT_SIZE (I).

Class: Elemental function

Result Type and Attributes: Same as I.

Result Value

- The result has the value obtained by shifting the bits of I by SHIFT positions.
- If SHIFT is positive, the shift is to the left; if SHIFT is negative, the shift is to the right; and, if SHIFT is zero, no shift is performed.
- Bits shifted out from the left or from the right, as appropriate, are lost.
- Vacated bits are filled with zeros.
- The bits are numbered 0 to BIT_SIZE(I)-1, from right to left.

Examples: ISHFT (3, 1) has the result 6. See "Integer Bit Model" on page 361.

ISHFTC (I, SHIFT, SIZE)

Performs a circular shift of the right-most bits; that is, bits shifted off one end are inserted again at the other end.

I   must be of type integer.

SHIFT must be of type integer. The absolute value of SHIFT must be less than or equal to SIZE.

SIZE (optional) must be of type integer. The value of SIZE must be positive and must not exceed BIT_SIZE (I). If SIZE is absent, it is as if it were present with the value of BIT_SIZE (I).

Class: Elemental function

Result Type and Attributes: Same as I.

Result Value: The result has the value obtained by shifting the SIZE right-most bits of I circularly by SHIFT positions. If SHIFT is positive, the shift is to the left; if SHIFT is negative, the shift is to the right; and, if SHIFT is zero, no shift is performed. No bits are lost. The unshifted bits are unaltered.

The bits are numbered 0 to BIT_SIZE(I)-1, from right to left.

Examples: ISHFTC (3, 2, 3) has the value 5. See "Integer Bit Model" on page 361.

KIND (X)

Returns the value of the kind type parameter of X.

X   may be of any intrinsic type.

Class: Inquiry function

Result Type and Attributes: Default integer scalar.

Result Value: The result has a value equal to the kind type parameter value of X.

See "Intrinsic Types" on page 23.

Examples: KIND (0.0) has the kind type parameter value of the default real type.

LBOUND (ARRAY, DIM)

Returns the lower bound of each dimension in an array, or the lower bound of a specified dimension.

ARRAY is the array whose lower bounds you want to determine. Its bounds must be defined; that is, it must not be a disassociated pointer or an allocatable array that is not allocated.

DIM (optional) is an integer scalar in the range $1 \leq DIM \leq rank(ARRAY)$. The corresponding actual argument must not be an optional dummy argument.

Class: Inquiry function

Result Type and Attributes: Default integer.

If DIM is present, the result is a scalar. If DIM is not present, the result is a one-dimensional array with one element for each dimension in ARRAY.

Result Value: Each element in the result corresponds to a dimension of ARRAY.

- If ARRAY is a whole array or array structure component, LBOUND(ARRAY,DIM) is equal to the lower bound for subscript DIM of ARRAY.

    The only exception is for a dimension that is zero-sized and ARRAY is not an assumed-size array of rank DIM, In such a case, the corresponding element in the result is one regardless of the value declared for the lower bound.

- If ARRAY is an array section or expression that is not a whole array or

array structure component, each element has the value one.

Examples

```
REAL A(1:10, -4:5, 4:-5)

    RES=LBOUND( A )
! The result is (/ 1, -4, 1 /).

    RES=LBOUND( A(:,:,:) )
    RES=LBOUND( A(4:10,-4:1,:) )
! The result in both cases is (/ 1, 1, 1 /)
! because the arguments are array sections.
```

LEN (STRING)

Returns the length of a character entity. The argument to this function need not be defined.

STRING must be of type character. It may be scalar or array valued.

Class: Inquiry function

Result Type and Attributes: Default integer scalar.

Result Value: The result has a value equal to the number of characters in STRING if it is scalar or in an element of STRING if it is array valued.

Examples: If C is declared by the statement

```
CHARACTER (11) C(100)
```

LEN (C) has the value 11.

Specific Name	Argument Type	Result Type	Pass As Arg?
LEN	default character	default integer	no

LEN_TRIM (STRING)

Returns the length of the character argument without counting trailing blank characters.

STRING must be of type character.

Class: Elemental function

Result Type and Attributes: Default integer.

Result Value: The result has a value equal to the number of characters remaining after any trailing blanks in STRING are removed. If the argument contains no nonblank characters, the result is zero.

Examples: LEN_TRIM ('ƀAƀBƀ') has the value 4. LEN_TRIM ('ƀƀ') has the value 0.

LGE (STRING_A, STRING_B)

Test whether a string is lexically greater than or equal to another string, based on the ASCII collating sequence.

STRING_A must be of type default character.

STRING_B must be of type default character.

Class: Elemental function

Result Type and Attributes: Default logical.

Result Value

- If the strings are of unequal length, the comparison is made as if the shorter string were extended on the right with blanks to the length of the longer string.

- If either string contains a character not in the ASCII character set, the result is undefined.
- The result is true if the strings are equal or if STRING_A follows STRING_B in the ASCII collating sequence; otherwise, the result is false. Note that the result is true if both STRING_A and STRING_B are of zero length.

Examples: LGE ('ONE', 'TWO') has the value .FALSE..

Specific Name	Argument Type	Result Type	Pass As Arg?
LGE	default character	default logical	no

LGT (STRING_A, STRING_B)

Test whether a string is lexically greater than another string, based on the ASCII collating sequence.

STRING_A must be of type default character.

STRING_B must be of type default character.

Class: Elemental function

Result Type and Attributes: Default logical.

Result Value

- If the strings are of unequal length, the comparison is made as if the shorter string were extended on the right with blanks to the length of the longer string.
- If either string contains a character not in the ASCII character set, the result is undefined.
- The result is true if STRING_A follows STRING_B in the ASCII collating

sequence; otherwise, the result is false. Note that the result is false if both STRING_A and STRING_B are of zero length.

Examples: LGT ('ONE', 'TWO') has the value .FALSE..

Specific Name	Argument Type	Result Type	Pass As Arg?
LGT	default character	default logical	no

LLE (STRING_A, STRING_B)

Test whether a string is lexically less than or equal to another string, based on the ASCII collating sequence.

STRING_A must be of type default character.

STRING_B must be of type default character.

Class: Elemental function

Result Type and Attributes: Default logical.

Result Value

- If the strings are of unequal length, the comparison is made as if the shorter string were extended on the right with blanks to the length of the longer string.
- If either string contains a character not in the ASCII character set, the result is undefined.
- The result is true if the strings are equal or if STRING_A precedes STRING_B in the ASCII collating sequence; otherwise, the result is false. Note that the result is true if both STRING_A and STRING_B are of zero length.

Examples: LLE ('ONE', 'TWO') has the value .TRUE..

Specific Name	Argument Type	Result Type	Pass As Arg?
LLE	default character	default logical	no

LLT (STRING_A, STRING_B)

Test whether a string is lexically less than another string, based on the ASCII collating sequence.

STRING_A must be of type default character.

STRING_B must be of type default character.

Class: Elemental function

Result Type and Attributes: Default logical.

Result Value

- If the strings are of unequal length, the comparison is made as if the shorter string were extended on the right with blanks to the length of the longer string.
- If either string contains a character not in the ASCII character set, the result is undefined.
- The result is true if STRING_A precedes STRING_B in the ASCII collating sequence; otherwise, the result is false. Note that the result is false if both STRING_A and STRING_B are of zero length.

Examples: LLT ('ONE', 'TWO') has the value .TRUE..

Specific Name	Argument Type	Result Type	Pass As Arg?
LLT	default character	default logical	no

Specific Name	Argument Type	Result Type	Pass As Arg?
CLOG	default complex	default complex	yes

LOG (X)

Natural logarithm.

X   must be of type real or complex.

- If X is real, its value must be greater than zero.
- If X is complex, its value must not be zero.

Class: Elemental function

Result Type and Attributes: Same as X.

Result Value

- It has a value approximating $\log_e X$.
- For complex arguments, LOG ((a,b)) approximates LOG (ABS((a,b))) + ATAN2((b,a)).

  If the argument type is complex, the result is the principal value of the imaginary part ω in the range $-\pi < \omega \leq \pi$. If the real part of the argument is less than zero and its imaginary part is zero, the imaginary part of the result approximates π.

Examples: LOG (10.0) has the value 2.3025851 (approximately).

Specific Name	Argument Type	Result Type	Pass As Arg?
ALOG	default real	default real	yes
DLOG	double precision real	double precision real	yes

LOG10 (X)

Common logarithm.

X   must be of type real. The value of X must be greater than zero.

Class: Elemental function

Result Type and Attributes: Same as X.

Result Value: The result has a value equal to $\log_{10} X$.

Examples: LOG10 (10.0) has the value 1.0.

Specific Name	Argument Type	Result Type	Pass As Arg?
ALOG10	default real	default real	yes
DLOG10	double precision real	double precision real	yes

LOGICAL (L, KIND)

Converts between objects of type logical with different kind type parameter values.

L   must be of type logical.

KIND (optional) must be a scalar integer initialization expression.

Class: Elemental function

Result Type and Attributes

- Logical.
- If KIND is present, the kind type parameter is that specified by KIND; otherwise, the kind type parameter is that of the default logical type.

Result Value: The value is that of L.

Examples: LOGICAL (L .OR. .NOT. L) has the value .TRUE. and is of type default logical, regardless of the kind type parameter of the logical variable L.

MATMUL (MATRIX_A, MATRIX_B)

Performs a matrix multiplication.

MATRIX_A is an array with a rank of one or two and a numeric or logical data type.

MATRIX_B is an array with a rank of one or two and a numeric or logical data type. It can be a different numeric type than MATRIX_A, but you cannot use one numeric matrix and one logical matrix.

At least one of the arguments must be of rank two. The size of the first or only dimension of MATRIX_B must be equal to the last or only dimension of MATRIX_A.

Class: Transformational function

Result Value: The result is an array. If one of the arguments is of rank one, the result has a rank of one. If both arguments are of rank two, the result has a rank of two.

The data type of the result depends on the data type of the arguments.

If MATRIX_A and MATRIX_B have a numeric data type, the array elements of the result are:

Value of Element (i,j) = SUM((row i of MATRIX_A) * (column j of MATRIX_B))

If MATRIX_A and MATRIX_B are of type logical, the array elements of the result are:

Value of Element (i,j) = ANY((row i of MATRIX_A) .AND. (column j of MATRIX_B))

Examples

```
! A is the array │ 1 2 3 │, B is the array │ 7 10 │
!                │ 4 5 6 │                  │ 8 11 │
!                                           │ 9 12 │
    RES = MATMUL(A, B)
! The result is │ 50   68 │
!               │ 122  167 │
```

MAX (A1, A2, A3, ...)

Maximum value.

- **A3,...** are optional arguments. Any array that is itself an optional dummy argument must not be passed as an optional argument to this function unless it is present in the calling procedure.
- All the arguments must have the same type, either integer or real, and they all must have the same kind type parameter.

Class: Elemental function

Result Type and Attributes: Same as the arguments. (Some specific functions return results of a particular type.)

Result Value: The value of the result is that of the largest argument.

Examples: MAX (-9.0, 7.0, 2.0) has the value 7.0.

If you evaluate MAX (10, 3, A), where A is an optional array argument in the calling procedure, PRESENT(A) must be true in the calling procedure.

Specific Name	Argument Type	Result Type	Pass As Arg?
AMAX0	default integer	default real	no
AMAX1	default real	default real	no
DMAX1	double precision real	double precision real	no
MAX0	default integer	same as argument	no
MAX1	default real	default integer	no

MAXEXPONENT (X)

Returns the maximum exponent in the model representing numbers of the same type and kind type parameter as the argument.

X   must be of type real. It may be scalar or array valued.

Class: Inquiry function

Result Type and Attributes: Default integer scalar.

Result Value: The result is the maximum exponent in the model representing numbers of the same kind and type as X.

Examples

MAXEXPONENT(X) = 128 for X of type real(4).

See "Real Data Model" on page 362.

MAXLOC (ARRAY, MASK)

Locates the first element of an array that has the maximum value of all elements or a set of elements.

ARRAY is an array of type integer or real.

MASK (optional) is an array of type logical that conforms to ARRAY in shape. If it is absent, the entire array is evaluated.

Class: Transformational function

Result Value: Normally, the result is an integer array of rank one and with a size equal to the rank of ARRAY. If there is no maximum value, perhaps because the array is zero-sized or the mask array has all .FALSE. values, the result value is processor-dependent.

The elements of the result form the subscript of the location of the maximum element of ARRAY, or the maximum of the elements designated by the mask. If more than one element is equal to this maximum value, the function finds the location of the first (in array element order).

Examples

```
! A is the array  |  4   9   8  -8 |
!                 |  2   1  -1   5 |
!                 |  9   4  -1   9 |
!                 | -7   5   7  -3 |

! What is the largest element in A?
    RES = MAXLOC(A)
! The result is | 3 1 | because 9 is located at A(3,1).
! Although there are other 9s, A(3,1) is the first one
! as we step through in column-major order.

! What is the largest element in A that is less than 7?
    RES = MAXLOC(A, MASK = A .LT. 7)
! The result is | 4 2 | because 5 is the largest value
! that satisfies the condition <value> .LT. 7, and 5
! first occurs at position (4,2).
```

MAXVAL (ARRAY, DIM, MASK)

Returns the maximum value of the elements in the array along a dimension corresponding to the true elements of MASK.

ARRAY is an array of type integer or real.

DIM (optional) is an integer scalar in the range 1 ≤ DIM ≤ rank(ARRAY). The corresponding actual argument must not be an optional dummy argument.

MASK (optional) is an array or scalar of type logical that conforms to ARRAY in shape. If it is absent, the entire array is evaluated.

Class: Transformational function

Result Value: The result is an array of rank rank(ARRAY)-1, with the same data type as ARRAY. If DIM is missing or if ARRAY is of rank one, the result is a scalar.

If DIM is specified, each element of the result value contains the maximum value of all the elements that satisfy the condition specified by MASK along each vector of the dimension DIM. The array element subscripts in the result are $(s_1, s_2, ..., s_{(DIM-1)}, s_{(DIM+1)}, ..., s_n)$, where n is the rank of ARRAY and DIM is the dimension specified by DIM.

If DIM is not specified, the function returns the maximum value of all applicable elements.

If ARRAY is zero-sized or the mask array has all .FALSE. values, the result value is the negative number of the largest magnitude, of the same type and kind type as ARRAY.

Examples

```
! A is the array  | -41  33 25 |
!                 |  12 -61 11 |

! What is the largest value in the entire array?
      RES = MAXVAL(A)
! The result is 33

! What is the largest value in each column?
      RES = MAXVAL(A, DIM=1)
! The result is | 12 33 25 |

! What is the largest value in each row?
      RES = MAXVAL(A, DIM=2)
! The result is | 33 12 |

! What is the largest value in each row, considering only
! elements that are less than 30?
      RES = MAXVAL(A, DIM=2, MASK = A .LT. 30)
! The result is | 25 12 |
```

MERGE (TSOURCE, FSOURCE, MASK)

Selects between two values, or corresponding elements in two arrays. A logical mask determines whether to take each result element from the first or second argument.

TSOURCE is the source array to use when the corresponding element in the mask is true. It is an expression of any data type.

FSOURCE is the source array to use when the corresponding element in the mask is false. It must have the same data type and shape as TSOURCE.

MASK is a logical expression that conforms to ARRAY in shape.

Class: Elemental function

Result Value: The result has the same shape and data type as TSOURCE and FSOURCE.

For each element in the result, the value of the corresponding element in MASK determines whether the value is taken from TSOURCE (if true) or FSOURCE (if false).

Examples

```
! TSOURCE is | A D G |, FSOURCE is | a d g |,
!            | B E H |             | b e h |
!            | C F I |             | c f i |
!
! and MASK is the array | T T T |
!                       | F F F |
!                       | F F F |

! Take the top row of TSOURCE, and the remaining elements
! from FSOURCE.
        RES = MERGE(TSOURCE, FSOURCE, MASK)
! The result is  | A D G |
!                | b e h |
!                | c f i |

! Evaluate IF (X .GT. Y) THEN
!             RES=6
!     \    ELSE
!             RES=12
!         END IF
! in a more concise form.
        RES = MERGE(6, 12, X .GT. Y)
```

MIN (A1, A2, A3, ...)

Minimum value.

- **A3,...** are optional arguments. Any array that is itself an optional dummy argument must not be passed as an optional argument to this function unless it is present in the calling procedure.
- All the arguments must have the same type, either integer or real, and they all must have the same kind type parameter.

Class: Elemental function

Result Type and Attributes: Same as the arguments. (Some specific functions return results of a particular type.)

Result Value: The value of the result is that of the smallest argument.

Examples: MIN (-9.0, 7.0, 2.0) has the value -9.0.

If you evaluate MIN (10, 3, A), where A is an optional array argument in the calling procedure, PRESENT(A) must be true in the calling procedure.

Specific Name	Argument Type	Result Type	Pass As Arg?
AMIN0	any integer	default real	no
AMIN1	default real	default real	no
DMIN1	double precision real	double precision real	no
MIN0	any integer	same as argument	no
MIN1	any real	default integer	no

MINEXPONENT (X)

Returns the minimum (most negative) exponent in the model representing the numbers of the same type and kind type parameter as the argument.

X   must be of type real. It may be scalar or array valued.

Class: Inquiry function

Result Type and Attributes: Default integer scalar.

Result Value: The result is the minimum exponent in the model representing numbers of the same kind and type as X.

Examples

MINEXPONENT(X) = -125 for X of type real(4).

See "Real Data Model" on page 362.

MINLOC (ARRAY, MASK)

Locates the first element of an array that has the minimum value of all elements or a set of elements.

ARRAY is an array of type integer or real.

MASK (optional) is an array of type logical that conforms to ARRAY in shape. If it is absent, the entire array is evaluated.

Class: Transformational function

Result Value: Normally, the result is an integer array of rank one, with a size equal to the rank of ARRAY. If there is no minimum value, perhaps because the array is zero-sized or the mask array has all .FALSE. values, the result value is processor-dependent.

The elements of the result form the subscript of the location of the minimum element of ARRAY, or the minimum of the elements designated by the mask. If more than one element is equal to this minimum value, the function finds the location of the first (in array element order).

Examples

```
! A is the array  |  4  9  8 -8 |
!                 |  2  1 -1  5 |
!                 |  9  4 -1  9 |
!                 | -7  5  7 -3 |

! What is the smallest element in A?
      RES = MINLOC(A)
! The result is | 4 1 | because -8 is located at A(4,1).

! What is the smallest element in A that is not -8?
```

```
      RES = MINLOC(A, MASK = A .NE. -8)
! The result is | 1 4 | because -7 is the next largest
! value after -8.
```

MINVAL (ARRAY, DIM, MASK)

Returns the minimum value of the elements in the array along a dimension corresponding to the true elements of MASK.

ARRAY is an array of type integer or real.

DIM (optional) is an integer scalar in the range $1 \leq$ DIM $\leq$ rank(ARRAY). The corresponding actual argument must not be an optional dummy argument.

MASK (optional) is an array or scalar of type logical that conforms to ARRAY in shape. If it is absent, the entire array is evaluated.

Class: Transformational function

Result Value: The result is an array of rank rank(ARRAY)-1, with the same data type as ARRAY. If DIM is missing or if ARRAY is of rank one, the result is a scalar.

If DIM is specified, each element of the result value contains the minimum value of all the elements that satisfy the condition specified by MASK along each vector of the dimension DIM. The array element subscripts in the result are (s_1, s_2, ..., $s_{(DIM-1)}$, $s_{(DIM+1)}$, ..., s_n), where n is the rank of ARRAY and DIM is the dimension specified by DIM.

If DIM is not specified, the function returns the minimum value of all applicable elements.

If ARRAY is zero-sized or the mask array has all .FALSE. values, the result value is the positive number of the largest

MOD •MODULO

magnitude, of the same type and kind type as ARRAY.

Examples

```
! A is the array │ -41  33 25 │
!                │  12 -61 11 │

! What is the smallest element in A?
      RES = MINVAL(A)
! The result is -61

! What is the smallest element in each column of A?
      RES = MINVAL(A, DIM=1)
! The result is │ -41 -61 11 │

! What is the smallest element in each row of A?
      RES = MINVAL(A, DIM=2)
! The result is │ -41 -61 │

! What is the smallest element in each row of A,
! considering only those elements that are
! greater than zero?
      RES = MINVAL(A, DIM=2, MASK = A .GT.0)
! The result is │ 25 11 │
```

MOD (A, P)

Remainder function.

A   must be of type integer or real.

P   must be of the same type and kind type parameter as A.

Class: Elemental function

Result Type and Attributes: Same as A.

Result Value

- If P ≠ 0, the value of the result is A - INT(A/P) * P.
- If P = 0, the result is undefined.

Examples

MOD (3.0, 2.0) has the value 1.0.
MOD (8, 5) has the value 3.
MOD (-8, 5) has the value -3.
MOD (8, -5) has the value 3.
MOD (-8, -5) has the value -3.

Specific Name	Argument Type	Result Type	Pass As Arg?
MOD	any integer	same as argument	yes
AMOD	default real	default real	yes
DMOD	double precision real	double precision real	yes

MODULO (A, P)

Modulo function.

A   must be of type integer or real.

P   must be of the same type and kind type parameter as A.

Class: Elemental function

Result Type and Attributes: Same as A.

Result Value

- Case (i): A is of type integer. If P ≠ 0, MODULO (A, P) has the value R such that A = Q * P + R, where Q is an integer.

  If P > 0, the inequalities $0 \leq R < P$ hold.

  If P < 0, $P < R \leq 0$ hold.

  If P = 0, the result is processor-dependent.

- Case (ii): A is of type real. If P ≠ 0, the value of the result is A - FLOOR (A / P) * P.

  If P = 0, the result is processor-dependent.

Examples

MODULO (8, 5) has the value 3.
MODULO (-8, 5) has the value 2.
MODULO (8, -5) has the value -2.

MODULO (-8, -5) has the value -3.

MVBITS (FROM, FROMPOS, LEN, TO, TOPOS)

Copies a sequence of bits from one data object to another.

FROM must be of type integer. It is an INTENT(IN) argument.

FROMPOS must be of type integer and nonnegative. It is an INTENT(IN) argument. FROMPOS + LEN must be less than or equal to BIT_SIZE (FROM).

LEN must be of type integer and nonnegative. It is an INTENT(IN) argument.

TO must be a variable of type integer with the same kind type parameter value as FROM and may be the same variable as FROM. It is an INTENT(INOUT) argument. TO is set by copying the sequence of bits of length LEN, starting at position FROMPOS of FROM to position TOPOS of TO. No other bits of TO are altered. On return, the LEN bits of TO starting at TOPOS are equal to the value that the LEN bits of FROM starting at FROMPOS had on entry.

The bits are numbered 0 to BIT_SIZE(I)-1, from right to left.

TOPOS must be of type integer and nonnegative. It is an INTENT(IN) argument. TOPOS + LEN must be less than or equal to BIT_SIZE (TO).

Class: Elemental subroutine

Examples: If TO has the initial value 6, the value of TO is 5 after the statement

```
CALL MVBITS (7, 2, 2, TO, 0)
```

See "Integer Bit Model" on page 361.

NEAREST (X,S)

Returns the nearest different processor-representable number in the direction indicated by the sign of S (toward positive or negative infinity).

X   must be of type real.

S   must be of type real and not equal to zero.

Class: Elemental function

Result Type and Attributes: Same as X.

Result Value: The result is the machine number different from and nearest to X in the direction of the infinity with the same sign as S.

Examples: NEAREST (3.0, 2.0) = 3.0 + $2.0^{(-22)}$. See "Real Data Model" on page 362.

NINT (A, KIND)

Nearest integer.

A   must be of type real.

KIND (optional) must be a scalar integer initialization expression.

Class: Elemental function

Result Type and Attributes

- Integer.
- If KIND is present, the kind type parameter is that specified by KIND; otherwise, the kind type parameter is that of the default integer type.

Result Value

- If A > 0, NINT (A) has the value INT (A + 0.5).
- If A ≤ 0, NINT (A) has the value INT (A - 0.5).
- The result is undefined if its value cannot be represented in the specified integer type.

Examples: NINT (2.789) has the value 3. NINT (2.123) has the value 2.

Specific Name	Argument Type	Result Type	Pass As Arg?
NINT	default real	default integer	yes
IDNINT	double precision real	default integer	yes

NOT (I)

Performs a logical complement.

I must be of type integer.

Class: Elemental function

Result Type and Attributes: Same as I.

Result Value: The result has the value obtained by complementing I bit-by-bit according to the following table:

```
I NOT (I)
---------
1    0
0    1
```

The bits are numbered 0 to BIT_SIZE(I)-1, from right to left.

Examples: If I is represented by the string of bits 01010101, NOT (I) has the string of bits 10101010. See "Integer Bit Model" on page 361.

PACK (ARRAY, MASK, VECTOR)

Takes some or all elements from an array and packs them into a one-dimensional array, under the control of a mask.

ARRAY is the source array, whose elements become part of the result. It can have any data type.

MASK must be of type logical and must be conformable with ARRAY. It determines which elements are taken from the source array. If it is a scalar, its value applies to all elements in ARRAY.

VECTOR (optional) is a padding array whose elements are used to fill out the result if there are not enough elements selected by the mask. It is a one-dimensional array that has the same data type as ARRAY and at least as many elements as there are true values in MASK. If MASK is a scalar with a value of .TRUE., VECTOR must have at least as many elements as there are array elements in ARRAY.

Class: Transformational function

Result Value: The result is always a one-dimensional array with the same data type as ARRAY.

The size of the result depends on the optional arguments:

- If VECTOR is specified, the size of the resultant array equals the size of VECTOR.
- Otherwise, it equals the number of true array elements in MASK, or the number of elements in ARRAY if MASK is a scalar with a value of .TRUE..

The array elements in ARRAY are taken in array element order to form the result. If the corresponding array element in MASK is .TRUE., the element from ARRAY is placed at the end of the result.

If any elements remain empty in the result (because VECTOR is present, and has more elements than there are .TRUE. values in MASK), the remaining elements in the result are set to the corresponding values from VECTOR.

Examples

```
! A is the array  | 0  7  0 |
!                 | 1  0  3 |
!                 | 4  0  0 |

! Take only the non-zero elements of this sparse array.
! If there are less than six, fill in -1 for the rest.
RES = PACK(A, MASK= A .NE. 0, VECTOR=(/-1,-1,-1,-1,-1,-1/)
! The result is (/ 1, 4, 7, 3, -1, -1 /).

! Elements 1, 4, 7, and 3 are taken in order from A
! because the value of MASK is true only for these
! elements. The -1s are added to the result from VECTOR
! because the length (6) of VECTOR exceeds the number
! of .TRUE. values (4) in MASK.
```

PRECISION (X)

Returns the decimal precision in the model representing real numbers with the same kind type parameter as the argument.

X must be of type real or complex. It may be scalar or array valued.

Class: Inquiry function

Result Type and Attributes: Default integer scalar.

Result Value: The result is:

```
INT( (DIGITS(X) - 1) * LOG10(RADIX(X)) )
```

Examples: PRECISION (X) = INT((24 - 1) * LOG10(2.)) = INT(6.92...) = 6 for X of type real(4). See "Real Data Model" on page 362.

PRESENT (A)

Determine whether an optional argument is present. If it is not present, you may only pass it as an optional argument to another procedure or pass it as an argument to PRESENT.

A is the name of an optional dummy argument that is accessible in the procedure in which the **PRESENT** function reference appears.

Class: Inquiry function

Result Type and Attributes: Default logical scalar.

Result Value: The result is .TRUE. if the actual argument is present (that is, if it was passed to the current procedure in the specified dummy argument), and .FALSE. otherwise.

Examples

```
      SUBROUTINE SUB (X, Y)
        REAL, OPTIONAL :: Y
        IF (PRESENT (Y)) THEN
! In this section, we can use y like any other variable.
          X = X + Y
          PRINT *, SQRT(Y)
        ELSE
! In this section, we cannot define or reference y.
          X = X + 5
! We can pass it to another procedure, but only if
! sub2 declares the corresponding argument as optional.
          CALL SUB2 (Z, Y)
        ENDIF
      END SUBROUTINE SUB
```

Related Information: "OPTIONAL" on page 300

PRODUCT

PRODUCT (ARRAY, DIM, MASK)

Multiplies together all elements in an entire array, or selected elements from all vectors along a dimension.

ARRAY is an array with a numeric data type.

DIM (optional) is an integer scalar in the range 1 ≤ DIM ≤ rank(ARRAY). The corresponding actual argument must not be an optional dummy argument.

MASK (optional) is a logical expression that conforms with ARRAY in shape. If MASK is a scalar, the scalar value applies to all elements in ARRAY.

Class: Transformational function

Result Value: If DIM is present, the result is an array of rank rank(ARRAY)-1 and the same data type as ARRAY. If DIM is missing, or if MASK has a rank of one, the result is a scalar.

The result is calculated by one of the following methods:

Method 1:
If only ARRAY is specified, the result is the product of all its array elements. If ARRAY is a zero-sized array, the result is equal to one.

Method 2:
If ARRAY and MASK are both specified, the result is the product of those array elements of ARRAY that have a corresponding true array element in MASK. If MASK has no elements with a value of .TRUE., the result is equal to one.

Method 3:
If DIM is also specified, the result value equals the product of the array elements

of ARRAY along dimension DIM that have a corresponding true array element in MASK.

Examples

Method 1:
```
! Multiply all elements in an array.
     RES = PRODUCT( (/2, 3, 4/) )
! The result is 24 because (2 * 3 * 4) = 24.

! Do the same for a two-dimensional array.
     RES = PRODUCT( (/2, 3, 4/), (/4, 5, 6/) )
! The result is 2880.  All elements are multiplied.
```

Method 2:
```
! A is the array (/ -3, -7, -5, 2, 3 /)
! Multiply all elements of the array that are > -5.
     RES = PRODUCT(A, MASK = A .GT. -5 )
! The result is -18 because (-3 * 2 * 3) = -18.
```

Method 3:
```
! A is the array | -2  5  7 |
!                |  3 -4  3 |
! Find the product of each column in A.
     RES = PRODUCT(A, DIM = 1)
! The result is | -6 -20 21 | because (-2 * 3) =  -6
!                                      ( 5 * -4) = -20
!                                      ( 7 *  3) = 21

! Find the product of each row in A.
     RES = PRODUCT(A, DIM = 2)
! The result is | -70 -36 |
! because (-2 *  5 * 7) = -70
!         ( 3 * -4 * 3) = -36

! Find the product of each row in A, considering
! only those elements greater than zero.
     RES = PRODUCT(A, DIM = 2, MASK = A .GT. 0)
! The result is | 35 9 | because ( 5 * 7) = 35
!                                ( 3 * 3) =  9
```

RADIX (X)

Returns the base of the model representing numbers of the same type and kind type parameter as the argument.

X   must be of type integer or real. It may be scalar or array valued.

Class: Inquiry function

Result Type and Attributes: Default integer scalar.

Result Value: The result is the base of the model representing numbers of the same kind and type as X.

Examples: Based on the models under "Data Representation Models" on page 361, the result is always 2.

RANDOM_NUMBER (HARVEST)

Returns one pseudorandom number or an array of pseudorandom numbers from the uniform distribution over the range $0 \le x < 1$.

HARVEST must be of type real. It is an INTENT(OUT) argument. It may be a scalar or array variable. It is set to pseudorandom numbers from the uniform distribution in the interval $0 \le x < 1$.

Class: Subroutine

Examples
```
REAL X, Y (10, 10)
! Initialize X with a pseudorandom number
CALL RANDOM_NUMBER (HARVEST = X)
CALL RANDOM_NUMBER (Y)
! X and Y contain uniformly distributed random numbers
```

RANDOM_SEED (SIZE, PUT, GET)

Restarts or queries the pseudorandom number generator used by RANDOM_NUMBER.

There must either be exactly one or no arguments present.

SIZE (optional) must be scalar and of type default integer. It is an INTENT(OUT) argument. It is set to the number of default type integers (N) that are needed to hold the value of the seed.

PUT (optional) must be a default integer array of rank one and size ≥ N. It is an INTENT(IN) argument. The seed for the current generator is transferred from it.

GET (optional) must be a default integer array of rank one and size ≥ N. It is an INTENT(OUT) argument. The seed for the current generator is transferred to it.

If no argument is present, the seed is set to a processor-dependent value.

Class: Subroutine

Examples
```
CALL RANDOM_SEED
   ! Current generator sets its seed to 1d0
CALL RANDOM_SEED (SIZE = K)
   ! Sets K = 64 / BIT_SIZE( 0 )
CALL RANDOM_SEED (PUT = SEED (1 : K))
   ! Transfer seed to current generator
CALL RANDOM_SEED (GET = OLD (1 : K))
   ! Transfer seed from current generator
```

RANGE (X)

Returns the decimal exponent range in the model representing integer or real numbers with the same kind type parameter as the argument.

X   must be of type integer, real, or complex. It may be scalar or array valued.

Class: Inquiry function

Result Type and Attributes: Default integer scalar.

Result Value

1. For an integer argument, the result is:

   INT(LOG10(HUGE(X)))

2. For a real or complex argument, the result is:

   INT(MIN(LOG10(HUGE(X)), -LOG10(TINY(X))))

Examples: X is of type real(4):

   HUGE(X) = 0.34E+39
   TINY(X) = 0.11E-37
   RANGE(X) = 37

See "Data Representation Models" on page 361.

REAL (A, KIND)

Convert to real type.

A   must be of type integer, real, or complex.

KIND (optional) must be a scalar integer initialization expression.

Class: Elemental function

Result Type and Attributes

- Real.
- Case (i):
  If A is of type integer or real and KIND is present, the kind type parameter is that specified by KIND.
  If A is of type integer or real and KIND is not present, the kind type parameter is the kind type parameter of the default real type.
- Case (ii):
  If A is of type complex and KIND is present, the kind type parameter is that specified by KIND.
  If A is of type complex and KIND is not present, the kind type parameter is the kind type parameter of A.

Result Value

- Case (i): If A is of type integer or real, the result is equal to a kind-dependent approximation to A.
- Case (ii): If A is of type complex, the result is equal to a kind-dependent approximation to the real part of A.

Examples: REAL (-3) has the value -3.0. REAL ((3.2, 2.1)) has the value 3.2.

Specific Name	Argument Type	Result Type	Pass As Arg?
REAL	default integer	default real	no
FLOAT	default integer	default real	no
SNGL	double precision real	default real	no

REPEAT (STRING, NCOPIES)

Concatenate several copies of a string.

STRING must be scalar and of type character.

NCOPIES must be scalar and of type integer. Its value must not be negative.

Class: Transformational function

Result Type and Attributes: Character scalar with a length equal to NCOPIES * LENGTH(STRING), with the same kind type parameter as STRING.

Result Value: The value of the result is the concatenation of NCOPIES copies of STRING.

Examples: REPEAT ('H', 2) has the value 'HH'. REPEAT ('XYZ', 0) has the value of a zero-length string.

RESHAPE (SOURCE, SHAPE, PAD, ORDER)

Constructs an array of a specified shape from the elements of a given array.

SOURCE is an array of any type, which supplies the elements for the result array.

SHAPE defines the shape of the result array. It is an integer array of up to seven elements, with rank one and of a constant size. All elements are either positive integers or zero.

PAD (optional) is used to fill in extra values if SOURCE is reshaped into a larger array. It is an array of the same data type as SOURCE. If it is absent or is a zero-sized array, you can only make SOURCE into another array of the same size or smaller.

ORDER (optional) is an integer array of rank one with a constant size. Its elements must be a permutation of (1,2,...,SIZE(SHAPE)). You can use it to insert elements in the result in an order of dimensions other than the normal (1,2,...,rank(RESULT)).

Class: Transformational function

Result Value: The result is an array with shape SHAPE. It has the same data type as SOURCE.

The array elements of SOURCE are placed into the result in the order of dimensions as specified by ORDER, or in the usual order for array elements if ORDER is not specified.

The array elements of SOURCE are followed by the array elements of PAD in array element order, and followed by additional copies of PAD until all of the elements of the result are set.

Examples

```
! Turn a rank-1 array into a 3x4 array of the
! same size.
RES= RESHAPE( (/A,B,C,D,E,F,G,H,I,J,K,L/), (/3,4/)
! The result is | A D G J |
!               | B E H K |
!               | C F I L |

! Turn a rank-1 array into a larger 3x5 array.
! Keep repeating -1 and -2 values for any
! elements not filled by the source array.
! Fill the rows first, then the columns.
RES= RESHAPE( (/1,2,3,4,5,6/), (/3,5/), &
  (/-1,-2/), (/2,1/) )
! The result is | 1  2  3  4  5 |
!               |    6 -1 -2 -1 -2 |
!               |   -1 -2 -1 -2 -1 |
```

Related Information: "SHAPE (SOURCE)" on page 404.

RRSPACING (X)

Returns the reciprocal of the relative spacing of the model numbers near the argument value.

X   must be of type real.

Class: Elemental function

Result Type and Attributes: Same as X.

Result Value: The result is:

ABS(FRACTION(X)) * FLOAT(RADIX(X))$^{DIGITS(X)}$

Examples: RRSPACING (-3.0) = 0.75 * 2^{24}. See "Real Data Model" on page 362.

SCALE (X,I)

Returns the scaled value: $X * RADIX(X)^I$

X   must be of type real.

I   must be of type integer.

Class: Elemental function

Result Type and Attributes: Same as X.

Result Value: The result is determined from the following:

$X * RADIX(X)^I$

$SCALE (X, I) = X * (RADIX(X)^I)$

Examples: SCALE (4.0, 3) = 4.0 * (2^3) = 32.0. See "Real Data Model" on page 362.

SCAN (STRING, SET, BACK)

Scan a string for any one of the characters in a set of characters.

STRING must be of type character.

SET must be of type character with the same kind type parameter as STRING.

BACK (optional) must be of type logical.

Class: Elemental function

Result Type and Attributes: Default integer.

Result Value

- Case (i): If BACK is absent or is present with the value .FALSE. and if STRING contains at least one character that is in SET, the value of the result is the position of the left-most character of STRING that is in SET.

- Case (ii): If BACK is present with the value .TRUE. and if STRING contains at least one character that is in SET, the value of the result is the position of the right-most character of STRING that is in SET.
- Case (iii): The value of the result is zero if no character of STRING is in SET or if the length of STRING or SET is zero.

Examples

- Case (i): SCAN ('FORTRAN', 'TR') has the value 3.
- Case (ii): SCAN ('FORTRAN', 'TR', BACK = .TRUE.) has the value 5.
- Case (iii): SCAN ('FORTRAN', 'BCD') has the value 0.

SELECTED_INT_KIND (R)

Returns a value of the kind type parameter of an integer data type that represents all integer values n with $-10^R < n < 10^R$.

R   must be a scalar of type integer.

Class: Transformational function

Result Type and Attributes: Default integer scalar.

Result Value

- The result has a value equal to the value of the kind type parameter of an integer data type that represents all values n in the range values n with $-10^R < n < 10^R$, or if no such kind type parameter is available, the result is -1.
- If more than one kind type parameter meets the criteria, the value returned is

the one with the smallest decimal exponent range.

Related Information: See "Type Parameters and Specifiers" on page 21.

SELECTED_REAL_KIND (P, R)

Returns a value of the kind type parameter of a real data type with decimal precision of at least P digits and a decimal exponent range of at least R.

P (optional) must be scalar and of type integer.

R (optional) must be scalar and of type integer.

Class: Transformational function

Result Type and Attributes: Default integer scalar.

Result Value

- The result has a value equal to a value of the kind type parameter of a real data type with decimal precision, as returned by the function PRECISION, of at least P digits and a decimal exponent range, as returned by the function RANGE, of at least R, or if no such kind type parameter is available,
  - If the precision is not available, the result is -1.
  - If the exponent range is not available, the result is -2.
  - If neither is available, the result is -3.
- If more than one kind type parameter value meets the criteria, the value returned is the one with the smallest decimal precision, unless there are several such values, in which case, the

smallest of these kind values is returned.

Related Information: See "Type Parameters and Specifiers" on page 21.

SET_EXPONENT (X,I)

Returns the number whose fractional part is the fractional part of the model representation of X, and whose exponent part is I.

X   must be of type real.

I   must be of type integer.

Class: Elemental function

Result Type and Attributes: Same as X.

Result Value

- If X = 0 the result is zero.
- Otherwise, the result is:

  $\text{FRACTION}(X) * \text{RADIX}(X)^I$

Examples: SET_EXPONENT (10.5, 1) = 0.65625 * 2.0^1 = 1.3125 See "Real Data Model" on page 362.

SHAPE (SOURCE)

Returns the shape of an array or scalar.

SOURCE is an array or scalar of any data type. It must not be a disassociated pointer, allocatable array that is not allocated, or assumed-size array.

Class: Inquiry function

Result Value: The result is a one-dimensional default integer array whose elements define the shape of SOURCES.

The extent of each dimension in SOURCES is returned in the corresponding element in the result array.

Related Information: "RESHAPE (SOURCE, SHAPE, PAD, ORDER)" on page 401.

Examples

```
! A is the array  | 7 6 3 1 |
!                 | 2 4 0 9 |
!                 | 5 7 6 8 |
!
     RES = SHAPE( A )
! The result is | 3  4 | because A is a rank-2 array
! with 3 elements in each column and 4 elements in
! each row.
```

SIGN (A, B)

Absolute value of A times the sign of B.

A   must be of type integer or real.

B   must be of the same type and kind type parameter as A.

Class: Elemental function

Result Type and Attributes: Same as A.

Result Value

- The value of the result is |A| if B ≥ 0
- The value of the result is -|A| if B < 0

Examples: SIGN (-3.0, 2.0) has the value 3.0.

Specific Name	Argument Type	Result Type	Pass As Arg?
SIGN	default real	default real	yes
ISIGN	default integer	same as argument	yes
DSIGN	double precision real	double precision real	yes

SIN (X)

Sine function.

X   must be of type real or complex. If X is real, it is regarded as a value in radians. If X is complex, its real part is regarded as a value in radians.

Class: Elemental function

Result Type and Attributes: Same as X.

Result Value: It approximates sin(X).

Examples: SIN (1.0) has the value 0.84147098 (approximately).

Specific Name	Argument Type	Result Type	Pass As Arg?
SIN	default real	default real	yes
DSIN	double precision real	double precision real	yes
CSIN	default complex	default complex	yes

SINH (X)

Hyperbolic sine function.

X   must be of type real.

Class: Elemental function

Result Type and Attributes: Same as X.

Result Value: The result has a value equal to sinh(x).

Examples: SINH (1.0) has the value 1.1752012 (approximately).

Specific Name	Argument Type	Result Type	Pass As Arg?
SINH	default real	default real	yes
DSINH	double precision real	double precision real	yes

SIZE (ARRAY, DIM)

Returns the extent of an array along a specified dimension or the total number of elements in the array.

ARRAY is an array of any data type. It must not be a scalar, disassociated pointer, or allocatable array that is not allocated. It can be an assumed-size array if DIM is present and has a value that is less than the rank of ARRAY.

DIM (optional) is an integer scalar in the range $1 \le DIM \le rank(ARRAY)$.

Class: Inquiry function

Result Type and Attributes: Default integer scalar.

Result Value: The result equals the extent of ARRAY along dimension DIM; or, if DIM is not specified, it is the total number of array elements in ARRAY.

Examples

```
! A is the array  | 1 -4  7 -10 |
!                 | 2  5 -8  11 |
!                 | 3  6  9 -12 |

      RES = SIZE( A )
! The result is 12 because there are 12 elements in A.

      RES = SIZE( A, DIM = 1 )
! The result is 3 because there are 3 rows in A.

      RES = SIZE( A, DIM = 2 )
! The result is 4 because there are 4 columns in A.
```

SPACING (X)

Returns the absolute spacing of the model numbers near the argument value.

X   must be of type real.

Class: Elemental function

Result Type and Attributes: Same as X.

Result Value: If X is not 0, the result is:

RADIX(X)$^{\text{EXPONENT(X) - DIGITS(X)}}$

If X is 0, the result is the same as that of TINY(X).

Examples: SPACING (3.0) = $2.0^{2 \cdot 24}$ = $2.0^{(-22)}$ See "Real Data Model" on page 362.

SPREAD (SOURCE, DIM, NCOPIES)

Replicates an array in an additional dimension by making copies of existing elements along that dimension.

SOURCE can be an array or scalar. It can have any data type. The rank of SOURCE has a maximum value of 6.

DIM is an integer scalar in the range $1 \le \text{DIM} \le \text{rank(SOURCE)}+1$. Unlike most other array intrinsic functions, **SPREAD** requires the DIM argument.

NCOPIES is an integer scalar. It becomes the extent of the extra dimension added to the result.

Class: Transformational function

Result Type and Attributes: The result is an array of rank rank(SOURCE)+1 and with the same type and type parameters as SOURCE.

Result Value: If SOURCE is a scalar, the result is a one-dimensional array with NCOPIES elements, each with value SOURCE.

If SOURCE is an array, the result is an array of rank rank(SOURCE) + 1. Along dimension DIM, each array element of the result is equal to the corresponding array element in SOURCE.

If NCOPIES is less than or equal to zero, the result is a zero-sized array.

Examples

```
! A is the array (/ -4.7, 6.1, 0.3 /)

      RES = SPREAD( A, DIM = 1, NCOPIES = 3 )
! The result is   | -4.7 6.1 0.3 |
!                 | -4.7 6.1 0.3 |
!                 | -4.7 6.1 0.3 |
! DIM=1 extends each column.  Each element in RES(:,1)
! becomes a copy of A(1), each element in RES(:,2) becomes
! a copy of A(2), and so on.

      RES = SPREAD( A, DIM = 2, NCOPIES = 3 )
! The result is   | -4.7 -4.7 -4.7 |
!                 |  6.1  6.1  6.1 |
!                 |  0.3  0.3  0.3 |
! DIM=2 extends each row.  Each element in RES(1,:)
! becomes a copy of A(1), each element in RES(2,:)
! becomes a copy of A(2), and so on.

      RES = SPREAD( A, DIM = 2, NCOPIES = 0 )
! The result is (/ /) (a zero-sized array).
```

SQRT (X)

Square root.

X   must be of type real or complex. Unless X is complex, its value must be greater than or equal to zero.

Class: Elemental function

Result Type and Attributes: Same as X.

Result Value

- It has a value equal to the square root of X.
- If the result type is complex, its value is the principal value with the real part greater than or equal to zero. If the real part is zero, the imaginary part is greater than or equal to zero.

Examples: SQRT (4.0) has the value 2.0.

Specific Name	Argument Type	Result Type	Pass As Arg?
SQRT	default real	default real	yes
DSQRT	double precision real	double precision real	yes
CSQRT	default complex	default complex	yes

SUM (ARRAY, DIM, MASK)

Calculates the sum of selected elements in an array.

ARRAY is an array of numeric type, whose elements you want to sum.

DIM (optional) is an integer scalar in the range 1 ≤ DIM ≤ rank(ARRAY). The corresponding actual argument must not be an optional dummy argument.

MASK (optional) is a logical expression. If it is an array, it must conform with ARRAY in shape. If MASK is a scalar, the scalar value applies to all elements in ARRAY.

Class: Transformational function

Result Value: If DIM is present, the result is an array of rank rank(ARRAY)-1, with the same data type as ARRAY. If DIM is missing, or if MASK has a rank of one, the result is a scalar.

The result is calculated by one of the following methods:

Method 1:
   If only ARRAY is specified, the result equals the sum of all the array elements of ARRAY. If ARRAY is a zero-sized array, the result equals zero.

Method 2:
   If ARRAY and MASK are both specified, the result equals the sum of the array elements of ARRAY that have a corresponding array element in MASK with a value of .TRUE.. If MASK has no elements with a value of .TRUE., the result is equal to zero.

Method 3:
   If DIM is also specified, the result value equals the sum of the array elements of

SYSTEM_CLOCK

ARRAY along dimension DIM that have a corresponding true array element in MASK.

Examples: Method 1:

```
! Sum all the elements in an array.
      RES = SUM( (/2, 3, 4 /) )
! The result is 9 because (2+3+4) = 9
```

Method 2:

```
! A is the array (/ -3, -7, -5, 2, 3 /)
! Sum all elements that are greater than -5.
      RES = SUM( A, MASK = A .GT. -5 )
! The result is 2 because (-3 + 2 + 3) = 2
```

Method 3:

```
! B is the array | 4 2 3 |
!                | 7 8 5 |

! Sum the elements in each column.
      RES = SUM(B, DIM = 1)
! The result is | 11 10 8 | because (4 + 7) = 11
!                              (2 + 8) = 10
!                              (3 + 5) =  8

! Sum the elements in each row.
      RES = SUM(B, DIM = 2)
! The result is | 9 20 | because (4 + 2 + 3) =  9
!                              (7 + 8 + 5) = 20

! Sum the elements in each row, considering only
! those elements greater than two.
      RES = SUM(B, DIM = 2, MASK = B .GT. 2)
! The result is | 7 20 | because (4 + 3) =  7
!                              (7 + 8 + 5) = 20
```

SYSTEM_CLOCK (COUNT, COUNT_RATE, COUNT_MAX)

Returns integer data from a real-time clock.

COUNT (optional) must be scalar and of type default integer. It is an INTENT(OUT) argument. It is set to a processor-dependent value based on the current value of the processor clock or to -HUGE (0) if there is no clock. The processor-dependent value is incremented by one for each clock count until the value COUNT_MAX is reached

and is reset to zero at the next count. It lies in the range of 0 to COUNT_MAX if there is a clock.

COUNT_RATE (optional) must be scalar and of type default integer. It is an INTENT(OUT) argument. It is set to a processor-dependent approximation of the number of processor clock counts per second, or to zero if there is no clock.

COUNT_MAX (optional) must be scalar and of type default integer. It is an INTENT(OUT) argument. It is set to the maximum value that COUNT can have, or to zero if there is no clock.

Class: Subroutine

Examples

```
! The following example shows how to interpret values
! returned by the subroutine SYSTEM_CLOCK. The processor
! clock is a 24-hour clock. After the call to SYSTEM_CLOCK,
! the COUNT contains the day time expressed in clock ticks
! per second. The number of ticks per second is available
! in the COUNT_RATE. The COUNT_RATE value is processor-
! dependent.

INTEGER, DIMENSION(8) :: IV
TIME_SYNC: DO
CALL DATE_AND_TIME(VALUES=IV)
IHR  = IV(5)
IMIN = IV(6)
ISEC = IV(7)
CALL SYSTEM_CLOCK(COUNT=IC, COUNT_RATE=IR, COUNT_MAX=IM)
CALL DATE_AND_TIME(VALUES=IV)

IF ((IHR == IV(5)) .AND. (IMIN == IV(6)) .AND. &
   (ISEC == IV(7))) EXIT TIME_SYNC

END DO TIME_SYNC

IDAY_SEC = 3600*IHR + IMIN*60 + ISEC
IDAY_TICKS = IDAY_SEC * IR

IF (IDAY_TICKS /= IC) THEN
   STOP 'clock error'
ENDIF
END
```

TAN (X)

Tangent function.

X   must be of type real.

Class: Elemental function

Result Type and Attributes: Same as X.

Result Value: The result approximates tan(X), where X has a value in radians.

Examples: TAN (1.0) has the value 1.5574077 (approximately).

Specific Name	Argument Type	Result Type	Pass As Arg?
TAN	default real	default real	yes
DTAN	double precision real	double precision real	yes

TANH (X)

Hyperbolic tangent function.

X   must be of type real.

Class: Elemental function

Result Type and Attributes: Same as X.

Result Value: The result has a value equal to tanh(X).

Examples: TANH (1.0) has the value 0.76159416 (approximately).

Specific Name	Argument Type	Result Type	Pass As Arg?
TANH	default real	default real	yes
DTANH	double precision real	double precision real	yes

TINY (X)

Returns the smallest positive number in the model representing numbers of the same type and kind type parameter as the argument.

X   must be of type real. It may be scalar or array valued.

Class: Inquiry function

Result Type and Attributes: Scalar with the same type as X.

Result Value: The result is:

$$\text{RADIX}(X)^{(\text{MINEXPONENT}(X)-1)} \text{ for real } X$$

Examples: TINY (X) = float(2)$^{(-126)}$ = 1.17549351e-38 See "Real Data Model" on page 362.

TRANSFER (SOURCE, MOLD, SIZE)

Returns a result with a physical representation identical to that of SOURCE but interpreted with the type and type parameters of MOLD.

It performs a low-level conversion between types without any sign extension, rounding, blank padding, or other alteration that may occur using other methods of conversion.

TRANSPOSE

SOURCE is the data entity whose bitwise value you want to transfer to a different type. It may be of any type and may be scalar or array valued.

MOLD is a data entity that has the type characteristics you want for the result. It may be of any type and may be scalar or array valued. Its value is not used, only its type characteristics.

SIZE (optional) is the number of elements for the output result. It must be a scalar integer. The corresponding actual argument must not be an optional dummy argument.

Class: Transformational function

Result Type and Attributes: The same type and type parameters as MOLD.

If MOLD is a scalar and SIZE is absent, the result is a scalar.

If MOLD is array valued and SIZE is absent, the result is array valued and of rank one, with the smallest size that is physically large enough to hold SOURCE.

If SIZE is present, the result is array valued of rank one and size SIZE.

Result Value: The physical representation of the result is the same as SOURCE, truncated if the result is smaller or with an undefined trailing portion if the result is larger.

Because the physical representation is unchanged, it is possible to undo the results of TRANSFER as long as the result is not truncated:

```
REAL(4) X = 3.141
DOUBLE PRECISION I, J(6) = (/1,2,3,4,5,6/)

! Because x is transferred to a larger representation
! and then back, its value is unchanged.
    X = TRANSFER( TRANSFER( X, I ), X )

! j is transferred into a real(4) array large enough to
! hold all its elements, then back into an array of
! its original size, so its value is unchanged too.
    J = TRANSFER( TRANSFER( J, X ), J, SIZE=SIZE(J) )
```

TRANSFER ((/1.1,2.2,3.3/), (/(0.0,0.0)/)) is a complex rank-one array of length two whose first element has the value (1.1, 2.2) and whose second element has a real part with the value 3.3. The imaginary part of the second element is undefined.

TRANSFER ((/1.1,2.2,3.3/), (/(0.0,0.0)/), 1) has the value (/(1.1,2.2)/).

TRANSPOSE (MATRIX)

Transposes a two-dimensional array, turning each column into a row and each row into a column.

MATRIX is an array of any data type, with a rank of two.

Class: Transformational function

Result Value: The result is a two-dimensional array of the same data type as MATRIX.

The shape of the result is (n,m) where the shape of MATRIX is (m,n). For example, if the shape of MATRIX is (2,3), the shape of the result is (3,2).

Each element (i,j) in the result has the value MATRIX (j,i) for i in the range 1-n and j in the range 1-m.

Examples

```
! A is the array  | 0 -5  8 -7 |
!                 | 2  4 -1  1 |
!                 | 7  5  6 -6 |
! Transpose the columns and rows of A.
      RES = TRANSPOSE( A )
! The result is   | 0  2  7 |
!                 |-5  4  5 |
!                 | 8 -1  6 |
!                 |-7  1 -6 |
```

TRIM (STRING)

Returns the argument with trailing blank characters removed.

STRING must be of type character and must be a scalar.

Class: Transformational function

Result Type and Attributes: Character with the same kind type parameter value as STRING and with a length that is the length of STRING less the number of trailing blanks in STRING.

Result Value

- The value of the result is the same as STRING, except trailing blanks are removed.
- If STRING contains no nonblank characters, the result has zero length.

Examples: TRIM ('ƅAƅBƅƅ') has the value 'ƅAƅB'.

UBOUND (ARRAY, DIM)

Returns the upper bounds of each dimension in an array, or the upper bound of a specified dimension.

ARRAY is the array whose upper bounds you want to determine. Its bounds must be defined; that is, it must not be a disassociated pointer or an allocatable array that is not allocated, and if its size is assumed, you can only examine one dimension.

DIM (optional) is an integer scalar in the range $1 \leq \text{DIM} \leq \text{rank(ARRAY)}$. The corresponding actual argument must not be an optional dummy argument.

Class: Inquiry function

Result Type and Attributes: Default integer.

If DIM is present, the result is a scalar. If DIM is not present, the result is a one-dimensional array with one element for each dimension in ARRAY.

Result Value: Each element in the result corresponds to a dimension of ARRAY. If ARRAY is a whole array or array structure component, these values are equal to the upper bounds. If ARRAY is an array section or expression that is not a whole array or array structure component, the values represent the number of elements in each dimension, which may be different than the declared upper bounds of the original array. If a dimension is zero-sized, the corresponding element in the result is zero, regardless of the value of the upper bound.

Examples

```
! This array illustrates the way UBOUND works with
! different ranges for dimensions.
      REAL A(1:10, -4:5, 4:-5)

      RES=UBOUND( A )
! The result is (/ 10, 5, 0 /).

      RES=UBOUND( A(:,:,:) )
! The result is (/ 10, 10, 0 /) because the argument is
! is an array section.

      RES=UBOUND( A(4:10,-4:1,:) )
! The result is (/ 7, 6, 0 /), because for an array section,
! it is the number of elements that is significant.
```

UNPACK (VECTOR, MASK, FIELD)

Takes some or all elements from a one-dimensional array and rearranges them into another, possibly larger, array.

VECTOR is a one-dimensional array of any data type. There must be at least as many elements in VECTOR as there are .TRUE. values in MASK.

MASK is a logical array that determines where the elements of VECTOR are placed when they are unpacked.

FIELD must have the same shape as the mask argument, and the same data type as VECTOR. Its elements are inserted into the result array wherever the corresponding MASK element has the value .FALSE..

Class: Transformational function

Result Value: The result is an array with the same shape as MASK and the same data type as VECTOR.

The elements of the result are filled in array-element order: if the corresponding element in MASK is .TRUE., the result element is filled by the next element of

VECTOR; otherwise, it is filled by the corresponding element of FIELD.

Examples

```
! VECTOR is the array (/ 5, 6, 7, 8 /),
! MASK is | F T T |, FIELD is | -1 -4 -7 |
!         | T F F |           | -2 -5 -8 |
!         | F F T |           | -3 -6 -9 |

! Turn the one-dimensional vector into a two-dimensional
! array.  The elements of VECTOR are placed into the .TRUE.
! positions in MASK, and the remaining elements are
! made up of negative values from FIELD.
      RES = UNPACK( VECTOR, MASK, FIELD )
! The result is | -1  6  7 |
!               |  5 -5 -8 |
!               | -3 -6  8 |

! Do the same transformation, but using all zeros for the
! replacement values of FIELD.
      RES = UNPACK( VECTOR, MASK, FIELD = 0 )
! The result is | 0 6 7 |
!               | 5 0 0 |
!               | 0 0 8 |
```

VERIFY (STRING, SET, BACK)

Verify that a set of characters contains all the characters in a string by identifying the position of the first character in a string of characters that does not appear in a given set of characters.

STRING must be of type character.

SET must be of type character with the same kind type parameter as STRING.

BACK (optional) must be of type logical.

Class: Elemental function

Result Type and Attributes: Default integer.

Result Value

- Case (i): If BACK is absent or present with the value .FALSE. and if STRING contains at least one character that is not in SET, the value of the result is the

position of the left-most character of
STRING that is not in SET.

- Case (ii): If BACK is present with the
  value .TRUE. and if STRING contains at
  least one character that is not in SET,
  the value of the result is the position of
  the right-most character of STRING that
  is not in SET.
- Case (iii): The value of the result is
  zero if each character in STRING is in
  SET or if STRING has zero length.

Examples

- Case (i): VERIFY ('ABBA', 'A') has the
  value 2.
- Case (ii): VERIFY ('ABBA', 'A',
  BACK = .TRUE.) has the value 3.
- Case (iii): VERIFY ('ABBA', 'AB') has
  the value 0.

Appendix A. FORTRAN 77 Compatibility

Except as noted here, the Fortran 90 standard is an upward-compatible extension to the preceding Fortran International Standard, ISO 1539-1:1980, informally referred to as FORTRAN 77. Any standard-conforming FORTRAN 77 program remains standard-conforming under the Fortran 90 standard, except as noted under item 4 below regarding intrinsic procedures. The Fortran 90 standard restricts the behavior of some features that are processor-dependent in FORTRAN 77. Therefore, a standard-conforming FORTRAN 77 program that uses one of these processor-dependent features may have a different interpretation under the Fortran 90 standard, yet remain a standard-conforming program. The following FORTRAN 77 features have different interpretations in Fortran 90:

1. FORTRAN 77 permitted a processor to supply more precision derived from a real constant than can be contained in a real datum when the constant is used to initialize a double precision data object in a **DATA** statement. Fortran 90 does not permit a processor this option.

2. If a named variable that is not in a common block is initialized in a **DATA** statement and does not have the **SAVE** attribute specified, FORTRAN 77 left its **SAVE** attribute processor-dependent. The Fortran 90 standard specifies that this named variable has the **SAVE** attribute.

3. FORTRAN 77 required that the number of characters required by the input list must be less than or equal to the number of characters in the record during formatted input. The Fortran 90 standard specifies that the input record is logically padded with blanks if there are not enough characters in the record, unless the **PAD='NO'** specifier is indicated in an appropriate **OPEN** statement.

4. The Fortran 90 standard has more intrinsic functions than FORTRAN 77, in addition to a few intrinsic subroutines. Therefore, a standard-conforming FORTRAN 77 program may have a different interpretation under Fortran 90 if it invokes a procedure having the same name as one of the new standard intrinsic procedures, unless that procedure is specified in an **EXTERNAL** statement.

Obsolescent Features

As the Fortran language evolves, it is only natural that the usefulness of some older features are better handled by newer features geared toward today's programming needs. At the same time, the considerable investment in legacy Fortran code suggests that it would be insensitive to customer needs to decommit any FORTRAN 77 features at this time. For this reason, Fortran 90 is a fully upward compatible standard with the FORTRAN 77 standard.

Fortran 90 defines two categories of outmoded features, deleted features and obsolescent features. Deleted features are FORTRAN 77 features that are considered to be largely unused and so are not supported in Fortran 90. There are no deleted features in Fortran 90.

Obsolescent features are FORTRAN 77 features that are still frequently used today, but whose use can be better delivered by newer features and methods. Although obsolescent features are, by definition, supported in the Fortran 90 standard, some of these features may be marked as deleted in the next Fortran standard. Although a processor may still support deleted features as extensions to the language, you may want to take steps now to modify your existing code to use better methods.

Fortran 90 indicates the following FORTRAN 77 features obsolescent:

- Arithmetic **IF**

  Recommended method: Use the logical **IF** statement, **IF** construct, or **CASE** construct.

- **DO** control variables and expressions of type real

  Recommended method: Use variables and expression of type integer.

- **PAUSE** statement

  Recommended method: Use the **READ** statement.

- Alternate return specifiers

  Recommended method: Evaluate a return code in a **CASE** construct or a computed **GO TO** statement on return from the procedure.

  ```
  ! FORTRAN 77

    CALL SUB(A,B,C,*10,*20,*30)

  ! Fortran 90

    CALL SUB(A,B,C,RET_CODE)
    SELECT CASE (RET_CODE)
      CASE (1)
        ⋮
      CASE (2)
        ⋮
      CASE (3)
        ⋮
    END SELECT
  ```

- **ASSIGN** and assigned **GO TO** statements

  Recommended method: Use internal procedures.

- Branching to an **END IF** statement from outside the **IF** block

  Recommended method: Branch to the statement that follows the **END IF** statement.

- Shared loop termination and termination on a statement other than **END DO** or **CONTINUE**

  Recommended method: Use an **END DO** or **CONTINUE** statement to terminate each loop.

- **H** edit descriptor

  Recommended method: Use the character constant edit descriptor.

Glossary

This glossary defines terms that are commonly used in this book.

A

actual argument. An expression, variable, procedure, or alternate return specifier that is specified in a procedure reference.

alphabetic character. A letter or other symbol, excluding digits, used in a language. Usually the uppercase and lowercase letters A through Z plus other special symbols (such as _) allowed by a particular language.

alphanumeric. Pertaining to a character set that contains letters, digits, and usually other characters, such as punctuation marks and mathematical symbols.

American National Standards Institute (ANSI). An organization sponsored by the Computer and Business Equipment Manufacturers Association through which accredited organizations create and maintain voluntary industry standards.

argument. An actual argument or a dummy argument.

argument association. The relationship between an actual argument and a dummy argument during the execution of a procedure reference.

arithmetic constant. A constant of type integer, real, or complex.

arithmetic expression. One or more arithmetic operators and arithmetic primaries, the evaluation of which produces a numeric value. An arithmetic expression can be an unsigned arithmetic constant, the name of an arithmetic constant, or a reference to an arithmetic variable, function reference, or a combination of such primaries formed by using arithmetic operators and parentheses.

arithmetic operator. A symbol that directs the performance of an arithmetic operation. The intrinsic arithmetic operators are:

```
+      addition
-      subtraction
*      multiplication
/      division
**     exponentiation
```

array. An entity that contains an ordered group of scalar data. All objects in an array have the same data type and type parameters.

array declarator. The part of a statement that describes an array used in a program unit. It indicates the name of the array, the number of dimensions it contains, and the size of each dimension.

array element. A single data item in an array, identified by the array name followed by one or more integer expressions called subscript expressions that indicate its position in the array.

array name. The name of an ordered set of data items.

array pointer. A pointer to an array.

array section. A subobject that is an array and is not a structure component.

assignment statement. An assignment statement can be intrinsic or defined. An intrinsic assignment stores the value of the right operand in the storage location of the left operand.

attribute. A property of a data object that may be specified in a type declaration statement, attribute specification statement, or through a default setting.

B

blank common. An unnamed common block.

block data subprogram. A subprogram headed by a **BLOCK DATA** statement and used to initialize variables in named common blocks.

C

character constant. A string of one or more alphabetic characters enclosed in apostrophes or double quotation marks.

character expression. A character object, a character-valued function reference, or a sequence of them separated by the concatenation operator, with optional parentheses.

character operator. A symbol that represents an operation, such as concatenation (//) to be performed on character data.

character string. A sequence of consecutive characters.

character substring. A contiguous portion of a character string.

character type. A data type that consists of alphanumeric characters. See also *data type*.

collating sequence. The sequence in which characters are ordered within the computer for sorting, combining, or comparing.

comment. A language construct for the inclusion of text in a program that has no effect on the execution of the program.

common block. A storage area that may be referred to by a calling program and one or more subprograms.

complex constant. An ordered pair of real or integer constants separated by a comma and enclosed in parentheses. The first constant of

the pair is the real part of the complex number; the second is the imaginary part.

complex number. A number consisting of an ordered pair of real numbers, expressible in the form **a+bi**, where **a** and **b** are real numbers and **i** squared equals -1.

complex type. A data type that represents the values of complex numbers. The value is expressed as an ordered pair of real data items separated by a comma and enclosed in parentheses. The first item represents the real part of the complex number; the second represents the imaginary part.

conformance. An executable program conforms to the Fortran 90 Standard if it uses only those forms and relationships described therein and if the executable program has an interpretation according to the Fortran 90 Standard. A program unit conforms to the Fortran 90 Standard if it can be included in an executable program in a manner that allows the executable program to be standard-conforming. A processor conforms to the standard if it executes standard-conforming programs in a manner that fulfills the interpretations prescribed in the standard.

connected unit. A unit that is connected either through preconnection or explicitly via the **OPEN** statement to a named file.

constant. A data object with a value that does not change. Contrast with *variable*. The three classes of constants specify numbers (arithmetic), truth values (logical), and character data (character).

construct. A sequence of statements starting with a **SELECT CASE, DO, IF,** or **WHERE** statement and ending with the corresponding terminal statement.

continuation line. Continues a statement beyond its initial line.

control statement. A statement that is used to alter the continuous sequential invocation of statements; a control statement may be a conditional statement, such as **IF**, or an imperative statement, such as **STOP**.

D

data object. A variable, constant, or subobject of a constant.

data transfer statement. A **READ**, **WRITE**, or **PRINT** statement.

data type. The properties and internal representation that characterize data and functions. The intrinsic types are integer, real, complex, logical, and character.

definable. A variable is definable if its value can be changed by the appearance of its name or designator on the left of an assignment statement.

delimiters. A pair of parentheses or slashes (or both) used to enclose syntactic lists.

derived type. A type whose data have components, each of which is either of intrinsic type or of another derived type.

digit. A character that represents a nonnegative integer. For example, any of the numerals from 0 through 9.

DO loop. A range of statements invoked repetitively by a **DO** statement.

DO variable. A variable, specified in a **DO** statement, that is initialized or incremented prior to each occurrence of the statement or statements within a **DO** range. It is used to control the number of times the statements within the range are executed.

double precision constant. A constant of type real with greater precision than the default real precision.

dummy argument. An entity whose name appears in the parenthesized list following the procedure name in a **FUNCTION, SUBROUTINE, ENTRY**, or statement function statement.

E

elemental. An adjective applied to an intrinsic operation, procedure or assignment that is applied independently to elements of an array or corresponding elements of a set of conformable arrays and scalars.

embedded blanks. Blanks that are surrounded by any other characters.

entity. A general term for the following: a program unit, procedure, operator, interface block, common block, external unit, statement function, type, named variable, expression, component of a structure, named constant, statement label, construct, or namelist group.

executable program. A program that can be executed as a self-contained procedure. It consists of a main program and, optionally, modules, subprograms and non-Fortran external procedures.

executable statement. A statement that causes an action to be taken by the program; for example, to calculate, test conditions, or alter normal sequential execution.

existing unit. A valid unit number that is system-specific.

explicit interface. For a procedure referenced in a scoping unit, the property of being an internal procedure, module procedure, intrinsic procedure, external procedure that has an interface block, recursive procedure reference in its own scoping unit, or dummy procedure that has an interface block.

expression. A sequence of operands, operators, and parentheses. It may be a variable, constant, function reference, or it may represent a computation.

external procedure. A procedure that is defined by an external subprogram or by a means other than Fortran.

F

field. An area in a record used to contain a particular category of data.

file. A sequence of records. If the file is located in internal storage, it is an internal file; if it is on an input/output device, it is an external file.

floating-point number. A real number represented by a pair of distinct numerals. The real number is the product of the fractional part, one of the numerals, and a value obtained by raising the implicit floating-point base to a power indicated by the second numeral.

format. (1) A defined arrangement of such things as characters, fields, and lines, usually used for displays, printouts, or files. (2) To arrange such things as characters, fields, and lines.

formatted data. Data that is transferred between main storage and an input/output device according to a specified format. See also *list-directed data* and *unformatted data*.

Fortran (FORmula TRANslation). A high-level programming language used primarily for scientific, engineering, and mathematical applications.

function. A procedure that returns the value of a single variable and that usually has a single exit. See also *function subprogram*, *intrinsic function*, and *statement function*.

G

generic identifier. A lexical token that appears in an **INTERFACE** statement and is associated with all the procedures in an interface block.

H

host. A main program or subprogram that contains an internal procedure is called the host of the internal procedure. A module that contains a module procedure is called the host of the module procedure.

host association. The process by which an internal subprogram, module subprogram, or derived-type definition accesses the entities of its host.

I

implicit interface. A procedure referenced in a scoping unit other than its own is said to have an implicit interface if the procedure is an external procedure that does not have an interface block, a dummy procedure that does not have an interface block, or a statement function.

implied DO. An indexing specification (similar to a **DO** statement, but without specifying the word **DO**) with a list of data elements, rather than a set of statements, as its range.

input/output (I/O). Pertaining to either input or output, or both.

input/output list. A list of variables in an input or output statement specifying the data to be read or written. An output list can also contain a constant, an expression involving operators or function references, or an expression enclosed in parentheses.

integer constant. An optionally signed digit string that contains no decimal point.

interface block. A sequence of statements from an **INTERFACE** statement to the corresponding **END INTERFACE** statement.

interface body. A sequence of statements in an interface block from a **FUNCTION** or **SUBROUTINE** statement to the corresponding **END** statement.

intrinsic. An adjective applied to types, operations, assignment statements, and procedures that are defined by Fortran 90 and can be used in any scoping unit without further definition or specification.

K

keyword. (1) A statement keyword is a word that is part of the syntax of a statement and that may be used to identify the statement. (2) An argument keyword specifies a name for a dummy argument.

kind type parameter. A parameter whose values label the available kinds of an intrinsic type.

L

lexical token. A sequence of characters with an indivisible interpretation.

list-directed. A predefined input/output format that depends on the type, type parameters, and values of the entities in the data list.

literal. A symbol or a quantity in a source program that is itself data, rather than a reference to data.

logical constant. A constant with a value of either `true` or `false`.

logical operator. A symbol that represents an operation on logical expressions:

```
.NOT.    (logical negation)
.AND.    (logical conjunction)
.OR.     (logical union)
.EQV.    (logical equivalence)
.NEQV.   (logical nonequivalence)
```

loop. A statement block that executes repeatedly.

M

main program. The first program unit to receive control when a program is run. Contrast with *subprogram*.

module. A program unit that contains or accesses definitions to be accessed by other program units.

N

name. A lexical token consisting of a letter followed by up to 30 alphanumeric characters (letters, digits, and underscores). Note that in FORTRAN 77, this was called a symbolic name.

named common. A separate, named common block consisting of variables.

nest. To incorporate a structure or structures of some kind into a structure of the same kind. For example, to nest one loop (the nested loop) within another loop (the nesting loop); to nest one subroutine (the nested subroutine) within another subroutine (the nesting subroutine).

nonexecutable statement. A statement that describes the characteristics of a program unit, data, editing information, or statement functions, but does not cause any action to be taken by the program.

nonexisting file. A file that does not physically exist on any accessible storage medium.

numeric constant. A constant that expresses an integer, real, or complex number.

P

pad. To fill unused positions in a field or character string with dummy data, usually zeros or blanks.

pointer. A variable that has the **POINTER** attribute. A pointer must not be referenced or defined unless it is pointer associated with a target. If it is an array, it does not have a shape unless it is pointer-associated.

preconnected file. A file that is connected to a unit at the beginning of execution of the executable program.

predefined convention. The implied type and length specification of a data object, based on the initial character of its name when no explicit specification is given. The initial characters I through N imply type integer; the initial characters A through H, and O through Z imply type real.

present. A dummy argument is present in an instance of a subprogram if it is associated with an actual argument and the actual argument is a dummy argument that is present in the invoking procedure or is not a dummy argument of the invoking procedure.

primary. The simplest form of an expression: an object, array constructor, structure constructor, function reference, or expression enclosed in parentheses.

procedure. A computation that may be invoked during program execution. It may be a function or subroutine. It may be an intrinsic procedure, external procedure, module procedure, internal procedure, dummy procedure, or statement function. A subprogram may define more than one procedure if it contains **ENTRY** statements.

program unit. A main program or subprogram.

R

random access. An access method in which records can be read from, written to, or removed from a file in any order.

real constant. A string of decimal digits that expresses a real number. A real constant must contain a decimal point, a decimal exponent, or both.

record. A sequence of values that is treated as a whole within a file.

relational expression. An expression that consists of an arithmetic or character expression, followed by a relational operator, followed by another arithmetic or character expression.

relational operator. The words or symbols used to express a relational condition or a relational expression:

```
.GT.      greater than
.GE.      greater than or equal to
.LE.      less than or equal to
.EQ.      equal to
.NE.      not equal to
```

result variable. The variable that returns the value of a function.

S

scalar. (1) A single datum that is not an array. (2) Not having the property of being an array.

scale factor. A number indicating the location of the decimal point in a real number (and, on input, if there is no exponent, the magnitude of the number).

scope. That part of an executable program within which a lexical token has a single interpretation.

scoping unit. (1) A derived-type definition. (2) An interface body, excluding any derived-type definitions and interface bodies contained within it. (3) A program unit or subprogram, excluding derived-type definitions, interface bodies, and subprograms contained within it.

sequential access. An access method in which records are read from, written to, or removed from a file based on the logical order of the records in the file.

specification statement. One of the set of statements that provides information about the data used in the source program. The statement could also supply information to allocate data storage.

statement. A language construct that represents a step in a sequence of actions or a set of declarations. Statements fall into two broad classes: executable and nonexecutable.

statement function. A name, followed by a list of dummy arguments, that is equated with an intrinsic or derived-type expression, and that can be used as a substitute for the expression throughout the program.

statement label. A number from one through five digits that is used to identify a statement. Statement labels can be used to transfer control, to define the range of a **DO**, or to refer to a **FORMAT** statement.

storage association. The relationship between two storage sequences if a storage unit of one is the same as the storage unit of the other.

structure. A scalar data object of derived type.

structure component. The part of a data object of derived-type corresponding to a component of its type.

subobject. A portion of a named data object that may be referenced or defined independently of other portions. It can be an array element, array section, structure component, or substring.

subprogram. A function subprogram or a subroutine subprogram. Note that in FORTRAN 77, a block data program unit was called a subprogram.

subroutine. A procedure that is invoked by a **CALL** statement or defined assignment statement.

subscript. A subscript quantity or set of subscript quantities enclosed in parentheses and used with an array name to identify a particular array element.

substring. A contiguous portion of a scalar character string. (Although an array section can specify a substring selector, the result is not a substring.)

T

target. A named data object specified to have the **TARGET** attribute, a data object created by an **ALLOCATE** statement for a pointer, or a subobject of such an object.

type declaration statement. Specifies the type, length, and attributes of objects and functions. Objects can be assigned initial values.

U

unformatted record. A record that is transmitted unchanged between internal and external storage.

unit. A means of referring to a file to use in input/output statements. A unit can be connected or not connected to a file. If connected, it refers to a file. The connection is symmetric: that is, if a unit is connected to a file, the file is connected to the unit.

use association. The association of names in different scoping units specified by a **USE** statement.

V

variable. A data object whose value can be defined and redefined during the execution of an executable program. It may be a named data object, array element, array section, structure component, or substring. Note that in FORTRAN 77, a variable was always scalar and named.

Z

zero-length character. A character object that has a length of 0 and is always defined.

zero-sized array. An array that has a lower bound that is greater than its corresponding upper bound. The array is always defined.

Index

Special Characters

D

D (double precision) editing 154
DABS specific name 364
DACOS specific name 365
DASIN specific name 368
data edit descriptors 149, 252
data objects 22
DATA statement 216
data transfer statement
    PRINT statement 307
    READ statement 315
    WRITE statement 353
data types 21
    conversion rules 70
    derived 28—33
    intrinsic 23—28
    predefined conventions 34
DATAN specific name 369
DATAN2 specific name 370
DATE_AND_TIME intrinsic subroutine 374
DBLE intrinsic function 375
DCOS specific name 372
DCOSH specific name 372
DDIM specific name 376
DEALLOCATE statement 221
declarators
    array 43
    scoping level 102
default typing 34
deferred-shape arrays 47
defined assignment 119
defined operations 75
defined operators 118
definition status 34
DELIM specifier
    of INQUIRE statement 274
    of OPEN statement 298
derived types 28—33
    array structure components 57
    determining the type 30
    scalar structure components 31
    structure components 30
    structure constructor 32
derived-type statement 223
designators
    for array elements 51

designators *(continued)*
    for components 31
DEXP specific name 378
digits 11
DIGITS intrinsic function 375
DIM intrinsic function 375
DIM specific name 376
DIMENSION attribute 224
dimension bound expression 41
dimensions of an array 42
DINT specific name 366
direct access 142
DIRECT specifier
    of INQUIRE statement 273
disconnection 144
disjunction, logical 73, 74
division arithmetic operator 69
DLOG specific name 388
DLOG10 specific name 388
DMAX1 specific name 390
DMIN1 specific name 392
DMOD specific name 394
DNINT specific name 367
DO loop 93—97, 225
DO statement 93, 225
DO WHILE construct 97
DO WHILE loop 227
DO WHILE statement 227
DOT_PRODUCT array intrinsic function 376
double precision (D) editing 154
DOUBLE PRECISION type declaration
    statement 229
double quotation mark ("") editing 165
DPROD intrinsic function 376
DPROD specific name 376
DSIGN specific name 404
DSIN specific name 405
DSINH specific name 405
DSQRT specific name 407
DTAN specific name 409
DTANH specific name 409
dummy argument 131
    asterisk as 137
    intent 133
    procedure as 136
    variable as 134

dummy procedure   136

E

E (real with exponent) editing   154
edit descriptors
    character string   151, 254
    control (nonrepeatable)   150, 253
    data (repeatable)   149, 252
    numeric   151
editing   151—169
    ' (apostrophe)   165
    : (colon)   165
    / (slash)   164
    " (double quotation mark)   165
    A (character)   152
    B (binary)   153
    BN (blank null)   165
    BZ (blank zero)   165
    character-string   165
    complex   152
    D (double precision)   154
    E (real with exponent)   154
    EN   155
    ES   156
    F (real without exponent)   157
    G (general)   158
    H   166
    I (integer)   160
    L (logical)   161
    O (octal)   162
    P (scale factor)   167
    S, SS, and SP (sign control)   168
    T, TL, TR, and X (positional)   168
    Z (hexadecimal)   163
elemental intrinsic procedures   359
ELSE block   88, 89
ELSE IF block   88
ELSE IF statement   88, 233
ELSE statement   89, 232
ELSEWHERE statement   234
EN editing   155
END DO statement   93, 237
END IF statement   88, 237
END INTERFACE statement   112, 239
END SELECT statement   237

END specifier
    of READ statement   317
END statement   235
END TYPE statement   240
END WHERE statement   237
end-of-file conditions   147
end-of-record conditions   147
endfile records   141
ENDFILE statement   241
entities   102
entry association   258
entry name   243
ENTRY statement   243
EOR specifier
    of READ statement   318
EOSHIFT array intrinsic function   377
EPSILON intrinsic function   378
equivalence
    association   246
    logical   74
    restriction on COMMON and   207
EQUIVALENCE statement   246
.EQV. logical operator   74
ERR specifier
    of BACKSPACE statement   191
    of CLOSE statement   203
    of ENDFILE statement   241
    of INQUIRE statement   271
    of OPEN statement   295
    of READ statement   317
    of REWIND statement   326
    of WRITE statement   355
error conditions   147
ES editing   156
executable program   108
execution sequence   18
execution_part   121
EXIST specifier
    of INQUIRE statement   272
EXIT statement   248
EXP intrinsic function   378
EXP specific name   378
explicit interface   112
explicit typing   33
explicit-shape arrays   44
EXPONENT intrinsic function   378

exponentiation arithmetic operator 69
expressions
    arithmetic 68
    character 71
    constant 65
    dimension bound 41
    general 68
    initialization 66
    logical 73
    primary 75
    relational 72
    restricted 66
    specification 67
    subscript 51
extended intrinsic operations 75
EXTERNAL attribute 250
external files 142
    direct access 142
    sequential access 142
external function 257

F

F (real without exponent) editing 157
factor
    arithmetic 69
    logical 74
field 151
file position
    after BACKSPACE statement 191
    after ENDFILE statement 241
    after REWIND statement 326
    before and after data transfer 146
    of an external file 142
file positioning statement
    BACKSPACE statement 191
    ENDFILE statement 241
    REWIND statement 326
FILE specifier
    of INQUIRE statement 271
    of OPEN statement 295
files
    external 142
    internal 143
fixed form 14
FLOAT specific name 401

FLOOR intrinsic function 379
FMT specifier
    of PRINT statement 307
    of READ statement 316
    of WRITE statement 354
FORM specifier
    of INQUIRE statement 271
    of OPEN statement 296
format
    fixed form 14
    free form 16
format codes 151
format control 169
format specification
    character 255
    interaction with input/output list 169
FORMAT statement 252
format-directed formatting 149
formatted records 141
FORMATTED specifier
    of INQUIRE statement 273
formatting 149
    format-directed 149
    list-directed 170
    namelist 173
FRACTION intrinsic function 379
free form 16
function
    intrinsic 359
    reference 128
    statement 333
    subprogram 127
    value 128
FUNCTION statement 257

G

G (general) editing 158
general (G) editing 158
general expression 68
generic name of an intrinsic function 129
global entities 102
GO TO statement
    assigned 260
    computed 262
    unconditional 263

T

T (positional) editing   168
TAN intrinsic function   409
TAN specific name   409
TANH intrinsic function   409
TANH specific name   409
TARGET attribute   338
   TYPE type declaration statement   339
terminal statement   93
TINY intrinsic function   409
TL (positional) editing   168
TR (positional) editing   168
TRANSFER intrinsic function   409, 66, 67
transfer of control   18
   in a DO loop   95
transformational intrinsic functions   360
TRANSPOSE array intrinsic function   410
TRIM intrinsic function   411, 66, 67
type declaration   343
   CHARACTER   199
   COMPLEX   209
   DOUBLE PRECISION   229
   INTEGER   276
   LOGICAL   285
   REAL   321
   TYPE   339
type parameters and specifiers   21—22
type specifiers   21
type, determining   33

U

UBOUND array intrinsic function   411
unambiguous references   116
unary operations   63
unconditional GO TO statement   263
unformatted records   141
UNFORMATTED specifier
   of INQUIRE statement   273
UNIT specifier
   of BACKSPACE statement   191
   of CLOSE statement   203
   of ENDFILE statement   241
   of INQUIRE statement   270
   of OPEN statement   295

UNIT specifier *(continued)*
   of READ statement   315
   of REWIND statement   326
   of WRITE statement   353
units   144
UNPACK array intrinsic function   412
use association   106, 348
USE statement   348

V

value separators   170
variable   22
vector subscripts   56
VERIFY intrinsic function   412

W

WHERE construct   81
WHERE statement   351
whole array   41
WRITE specifier
   of INQUIRE statement   274
WRITE statement   353

X

X (positional) editing   168

Z

Z (hexadecimal) editing   163
zero-length string   27
zero-sized array   42

Fortran began at IBM. Since the 1950s, IBM has continued to demonstrate leadership in developing Fortran compilers.

Among IBM's Fortran products, **XL Fortran for AIX** provides today's Fortran programmer with a powerful UNIX compiler. Since XL Fortran Version 3, IBM has provided native Fortran 90 support. All the features described in *Fortran 90: A Reference Guide* are included in XL Fortran.

The optimization features of XL Fortran are designed to harness the power of the RISC System/6000.

> *The compiler does an outstanding job at optimization and generates code that can run at close to the theoretical peak performance of the machine for certain problems. The ability of the compiler to optimize and generate efficient code is unsurpassed in the industry.*

> Professor Jack Dongarra
> Distinguished Professor, University of Tennessee
> Distinguished Scientist, Oak Ridge National Laboratory

In addition, XL Fortran now provides an integrated development environment (including building and debugging tools).

For more details on XL Fortran and ordering information, look at the IBM Software Home Page on the World Wide Web: `http://www.torolab.ibm.com/`

You can also send e-mail enquiries to *fortran_info@vnet.ibm.com*